TRANSPORT IN BRITAIN

Transport in Britain

From Canal Lock to Gridlock

Philip Bagwell and Peter Lyth

Hambledon and London

London and New York

Hambledon and London
102 Gloucester Avenue
London, NW1 8HX

838 Broadway
New York
NY 10003–4812

First Published 2002

ISBN 1 85285 263 1

Typeset by Carnegie Publishing, Lancaster
Printed on acid-free paper and bound in
Great Britain by Cambridge University Press

Contents

Illustrations

Between Pages 176 and 177

Preface

In the autumn of 2000, as we were writing this book, British transport policy finally blew up in the government's face. Problems which had festered for decades erupted in crisis: a series of well-publicised train crashes on Britain's underfunded and recently privatised railways coincided with a Poujadist-style uprising of farmers and lorry-drivers, angry at the high price of petrol and diesel fuel. The latter felt that the government was imposing too high a tax on fuel, compared to tax on their colleagues in continental Europe. The travelling public felt that they were paying too much for a wretched and dangerous rail service. To make matters worse for the hapless government, the weather conspired against it and Britain had the worst floods for half a century; Britons were wet, angry and immobilised.

It does not matter that it happened to be a Labour government which was on the receiving end of these blows, although there is a certain irony in the fact the Prime Minister and his colleagues had more or less ignored transport issues in favour of what they considered to be more pressing concerns. It does not matter because transport and transport policy had long been disregarded in Britain, by Conservative and Labour governments alike.

The result of this neglect is that Britain, which once gave the world the steam locomotive, now has a sadly dilapidated transport system. Whether on the roads, the railways or the appallingly overcrowded London Underground, the evidence of underinvestment and bad planning – or no planning at all – is all too clear.

In this book we trace the history of transport in Britain over the last two and a half centuries and endeavour to find out how we got into this mess.

Acknowledgements

The authors would like to express their appreciation to John Armstrong for bringing them together to write this book. They would also like to thank him for reading through various sections of the manuscript and making helpful comments.

Philip Bagwell is grateful to his wife Rosemary for discussing with him both the details of the book and its conclusions. His neighbour, Ken Hester, with long experience working for British Rail and London Underground, and a prodigious memory for detail, was an invaluable source of reference and of verbal history to supplement the written record. Philip thanks Vernon Hince, Assistant General Secretary of the Rail, Maritime and Transport Workers' Union, for information about the deployment of trackmen following the privatisation of BR. Richard Cheffins, head of the State Paper Room of the old British Library, and since the transfer to the new building in Euston Road in charge of the Science and Technology and Official Publications Library, often put Philip on the right track to find needed information. There also Mike Stanbridge pointed out which Royal Commission or Select Report was most relevant to the job in hand, while Patrick Casey at the enquiry desk suggested useful ways to cast new light on past events. Jon Sims, Eveleen Rooney and Adrian Cornish at the Westminster Reference Library proved a sure guide through the maze of European Commission papers in helping to discover whether or not Britain's membership of the EU made the detachment of Railtrack from the rest of the railways obligatory.

Peter Lyth would like to thank Gerald Crompton for his valuable comments and suggestions, and Terry Gourvish for many useful discussions on transport matters over the years. He would also like to thank his wife Ofra for her support and understanding while the book was being written.

The authors and publisher are grateful to Helen Gaw for detailed work on the book and the following for permission to reproduce illustrations: British Airways, 25, 26; the London Transport Museum, 22, 24, 27 and 28; the National Maritime Museum, 4.

Introduction

Transport is something that everyone takes for granted.[1] Travel is fundamental to the human condition and when we want to travel we simply cast around for the best means or 'mode' of transport to get us to our destination; it might be a bicycle, or a bus or an Airbus. Transport, however, has not always been so universally available. Two and a half centuries ago only a few people travelled at all and when they did it was only slowly because there was no vehicle which could exceed ten miles per hour overland. There was rarely any need to move any faster. Mobility was neither available nor as valued as it is today. The vast majority of people living in the British Isles spent their entire lives close to home. Those who did travel did so on business – perhaps a doctor or lawyer visiting patient or client on horseback – or else because they were going to war or on a pilgrimage. There was no tourism and certainly no mass travel. Working people did not have to commute because they lived within walking distance of their place of work, often in the same building. Some goods travelled considerable distances, by river barge or coaster, or by what passed for the road system in the eighteenth century, but most produce and manufactured goods were drawn from the locality.

This book is about how transport in Britain has changed since the middle of the eighteenth century and how we got to where we are today. There is a considerable literature on transport history. Turnpikes, canals and railways have been studied in detail. Less attention has been given to how transport has fitted into the national economy and how it has affected and determined the lives of ordinary Britons. In looking at five modes of transport, canals, coastal shipping, railways, road transport (horse-drawn and motor-driven) and domestic air transport, this book will be informed by four broad questions concerning transport and its place in modern society: what was its relationship to industrialisation; what was its technological significance; to what extent was it a planned system conceived and constructed by the state; and how did people 'consume' it. In other words, what has been the lot of the British traveller in the years since 1750?

There is little dispute about the importance of transport improvements in the Industrial Revolution, which began in the second half of the eighteenth century, although there has been disagreement as to whether they were a cause or a consequence of industrialisation. Supporters of the cause theory have argued that a reliable system of transport, which could move raw materials and finished goods efficiently, and at low cost, was necessary for the Industrial Revolution to take place in England.[2] This view has been criticised as too monocausal by other historians, who rightly see the need to adduce other factors besides transport in the growth of industrialisation in Britain.[3]

The railway represents the transport technology which is most closely associated with early nineteenth-century industrialisation in Britain. After all Britain gave the world the steam engine and the railways. This cannot be said of the next two transport technologies: the internal combustion and the electric traction motor. The internal combustion engine was invented in Germany and its application in the automobile was first launched as a form of mass transport in the United States in the last years before the outbreak of the First World War. In sharp distinction to its experience with the railways, Britain was slow to adopt the motor car on a large scale and its per capita car ownership and use was far below the American level until as late as the 1960s.[4] The electric traction motor was first developed for street cars in the United States and drew on developments in electrical engineering in America, Germany and Britain. It was first employed on British trams in the 1890s and at the same time was introduced as the power source for London's deep-tunnel underground railways, the modern Northern and Central Lines. It took substantially longer for electrical traction to be adopted for main line rail operations, although the Southern Railway did electrify its suburban network in the 1930s.

The adoption of electrical traction coincided with the first appearance of public transport as mass transport in Britain's cities: trams were cheap and widely patronised by commuting workers. This was not the case with air transport, the leading long-distance transport innovation of the twentieth century. Air transport is to a large extent the result of advances made in aeronautical technology during the two world wars. Flying is a fast and direct means of travelling and it is the only transport mode with these characteristics. Its role in Britain's domestic transport began in the 1930s, but it did not become a significant force until the introduction of jet propulsion thirty years later.

Despite transport's importance to the process of industrialisation, it is more than just another sector of the economy. Rather it is a piece of national infrastructure, of equal importance to schools, hospitals, the police force and other vital institutions without which modern society cannot function. It is its importance to the infrastructure that causes problems for governments and leads to differing interpretations of transport's role and purpose in different countries. The alternatives can be put simply. Either transport is a public service which cannot be expected to cover its costs out of revenue, but which nonetheless cannot be allowed to malfunction through lack of funds because of the wider impact of that failure (what economists would call 'negative externalities', such as traffic congestion and environmental pollution); or transport is an enterprise, or collection of enterprises, which should be subject to market forces like any other business and should not be allowed to become a permanent financial burden on the state. As we aim to show in this book, Britain has had a great deal of difficulty – certainly more than most other European countries – in making up its mind on this question. And all the evidence suggests, again in comparison with other European countries, that it is still deliberating.

Subscribing to the first view, we believe that a working transport system is a integral part of a nation's 'social overhead capital' and that it must be properly provided for before an economy can reach its full potential, industry can be efficient, and a modern society can act in harmony. This social overhead capital requires very large amounts of financial investment; more, in fact, than any single enterprise can be expected to raise. In addition the returns on this investment are likely to be many years in coming and will accrue to the whole community, rather than to individual investors. For this reason these investments are more often and more easily made by governments than by private companies. Against this background, it is clear that the British model of transport development over the last 250 years has been exceptional in its reliance on private capital. As was observed some years ago, in Britain 'it was almost entirely native private enterprise that found both the initiative and the capital to lay down the system of communications which was essential to the British industrial revolution'.[5]

In the nineteenth and early twentieth centuries, British policy on transport, such as it was, consisted of allowing the growth of all transport modes in an environment which was as competitive as possible. Little attempt was made to coordinate or integrate the modes, or to consider the impact that one might have on the other, for example that of the railways on the canal system, or, later, road transport on the railways. Allowing the private sector to develop Britain's transport system by identifying travellers' needs and providing the necessary services, the state presided over the creation of an extensive but haphazard and ill-planned network. In the twentieth century this emphasis on market forces, and the neglect of government planning, has had an unfortunate effect on the railways, which have suffered from the fact that road transport has not been required to pay the full cost of its operation.

This non-intervention, or lack of planning, contrasts strongly with the experience of Britain's two most important European neighbours, France and Germany. In these countries, despite mistakes in policy and the occasional technological wrong turn, transport's performance has historically been measured in much wider terms than the ability to survive in the market. These countries have approached the question of transport provision with more willingness to meet long-term economic and social objectives. The result has been a greater degree of balance between transport modes than is the case in Britain. While Britain's canals were allowed to deteriorate in the late nineteenth century, and its railways to fall into disrepute in the mid twentieth century, France and Germany continued to invest in these 'older' transport modes and thus relieved some of the pressure on road transport which had become so intolerable in Britain by the end of the twentieth century. The absence of any tradition of transport planning in Britain, and the tendency to finance transport modes independently on a case by case basis according to criteria determined by the Treasury, has meant that integrated transport policies, and policies which encourage multimodal strategies, are rare. To give but a single, glaring example: Heathrow Airport, which handles the largest traffic volume of any airport in Europe, and is the single most important entry point for people coming to Britain, still has no direct connection to a mainline railway, although the airport is now over fifty years old.[6]

As we will demonstrate, the modern British approach to transport has long antecedents. The reluctance of successive British governments, with a few exceptions, to initiate long-term planning to create an integrated transport system goes back two centuries to the 'canal age' and Britain's early railways. Since then there has always been in Britain a strong single-project approach to transport organisation – and a profound distrust in government of transport coordination and planning, usually on the grounds that it inhibits competition and leads to monopoly. The ill-effects of planning deficiencies in British transport have moreover been compounded by an uneven and generally low level of investment. With the exception of a few prestige projects like the Concorde supersonic airliner and the Channel Tunnel, transport infrastructure investment in Britain in the second half of the twentieth century has been markedly lower than that in other European nations. There is little doubt that this under-investment in transport has adversely effected the British economy. Britain's antiquated and creaking infrastructure has imposed capacity restraints on the economy not experienced by other European countries with higher levels of investment. Of even greater importance, it has exacted a heavy human cost in delay, stress, frustration and illness: the anxious mother rushing to collect her child from school; the frustrated businessman sitting in a stationary taxi in an inner-city traffic jam; the student waiting on the platform of a run-down station for a train delayed because of yet another signal failure; the family car moving at walking pace down a motorway because unavoidable maintenance work has closed half the lanes; and the London Underground passenger pressed like the proverbial sardine into the corner of an ill-ventilated Tube carriage by the sheer mass of fellow commuters. They are all victims of the British approach to transport.

To John Armstrong

1

Inland Navigation

Before the invention of the steam engine, the transport of goods required either wind or horse power. While the former was more or less confined to shipping, horse power could be deployed either on roads or towing barges on rivers and canals.[1] Water transport carried bulk goods at a significantly lower unit cost than was possible overland. Land transport was between three and four times more expensive than water transport on eight routes studied for the years between 1780 and 1800.[2] Rivers formed the basis of the internal transport system in pre-industrial Europe and, at a time when roads were bad or non-existent, they were the natural means of transporting people and produce.[3] According to the old adage, geography makes history; and, as far as transport history is concerned, geography was kind to Britain: its navigable rivers emptied into the sea at frequent and convenient points along an island coastline which was admirably suited for shipping. These rivers were the only highways when most of the low-lying country was forested or swampy, and it is hardly surprising that many of the earliest settlements were established on river banks.

Before the nineteenth century, five rivers and their tributaries carried much of the bulk cargo transported in England: the Thames, navigable above Oxford as far west as Cricklade, served London and the south; the Severn and other rivers flowing into the Bristol Channel served the west midlands and parts of Wales; the Mersey and the Dee encompassed South Lancashire, Cheshire and North Wales; the Humber and the Trent served south Yorkshire, Nottinghamshire and Derbyshire; and the rivers discharging into the Wash served the Fens as well as eastern counties such as Northamptonshire and Bedfordshire. In addition there were rivers of importance to peripheral areas, such as the Tyne in the north east and the Exe in east Devon.

The Severn was probably the most important of the five and, together with the Wye and the Warwickshire Avon, formed a vital transport artery in the west. Indeed it was largely because of its position close to the Severn estuary that the city of Bristol became a port of national importance long before Liverpool. The Severn owed this early prominence to the comparative absence of obstructions in its course and to a lively trade in Welsh flannel.

This cloth was brought down the river from Shrewsbury by London merchants who then shipped it to Europe, or across the Atlantic where it was made up into clothing for slaves.[4] Later the Severn's value as a transport facility was one of the reasons for the pioneering growth of coal and iron industries in Shropshire.[5] Meanwhile, in the east of England, the River Thames served as London's supply line. In the seventeenth century it carried building stone downstream from Bullingdon near Oxford, as well as hay, straw and grain from Henley, while from the coasters on the Thames estuary came, beans from Hull, oats from Lynn and Boston, coals from Newcastle.[6] Within London itself the river also carried large numbers of passengers: boat traffic on the Thames with barges, wherries and tilts was said to employ 40,000 people between Windsor and Gravesend in the early 1600s.[7]

While river transport was obviously important in England, its value was essentially at the regional level. It would be an exaggeration to say that the river systems described above represented anything approaching a national transport network. River transport also had its drawbacks. Apart from natural disruptions caused by flooding and droughts which made navigation alternatively dangerous or impossible,[8] rivers were littered with man-made obstacles such as fishermen's nets, and the sluices and weirs erected by millers to drive their water-wheels. River barges could be delayed for hours while a miller was persuaded, or bribed, to raise his weir long enough to allow a 'flash' that would equalise the water levels above and below it to allow a boatman's vessel through.[9]

Gradually a process of river improvement removed most of these impediments to navigation. Thanks to Dutch influence and skills, England's rivers had their banks reinforced, their navigable stretches extended through dredging, their courses straightened with cuts, and their changing elevation harnessed with locks.[10] Serious river improvement was begun at least as early as the second half of the sixteenth century. By an Act of Parliament in 1571 the corporation of the City of London was empowered to finance the improvement of the River Lea.[11] In 1698 another private Act enabled the 'undertakers of the navigation of the rivers Aire and Calder', in the West Riding of Yorkshire, to deepen and straighten these two important waterways.[12] In the eighteenth century, with industrial activity increasing in the north, the number of sanctioned river improvements rose apace and important developments, including the Mersey and Irwell Navigation (1720), the Weaver Navigation (1720 and 1760), and improvements to the Wear (1716, 1747 and 1759), encouraged the rapid growth of coal fields, the Yorkshire woollen and the Lancashire cotton industries. The impetus for river improvements was the need to provision major towns like London with cheaper food and, after the beginning of the eighteenth century, to supply vital raw materials such as iron, lead, timber, wool and, above all, coal to manufacturing industries. The need for cheap and reliable coal supplies, both for industry and domestic consumption, was the driving force behind many river improvements in the north, including the Aire and Calder, the Don, the Weaver and the Mersey, as well as further south, for example, in the Fenland.[13] Coal was probably the dominant influence on the development of the whole programme of inland navigation in England in the eighteenth century, canals and rivers alike.[14]

The key invention in the process of river improvement and later canal construction was the pound lock. This was a much more efficient method of negotiating gradients in a waterway than the crude flash lock it replaced. The pound lock, using the double mitre gate (instead of a vertically-operated sluice), was first employed in Britain by John Trew, who used mitre gates in the construction of a canal running parallel to the River Exe in the years 1564–67.[15] But, apart from the technological advance which it represented, the pound lock was also of economic and social significance since it facilitated the easy settlement of disputes between different river users over the control of its water. Those who used the waterway as a means of transport inevitably clashed with riverside communities that used it as a source of power, irrigation or fish supply; there was rarely enough volume of water to allow both the passage of boats and the powering of water-wheels, while leaving enough of the river undisturbed to serve as a catchment area for fishermen. The pound lock went a long way towards resolving this hitherto intractable conflict and allowed everybody to benefit from the river's resources.[16]

River improvement was complicated by the need to acquire the agreement of the riparian owners, regardless of whether it was just a question of strengthening the river's banks or of making a extensive cut across adjacent land. From the second half of the seventeenth century parliamentary sanction had to precede every individual act of improvement, with bursts of legislation authorising projects on the Aire and Calder, the Trent and the Dee. The first quarter of the eighteenth century saw corresponding parliamentary activity as companies were formed to improve the Derwent, the Idle, the Mersey and the Irwell – all close to coal fields and northern textile manufacturers. Gaining parliamentary approval for these projects could be a long and painstaking business as determined local opposition was overcome.[17] Farmers fought river improvements if they thought that cheaper transport between regions would lower the price of agricultural produce and thus their own profits. And merchants based on one river might oppose the improvement of a rival waterway for fear of losing trade. Thus in 1725 York traders fought a Bill to improve the Aire and Calder rivers because they feared a diversion of traffic from their own river, the Ouse. Attempts to make the River Derwent navigable in order to facilitate the transport of lead from mines in Derbyshire were delayed for a long time by Nottingham interests who wanted to restrict navigation on the Trent. A similiar story unfolded on the River Don. In 1697 Sheffield cutlers sought to improve the Don so that boats could navigate the section beyond Doncaster to Sheffield. Their products could then be sent downstream to the Ouse and so on to the Humber and Hull. But the initiative was defeated by Bawtry merchants who stood to lose their livelihood if the Don was used instead of the Trent and its tributary, the River Idle. It took until 1726 before the Don was made navigable as far as Tinsley, three miles short of Sheffield.[18]

By 1724, as a result of improvement, around 1160 miles of English rivers were navigable and, apart from mountainous areas, most of England and Wales was within fifteen miles of a navigable waterway (see Map 1).[19] The only region of major industrial significance which was not well-served by the growing network of river navigation was Birmingham and the Black Country. Perhaps not surprisingly it was this area which experienced rapid and concentrated canal construction in the second half of the eighteenth century.

Navigable rivers continued to play a role in the transport of goods in Britain up until the nineteenth century; but, although improvements removed many of bottlenecks, they were not a total solution to the growing transport needs of industry and there were limits to how much rivers could be improved. Apart from the eternal problems of droughts, flooding and silting, especially in the Wash, rivers could not cross the Pennine watershed that ran like a spine down the centre of northern England, in precisely those areas where new industries were springing up. By the second half of the eighteenth century the rapid increase in manufacturing was leading to a greater demand for fuel and raw materials. For example, the quantity of raw cotton imported into Great Britain for textile manufacturing rose fifteen times,[20] and the demands of the textile industry for coal were far beyond the capacity of river transport to supply them. Above all, the growing volume of inter-regional commerce required a form of freight transport that could better overcome the physical barriers between those regions. The answer was canals.

The superiority of the man-made canal over the navigable river, whether improved or not, consists in the fact that the water is free of currents and is retained within a channel of consistent width and depth, along the side of which runs a towpath where tractive power to the barges, usually horses, can be applied. British canals were undoubtedly monuments to the proficiency of eighteenth-century civil engineers, but it would be wrong to see them as examples of path-breaking technological ingenuity. The techniques used in their excavation, including the construction of aqueducts, locks,

| River or drainage navigation | Broad canal (locks exceeding 7ft in width) | Narrow canal |

Map 1. Inland Waterways in England in the 1840s.

sluices and reservoirs, were all known and mostly imported from continental Europe. So when we talk of the 'Canal Age' we are dealing with an evolution from the 'River Age' rather than a fundamental technological breakthrough in transport, such as was represented a half century later by the steam engine and railway.[21]

At the end of the eighteenth century there were about two thousand miles of waterway in England, consisting of a third naturally navigable rivers, a third improved rivers (the improvement taking place mostly between 1600 and 1760), and a third canals, built between 1760 and 1800.[22] Canals had been cut before 1760, but these tended merely to extend or connect rivers. In addition to clearing obstacles in the stream or deepening it, side cuts began to be made in river courses, straightening difficult bends or bypassing the more extravagant meanders. These cuts were miniature canals, often with pound locks to maintain the water supply, and the experience gained from their excavation served their builders as an apprenticeship in dead-water canal construction. Even in the 'Canal Age' many canals were little more than short links between navigable rivers, into which so much investment had been made in their improvement over the centuries. The first early modern British canal was probably the Elizabethan example mentioned above between Exeter and Topsham, carried out in the hope of revitalising Exeter as a seaport.[23] In the seventeenth century the leading expertise in canal construction was on the Continent, particularly in France, and it is clear that the British admired the French in this respect. In 1670 a delegation from the Royal Society sought instruction from the French engineers who had joined the Atlantic and Mediterranean by the Canal du Midi. This marvel of the age was nearly a hundred and fifty miles long and negotiated elevation changes in the region of six hundred feet by means of tunnels, aqueducts and one hundred locks. After its completion in 1681, the Canal du Midi became a regular feature on the Grand Tour, undertaken by English gentlemen such as the Duke of Bridgewater, who saw it in 1753.[24]

The 'Canal Age' in England began in 1757 when the twelve-mile Sankey Brook Navigation was opened in south Lancashire.[25] Two years before the corporation of Liverpool and some Liverpool merchants had obtained parliamentary approval to deepen three streams which flowed off the St Helens coalfields, merging to form the Sankey Brook before draining into the River Mersey near Warrington. The intention was to make the river sufficiently navigable to transport St Helens coal to Liverpool. Improvement of the Sankey Brook, however, was found to be impractical and the parliamentary approval was used instead to make an entirely separate cut, parallel to the river but at a higher elevation. This Sankey Brook Canal not only eased coal provision to the growing market in Liverpool but also to Cheshire salt manufacturers who increased their exports from Liverpool. The canal's chief backer was the Mersey saltmaster John Ashton, who needed the St Helens coal for his business.[26] This was to be a model for many English canal projects in the next fifty years: individual entrepreneurs supporting a local canal initiative to enhance their businesses. John Ashton must have been well-pleased with his investment, as the Sankey Brook Navigation was highly profitable and paid a dividend of 33.3 per cent on its capital for the next eighty years.[27]

The next two entrepreneurs to see the advantage of canals for their business were Francis Egerton, the third Duke of Bridgewater, and the pottery magnate Josiah Wedgwood. Bridgewater owned coalfields at Worsley, ten miles west of Manchester. The city and its booming textile industry was growing fast and needed his coal, but the cost of transport was high. The Sankey Brook Canal also threatened to price his Worsley coal out of the Manchester market with cheaper coal from St Helens. The duke decided to construct a canal of his own, linking Worsley to Salford, where his coal could be unloaded for 4d. per ton instead of 7d.[28] The Bridgewater Canal was planned and built in the remarkably short time of two years between 1759 and 1761 by John Gilbert and James Brindley. For its time it was an extraordinary piece of engineering, featuring an aqueduct at Barton to carry the canal across the River Irwell. It made Brindley, the 'illiterate millwright', into a national figure as canal engineer and builder.[29] Beginning as a subterranean waterway, the canal took its water directly out of Bridgewater's mine, the barges, having been loaded with coal, emerging into the daylight at a place known appropriately as Worsley Delph. Having drastically cut the price of coal delivery to Manchester, Bridgewater and Brindley began the construction of another canal between Manchester and the Mersey, in the face of opposition from the Irwell and Mersey Navigation proprietors. It was opened in 1767 and later Bridgewater even inaugurated a passenger boat service on it. Thanks to this canal, Manchester's exports were now channelled through the growing port of Liverpool instead of having to make the long and costly journey via Bridgnorth to the River Severn.

The Duke of Bridgewater's success in Lancashire inspired a burst of canal building. By 1772 the Mersey and the Severn were linked, followed by the Trent and the Mersey in 1777, and the Thames and the Severn in 1789. It was now possible to move bulky goods at low cost throughout central England, although a northern trans-Pennine canal was still lacking. The most ambitious undertaking was the Trent and Mersey or Grand Trunk Canal, begun in 1766 under the direction of the irrepressible Brindley, with backing from both Bridgewater and Wedgwood. Indeed Wedgwood was to be the Grand Trunk's official spokesman. As a businessman who appreciated the value of good transport, he was the canal's proposer and the chief agent in obtaining the Act of Parliament needed to dig it. His famous Etruria works at Burslem was to lie on the route of the canal, which subsequently revolutionised the inward shipment of coal and the Cornish clay he needed, and the outward shipment of his fragile chinaware.[30] Following the contours as far as possible, the Grand Trunk was nearly a hundred miles long from Preston Bridge to Derwent Mouth in Derbyshire, winding in a great U-shape across the waist of England. It had thirty-five locks up to Harecastle, a 1.6 mile tunnel through Harecastle Hill and then a further forty locks on the other side to bring it down to the level of the Trent. In addition there was a twenty-three arch aqueduct over the River Dove. It was opened in 1777, five years after Brindley's death.

The Grand Trunk (when added to the navigable stretches of the Trent and the Mersey) was the first commercially viable link between east and west, between Hull and Liverpool, benefiting everyone along its path – from Cheshire's salt-masters, to Staffordshire potters, to the brewers of Burton-on-Trent. Its impact on transport costs was immediate and freight rates between Manchester and Litchfield, for example, dropped from £4 per ton to £1.[31] While it was an impressive piece of engineering, however, it set an unfortunate precedent in its operational dimensions. The canal was wide at its western and eastern ends, but the middle section was built narrower, out of economy, and could only handle boats of narrow beam, that is 7ft wide, with a draught of around 4ft. Thus it established an alternative standard for British narrow boat canals, which all but made it impossible to create an integrated national canal system with the broader 14 ft gauge which was used on many other canals.[32]

By the late 1760s canal engineers like Brindley were considering how a national network could be created, joining London, Liverpool, Bristol and Hull in a cross formation, with Birmingham and the Black Country at its centre. The Grand Trunk provided its northern arms; its south-western arm was ready in 1772 with the opening of the Staffordshire and Worcestershire Canal. Shorter than the Grand Trunk and more easily engineered, this linked the Grand Trunk with the River Severn at Stourport and immediately improved the access of the Black Country to markets and raw materials.

The first canal-building boom, which ended with the trade recession that followed the American War of Independence, was succeeded by a second burst of activity in the 1790s. This second boom was characterised by the cutting of new canals which sought to improve on and compete with existing ones and also to provide better transport to agricultural regions.[33] It also tackled the remaining link that would be necessary to complete a 'cross' network: the south-eastern arm to London. The Coventry and Oxford canals had further eased transport around Birmingham, but there was less urgency to make the canal connection to London than with Manchester and Birmingham because the metropolis already had good river and sea connections. The Grand Junction, which stretched from the Oxford Canal just south of Rugby to the Thames at Richmond, was completed in 1805 after twelve years work, making the route from the midlands to London more direct and efficient. Brindley's successor in the role of national canal-builder was Thomas Telford, who favoured more direct routes than Brindley, with more locks, cuts and aqueducts. Indeed it is fair to say that, thanks to improved engineering, Telford and his colleagues were able to build rather more daring creations than the earlier Brindley canals. The Grand Junction was wider than the narrow gauge Oxford Canal, so its boats could not navigate the last link into Birmingham formed by the Oxford and Coventry canals, both of which were opened in 1790 and were typical Brindley canals. In theory, at least, the 'cross' was now complete; but in practice, because of the change of gauge between the Grand Junction and the Oxford canals, and the host of separate canal companies and river navigations, each charging their own tolls, it hardly approached the significance or utility of a national system. Indeed the basic characteristic – and weakness – of the English canal system was already manifest by the 1790s: it was a product of overlapping regional interests rather than a centrally-planned national network; and, however useful the canals were to be in transporting goods within a region, there would always be irksome and costly junctions throughout the system on longer journeys where goods had to be unloaded from barges and transferred to another gauge.

After the 'cross' only a few other major canals were built. The most important were the massive Liverpool and Leeds Canal across the north Pennines, Britain's longest at 143 miles, and the Kennet and Avon, which linked the Thames at Reading with the Somerset Avon and Bristol. The Liverpool and Leeds Canal took nearly fifty years to complete (1770–1816) and included a whole range of tunnels and aqueducts and cost £1,200,000. Besides connecting the wool centre of Leeds to the port of Liverpool, it ranged high to Skipton in north Yorkshire and then down the western slopes of the Pennines through the industrial districts of south Lancashire.

The remaining new canals built before the dawn of the railway age tended to have specific local commercial objectives, such as linking a coalfield or an industrial centre to a port or waterway. By 1830 there were over four thousand miles of navigable waterways, rivers and canals in Britain. Two areas in particular were well served by the canal age: the Potteries and Birmingham. One canal linked Birmingham to the Grand Trunk, and thus Liverpool, and another to the Grand Junction and thus London. Others

gave access to the Severn, and by way of Warwick joined it to the Oxford
Canal and the south. Birmingham was therefore the hub, in so far as there
was one, of the English canal network. By contrast, London gained far less
benefit from canal connections and had to wait for the railways before it
became the pivot of a national transport system – albeit one which was
very much skewed to the south east. Canals were an essentially northern
phenomenon in England and the industries which benefited most from
them were in south Lancashire, the West Riding of Yorkshire and the west
midlands. Apart from the Manchester Ship Canal, which was a late Victorian
enterprise, the 1830s saw the end of canal construction in England, the last
inland canal being completed in 1834.[34]

One of the most significant features of the Canal Age, from the perspective
of Britain's long-term transport history, is the fact that the vast majority of
canal companies, while representing a huge financial and logistical effort in
the construction of any canal, did not operate transport services on their
own account but relied entirely for their revenue on the tolls they levied
on the independent barge owners who used them.[35] They were in effect
passive capitalists. Of course their investment – their canals – required
management and maintenance, including some modest improvements from
time to time, but essentially they were the owners of transport infrastructure
rather than transport businesses. In this they differed in a vital respect from
the railway companies of the mid nineteenth century, which both built the
track and operated the trains which ran upon them. The effect of this
distinction was to give the canal companies a certain inflexibility in relation
to their railway rivals; while they spent their time in long and complex
negotiations over rates with barge operators, the railways were able to
respond to changes in demand directly by putting on more trains.

The basic techniques of canal building were neither new nor British, but
when the British canals were built in the late eighteenth and early nineteenth
century they were the marvels of their age. They represented the state of
the art in civil engineering, with their pound locks, aqueducts, cuttings
and tunnels. Indeed, to the lay observer, these long ribbons of still water
stretching across the countryside appeared to be the surest sign of man's
triumph over nature. Canal entrepreneurs themselves often possessed a wide
knowledge of science and technology as it was understood at the time – of
Newtonian physics, for example. It was these 'knowledgeable capitalists', as
they have been called, who, by engaging financially in a technologically
demanding business, made it possible for practising engineers, such as
Brindley, Smeaton, Telford and Rennie, to gain employment for their skills
and make distinguished careers for themselves.[36] Canals were among those
spectacular 'improvements' which prompted Arthur Young to conclude that

'by such noble undertakings is the present age peculiarly distinguished'.[37] Canal tunnels of up to three miles in length were not uncommon in hilly districts. This was an extraordinary accomplishment in labour organisation and survey work, but also typical of the private entrepreneurial approach to canal building in Britain. With commercial criteria dictating the shape of the tunnel, and in the interests of economy in construction, they were often made so narrow that there was not even space for a tow path. The boats had to be worked through by men who lay on their backs on the cargo and pushed against the sides of the tunnel with their feet.

The cutting of the canals required a logistical effort in labour organisation unprecedented in Britain's economic history. Manual workers, known as 'navvies' (from the word navigator), were drawn from throughout the north of England, as well as Ireland, Scotland and Wales, and organised for the task by contractors such as Brindley. Indeed Brindley's fame may well lie as much in his experience in organising large armies of men, armed with picks and shovels, as in his engineering skills. The social and economic phenomenon of the navvies began with the construction of the canals, and developed further with the building of the railways. The progress of these rough and ready gangs around the country, often through quiet rural backwaters where canals were to be excavated, had a lasting effect on labour mobility.[38]

How were the canals paid for? As we have seen, the Duke of Bridgewater's canal halved the price of coal in Manchester and prompted other business-men and landowners to risk their money on canal projects. Bridgewater, although he ran seriously into debt during the construction of the first canal from Worsley, proceeded on a sound financial basis. He already owned a coal mine, which made it easy to borrow money, and he had a good plan: by delivering his coal direct to Manchester he could sell it for a much lower price and still make 20 per cent profit on his investment. Early profitable canals like Bridgewater's prompted investors to get on board, much as they pursued other new technologies and dawning industries in later periods. Small investors followed in the trail of successful businessmen like Bridge-water and Wedgwood, who needed canals for their own transport. In 1792, for example, a meeting was held at Rochdale in Lancashire to consider the proposed construction of the Rochdale Canal, when no less than £60,000 was subscribed in an hour.[39]

For the most part, canal financing was raised locally from those business-men and landowners who stood to gain directly from the benefits the canal would bring, but who also could afford to wait the several years it took to excavate it before they saw the fruits of their investment.[40] These people might be friends, family or a well-disposed banker or merchant, but canals were also increasingly the product of corporate enterprise supported by local shareholders. The first step in this process was to call a meeting, elect a committee and appoint an engineer to make a survey and cost estimate. Later a petition would be drawn up and taken to Parliament. Legal and parliamentary expenses were high and money had to be spent compensating local river navigation interests: Bridgewater, for example, was forced to buy a controlling interest in the Mersey and Irwell Navigation before he could operate his canal.

During the 'Canal Mania' of the 1790s, while there were enough profitable canals to keep the bubble expanding, many had risky financing which ultimately ruined their investors. The Oxford and the Kennet and Avon Canals usually paid over 20 per cent dividend, while the Trent and Mersey paid a fantastic 75 per cent.[41] Shares in the Birmingham Canal, originally £140 each, were selling at £900 at the height of the 'mania' in 1792; and by 1825 an eighth share in this canal was selling for £355. A writer who picked out the ten most successful canals in 1825 calculated that they were then paying an average of 27.6 per cent.[42] On the other hand, many canals failed because of engineering difficulties or bad management in operation, or simply because their economic justification had never been properly examined at the outset and they were doomed from the start. 'Fully one half of the number of canals and probably considerably more than one half of the capital expenditure,' noted Jackman, 'realized returns that were inadequate in order to maintain the canals as effective agents for the work they were intended to accomplish.'[43]

The speculative spirit of the 'canal mania' spread the geographical basis of the capital raising process beyond the regional level so that many individuals with limited resources, and no particular interest in transport, fell victim to the temptation of quick profits from investment in canal shares. It is remarkable how much private capital was raised in England to finance canal construction, considering that it was in the nature of canal construction and operation that a quick return could hardly be expected. Under the forty-seven Acts relating to inland navigation between 1788 and 1795, over six million pounds was raised by subscription, and between 1790 and 1793, when low interest rates made capital cheap, fifty-three canal and navigation bills, involving an outlay of over five million pounds, were authorised by Parliament. Shares were transferable and were often offered for sale in local newspapers.[44] Thus canal companies, by popularising the sale of equity shares, bonds, and debentures, did much to lay the financial basis of future industrial development. 'When a navigable cut or canal has been made, the management of it becomes quite simple and easy', noted Adam Smith, recognising the utility of limited liability to canal-building, 'such undertakings, therefore, may be, and accordingly frequently are, very successfully managed by joint stock companies without any exclusive privilege'.[45]

The joint stock company, established by Act of Parliament, was not new in the eighteenth century, but the canal age familiarised the small investor with their utility and potential. Increasingly the joint stock company was to become the vehicle by which private capital undertook large construction projects and non-participant shareholders provided the capital funds. In an almost seamless transition, the canal investors of the 1790s were to become the railway shareholders of the 1830s and 1840s, when the huge capital requirements of the next transport mode were presented to the nation.

British canals were the first example of private capitalist enterprise applied to canal-building in Europe and they were closely tied to the course of the Industrial Revolution. They also embodied a significant replacement of labour with capital, a universal characteristic of industrialisation. The contemporary witness John Phillips described the effects of this when he observed new and old transport systems working side by side at Barton Bridge:

> seven or eight stout fellows labouring like slaves to drag a boat slowly up the Irwell, and one horse or mule, or sometimes two men at most, drawing five or six of the Duke's barges, linked together, at a great rate upon the canal.[46]

The economic impact of transport, including canals, in the early stages of British industrialisation has been extensively debated. The question of whether a modern system of transport was a necessary precondition for the industrial revolution to take place in England has been a point of issue between historians.[47] There is no dispute, however, over the fact that canals, navigable rivers and coastal shipping combined to create an all-water transport capability for moving bulk freight within industrialising regions, and to a lesser extent, between them. Canals widened the market for manufactured products by enhancing the speed and reliability of transport, and lowered the cost of obtaining raw materials, an important inducement for the growth of a number of new industries.[48] As canals cut the cost of shipping bulky articles, they also reduced industry's dependence on road transport. English roads at the end of the eighteenth century were in an appalling state, despite the turnpike Acts, and it would be another fifty years before Telford and McAdam were able to change that state of affairs.

By the early nineteenth century Telford was already stressing the function of canals as a means of transporting coal and raw materials to the coast and to industrial centres, as well as manure and fertiliser to farmers, and manufactured products to the market.[49] Coal figured in a great many decisions to build canals. Shortage of coal in Liverpool led to the Sankey Brook Canal, shortage in Manchester to the Bridgewater Canal. In Birmingham the completion of a canal to Wednesbury in 1767 caused the price of coal to drop from thirteen to seven shillings per ton.[50] 'A navigation', the Duke of Bridgewater remarked famously, 'should have coals at the heel of it', and indeed of the 165 Acts passed between 1758 and 1802 no fewer than ninety were for concerns whose primary goal was to transport coal.[51] The parliamentary authorisation for the Nottingham Canal, for example, in 1792, singled out coal shipments from the Duke of Newcastle's collieries. 'The importance of coal in stimulating improvements in transport was thus evident in Nottinghamshire and Derbyshire, as it was in the Black Country and Lancashire.'[52] The fuel of the Industrial Revolution had to be delivered faster, more cheaply and more efficiently before the industries that made that revolution could take shape, and canals were the first serious attempt to solve that problem. Indeed if the canals promoted the Industrial Revolution, it was because they eased the transport of coal.[53]

Besides coal, canal transport also had an impact on the cost of grain, fertiliser, including manure, iron ore, bricks, stone, cement and timber. Within twenty years of 1785–89 the output of bricks, for example, had expanded 80 per cent, proof of the effectiveness of the new canals in providing brickmakers with cheap transport for both their fuel and their finished product.[54]

Table 1

Comparative Freight Charges, 1 December 1792

Journey	By Land		By Canal	
	£	shillings	£	shillings
Manchester–Birmingham	4	0	1	10
Manchester–Stourport	4	13	1	10
Manchester–the Potteries	2	15		15
Liverpool–Wolverhampton	5	0	1	5
Liverpool–Stourport	5	0	1	10
Chester–Wolverhampton	3	10	1	15
Chester–Birmingham	3	10	2	0

Source: *Felix Farley's Bristol Journal,* 1 December 1792.[55]

Although canals were generally cut through sparsely populated and often hilly countryside, large towns were usually at each end. Commerce was between towns and canal construction reflected the new urbanisation which accompanied the Industrial Revolution in England. It is fair to say in fact that canal construction was, initially at least, a function of urban growth; if

Manchester had not got so big it would not have needed Bridgewater's coal. The growth of towns and cities led to a huge rise in demand for domestic fuel and the canals facilitated the supply to households as well as serving the factories. It seems that English urbanisation and the rise of the new industrial cities typically followed improvements in transport, often canals, such as Leeds, Leicester, Nottingham, Liverpool and Hull.[56]

On the more general question of the relationship between canal construction in the latter half of the eighteenth century and English industrialisation, the regional nature of the canals' economic impact needs to be stressed. Canals were usually excavated to meet the needs of local or regional industrial interests, very often the provision of raw materials or coal. They were the work of private businessmen, who while they may have had their sights on a national market for their manufactured goods, like Wedgwood, nonetheless remained rooted in a regional economy such as south Lancashire, the west midlands or the West Riding of Yorkshire. The new canals were a major contribution to this regional industrialisation; what they did not represent however, or at least not completely and certainly not by design, was the first layer of an integrated, national transportation system.[57]

As we have seen, British canals were built by private entrepreneurs harnessed to the financial novelty of the joint stock company. Unfortunately, a consequence of building the canals with private capital was that it was not done very efficiently. The large variety of widths, depths, engineering standards and company charges made the canal network that emerged in the first quarter of the nineteenth century less integrated and efficient than if it had been centrally planned by government.

Like the turnpikes, English canals were built by and for regional interests. Industrialisation was in any case a regional rather than a national phenomenon, and canals were built in answer to local demand.[58] Canal companies aimed to meet the specific needs of a region and often connected or replaced a local river navigation. The Bridgewater Canal was a substitute for the Mersey and Irwell river navigation, the Trent and Mersey Canal a better alternative to the awkward River Weaver navigation. This is not to deny their national importance. Clearly without northern aristocrats and businessmen, like Bridgewater and Wedgwood, no canals would have been built at all, and England would have been obliged to stagger on with a transport structure little changed since the departure of the Romans. But there is no doubt that the combination of local interest and private enterprise led to a canal system determined by the needs and financial capabilities of local business interests, and made the formation of a national plan or policy more difficult. In both the initial period following the opening of the Bridgewater Canal and the 'mania' of the 1790s, Britain pursued a *laissez-faire* policy towards canal-building. There was always direct capitalist interest in a new canal, with few goals beyond immediate profit. Bridgewater's enterprise typified the British canal era in that prosperous manufacturers or coal owners supplied the capital for local canal construction, and determined its route, as a calculated business risk. But then this should not surprise us, it was after all the economic and political background to the entire Industrial Revolution. The state played no role in the canal age other than passing legislation for canal construction on a piecemeal basis and preventing any one canal company from becoming a monopoly. Parliament, while granting specific Acts to facilitate the purchase of land for a cut, failed to direct or even take much interest in the overall shape of the emerging canal system. Had the state played a more active role in the creation of the British canal system, a more uniform and efficient national network might have emerged.[59] Possibly canals might have survived as more effective competitors to the railways in the nineteenth century – certainly that was the experience in other parts of the European Continent, including France, Germany and Holland.

From 1700 to 1760 twenty-nine Bills on waterways were promoted in Parliament of which three referred to canals, the remainder to river improvement. In the last forty years of the eighteenth century sixty-nine out of the eighty-five Acts for new waterways were for canals. In 1794 alone twelve canal Bills were recorded. Thereafter the pressure abated. From 1800 to 1830 there were forty applications for new waterways, but in the half century from 1830 until 1883, when the Manchester Ship Canal Bill was promoted for the first time, there were hardly any.[60] The Canal Age was of little more than seventy years duration.

What happened to the English canals? It is said that they were impoverished and ruined by the railways, but this is only a partial explanation at best. Certainly the railways did not take long to make an impact on their older rivals. The opening of the Manchester to Leeds Railway in 1840 led to a 70 per cent fall in cargo revenue on the Rochdale Canal within two years, and on the Grand Junction Canal revenues were halved within six years of the completion of the London and Birmingham Railway in 1838.[61] Traffic on the Nottingham Canal fell from 12,183 tons of goods in 1841–42 to 8965 tons in 1845–46. In the latter year the directors agreed to surrender to the railway and to amalgamate with the Ambergate, Nottingham, Boston, and Eastern Junction Railway, which opened in 1852.[62] By contrast, where the railways came late to a region, the local canal companies prospered longer. The key to the enduring profitability of the Swansea Canal in the Tawe Valley was the very late arrival of the Swansea Vale Railway there in 1861.[63] Railway ownership of canals started in the 1840s and by 1865 about a third of the canals in the country belonged to railway companies. By the end of the nineteenth century, of 3935 miles of navigable waterways, 140 miles had been converted into railways, 275 were derelict, leaving 3520 miles, of which 2256 miles were independent and 1264 railway-owned.[64] While it is easy to blame the railways for the canals' demise, the fact is that they only owned a minority of the canal companies. The remainder of independent companies failed to make the necessary level of investment that would have kept the network competitive. Nicholas Wood, writing in 1838, noted that 'canals, ever since their adoption have undergone little or no change ... in their general economy they may be said to have remained stationary'.[65] The general level of investment in canal improvement and modernisation after 1800 was simply 'too little and too late for the economy as a whole'.[66]

The difficulty for the canals after the arrival of the railways was that enlargement of their network was much more expensive and time-consuming, while the return on investment was bound to be less than with the railways. Almost immediately in the 1840s private investment in canals collapsed and a long period of neglect set in. Only a few canals, such as the Aire and Calder Navigation between Leeds and the Humber, carried out any serious improvements to locks and banks.[67] While the railways could more or less go anywhere, and the track could be extended to meet demand, the canals remained limited to the transport of low value bulk goods that could be moved more slowly, often in combination with coastal shipping. Until the advent of the railways the movement of high value goods which needed to be delivered swiftly still had to go by road and at a high cost. The railways triumphed because of their flexibility: they could move bulk goods like coal and deliver finished products to widely diverse markets. By comparison with the railway wagon, the canal barge was inflexible in that, if it was not fully laden, it was uneconomic to use. Small consignments had to go by land.

Had the English canal system been more integrated, and planned more from above, the system might have developed in symmetry with the railways, with the burden of transport more efficiently divided between them. Canals might, for example, have continued to carry a greater load of bulk goods into the twentieth century. But the unwillingness of local canal companies to amalgamate with others, as the railway companies did steadily throughout the rest of century, and the lack of a standardised gauge, made them poor partners for the newer technology. From London to Birmingham, one of the most critical distribution channels in the country, a barge still had to go through canals owned by five different companies at the end of the century; and, because of the differences between them in gauge and lock size, only the smallest barges could be used for a through journey. By 1900 English canals were in a lamentable state. Most were unprofitable and many of them were in an advanced stage of dilapidation. Some were even health hazards. In 1874 in Nottingham the Great Northern Canal Company was paid to cleanse the Nottingham Canal 'whose dangerously insanitary condition was caused by sewage which flowed in from the [River] Leen'.[68]

By the late 1880s less than twenty canal companies were still making worthwhile profits, and these were short links in industrial areas heavily dependent on the reliable movement of raw materials.[69] Most attempts to improve the performance of the longer canals in the nineteenth century failed. Companies degenerated into a policy of general obstruction, trying to use what remained of their power to force the railway companies either to buy them out or to cover their losses. The usual method was to threaten to oppose a railway Bill and then announce the price for withdrawing their opposition. The London and Birmingham Railway acquired control of the Birmingham Canal Navigation because the latter threatened in 1845 to seek powers to build a rival railway up the Stour Valley. The railway company was only able to overcome this threat by guaranteeing a certain return on the canal company's capital, making up any deficiency of revenue, which it did from 1874 right down to 1910 – at a total cost of £874,652.[70] While it may have been occasionally true, as is often claimed, that railway companies acquired canals in order to smother them,[71] the more likely motive was a railway buying off a canal company to be rid of a rival's blocking tactics. In fact legislation in 1845 and 1847 tried to keep the canals going by allowing them to vary their tolls; but, although canal companies increased competition with the railways by lowering their hitherto monopolistic rates, they made little effort to consolidate amongst themselves as the railways were already in the process of doing.

At the end of the nineteenth century there was a canal renewal movement in Britain which favoured canals being brought into state ownership, with a view to improving them to the level where they could compete with the railways. In 1906 a Royal Commission investigated the state of Britain's inland waterways and recommended in its 1909 report that the canals be taken into state ownership and that urgent widening and modernising work be undertaken, particularly on the canals radiating from Birmingham. Comparison with progress on the European Continent was common by the end of the century, but there was a fundamental difference between canals in Britain and those abroad. Given the difficulty of getting over the Pennine chain, English canals were inevitably plagued with a long series of locks – the Leeds and Liverpool Canal is the obvious example.[72] There is no equivalent in Britain of the long flat stretches of land in Holland, Belgium or North Germany; on the 230 miles of waterway between Hamburg and Berlin, for example, there were only three locks, while Britain averaged one for every mile of waterway. In Britain canal builders were compelled to reduce construction costs and economise on water by keeping lock widths narrow at the higher elevations in the centre of the country. Barges which navigated the lower reaches of a canal on the east or west side were too wide to get over the top. By contrast the continental Europeans were blessed with very large rivers, including the Rhine, Danube, Elbe and Rhone, which were potentially navigable for great distances by barges carrying up to 2000 tons. European canal builders had geography on their side when they planned the critical links between these imposing waterways. German inland navigation, where the state of Prussia was the chief canal-builder, consisted largely of canals which connected or lengthened existing navigable rivers; and, unlike the British system, the Germans used navigable and canalised rivers much more than dead-water canals.[73] In addition, because British canal construction was earlier, at a time when their only competitor across land was the horse-drawn wagon, they were not planned to compete – or cooperate – with the railways as were German or French canals. While in England railway competition destroyed the canals, in France and Germany canals were developed in coordinated fashion by the state, side by side with state-owned railways.[74] In Germany internal navigation increased 65 per cent from 1875 to 1885 and by the end of the century close to a quarter of all internal traffic in Germany was carried by water, at a time when both Britain and the Continent were experiencing an enormous expansion of railway traffic. In France, Belgium and Germany waterways were cheaper than rail, particularly for the carriage of coal. Tonnage on waterways grew in the last quarter of the nineteenth century in those three countries by between 73 per cent and 274 per cent compared to Britain, where it increased by only 8 per cent, despite the opening of the Manchester Ship Canal in 1894.[75]

What can we conclude about the British Canal Age between 1760 and 1830? First, it is hard to see it as representing anything approaching a technological breakthrough in transport or the basis for a national transport system; certainly it is not comparable to the Railway Age of the mid nineteenth century. The idea that canal excavation was little more than an inevitable step beyond river improvement is persuasive. The know-how needed for lock and sluice construction, and for boring tunnels and building aqueducts, was in the main not indigenous and had little relationship to the vital new technologies of the Industrial Revolution, particularly developments in metallurgy. On the other hand, the Canal Age did afford a new generation of entrepreneurs and engineers valuable experience in the organisation of men and money. Brindley and his colleagues learnt how to organise and exploit the labour of navvies, and the country learnt for the first time the meaning of labour mobility as these armies of workmen moved across the face of central England from canal to canal. Meanwhile the businessmen who backed canal projects in the late eighteenth century acquired the skills needed to raise finance for major infrastructure projects (and of course any other enterprise) through the mechanism of the joint stock company.

Secondly, canals were created within a regional context and their economic impact tended to be regional rather than national in character. This reflects the claim that industrialisation in Britain was a regional affair triggered at different stages during the course of the late eighteenth and early nineteenth century, and 'by no means a single, uninterrupted, and unitary, still less a nation-wide process'.[76] Canals boosted and consolidated intra-regional trade and industrial growth, very often to the point where industries appeared on or in close proximity to the canals themselves. Indeed they went a long way towards creating Britain's industrial regions. They were far less effective, however, as a transport medium at the national level and in the creation of a national market for the fruits of industrialisation – this task had to await the coming of the railways. Even in the supply of coal, canals were not able to generate a national market and had little noticeable effect on the price of coal in other, more distant regions of the country.[77]

Thirdly, canals were critical *within* regions for the delivery of coal, the fuel of industrialisation. Because coal fields were comparatively compact areas, a canal linking the collieries to major cities or industrial consumers had every prospect of being used intensively and made good financial sense. By contrast the transport by canal of agricultural produce, drawn from a much wider area and involving considerable overland transport before the canal journey could even begin, had less chance of success.[78] Similarly the distribution of manufactured goods from factory to customer did not lend itself so easily to canal transport as the final destination points were obviously widely spread.

An American geographer has said that British canals 'lasted far longer as a morphological entity than they did in the consciousness of Britons'.[79] It is interesting that nowadays, two hundred years since they were excavated, they hold an increasing attraction for so-called 'nostalgia tourists'. While their original role as freight carriers may have dwindled to almost nothing, the canals which are still operational have found a new role in passenger transport for families of holiday-makers on narrow boats.[80] As historical artefacts and evidence of the back-breaking labour needed to build them, they seem to hold a special fascination for the late twentieth-century layman; indeed a glance at the richly illustrated website of the 'Canal Junction' heritage association and tourist agency might even give one the impression that British canals are experiencing a new renaissance.[81]

2

Coastal Shipping

Up to the beginning of the nineteenth century, transport in Britain was divided according to the nature of whatever was being transported. This meant that passengers, and high-value goods which had to be delivered reasonably fast, usually went by road, while less urgent, low-value bulk goods went more slowly and cheaply by coastal ship, canal or navigable river.

From the geographical standpoint, transport by coastal ship is the natural and obvious way of moving people and goods around a narrow island like Britain. Amongst European nations, only Italy, Spain and Sweden have a similarly extensive coastline, and none of them has the advantage for transport of being an island. In the seventeenth century it was already recognised that England had more coastline per square mile of land than any other country in Europe.[1] The value of coastal transport around Britain, moreover, was enhanced by its rivers, the navigable portions of which flowed into the sea in a manner which allowed river and canal navigation to connect almost seamlessly with coastal shipping. The average size coaster in the eighteenth century was little larger than a nineteenth-century canal barge and was usually able to penetrate some distance inland on Britain's navigable rivers, transforming itself with ease from sea-borne to fresh-water vessel.[2] The coast was a major transport artery for Britain and sailing vessels could be seen in most of its waters, particularly on the more direct eastern side where the coasting trade was the chief means by which Londoners lived and prospered. Of course the geographical blessing was tempered with historical reality, and coastal shipping was vulnerable to war and weather to a far greater degree than overland transport. Coastal vessels could easily become targets for pirates or marauding enemy ships in times of war (a frequent state of affairs in the eighteenth century), or lost without trace in storms and gales.[3] Nevertheless, by the end of the eighteenth century coastal shipping was a indispensable part of Britain's transport infrastructure. Coastal vessels buzzed like worker bees in and out of the string of ports – London, Southampton, Exeter, Bristol, Swansea, Liverpool, Glasgow, Leith, Newcastle, Hull and Lynn – which lay at convenient intervals around the coastline, nearly all of them located to give good access to the burgeoning industrial heartlands of the interior.

Before the application of the steam engine to transport, coastal shipping, like its deep-water sister, relied on sailing vessels. Water-borne traffic was ubiquitous and coastal transport was a natural extension of inland navigation on rivers and canals. The advantage of coastal transport for cargo in the eighteenth century was obvious: a typical coaster transported fifty tons – a load that would have required no less than four hundred packhorses or twelve large wagons over land. The capital and running costs of horse-drawn land transport per ton mile were at least twice as high as those for coasters and the prices charged were correspondingly higher.[4] On the other hand, coastal shipping in the days before steam was susceptible to delays caused by bad weather or adverse winds and tides, and the time of arrival of goods sent by coaster was less easily predicted than that of goods carried over land. It was not uncommon for coastal colliers from Tyneside to be held up for weeks by a contrary wind, with the inevitable result that the price of coal in London was driven too high for the poor to buy it. Alternatively, a sudden change in the wind would bring dozens of collier brigs into the Pool of London, flooding the market with coal, precipitating a price collapse and ruining the merchants.

This unpredictability of delivery meant that British coastal transport before steam was really only valuable for goods which were bulky, non-perishable and of low unit value. Grain, ore, pig iron, timber, bricks, building stone and slate, fertiliser and manure, and most important, coal, were all transported to optimal advantage by sailing coaster, whereas small manufactured goods and perishable farm produce were better dispatched by wagon or packhorse despite the poor state of Britain's roads. The relatively low cost of coastal shipping in the late eighteenth century, combined with internal water-borne transport, is illustrated by a remarkable, yet apparently typical case from 1775: it paid the Horsehay Company (a Shropshire ironmaster) to deliver its pig iron to Chester (hardly sixty miles away by road) by carting it to the Severn and thence transporting it by trows (barges) to Bristol, where an agent, John James, put it on a vessel that sailed round the Welsh coast to the Dee.[5]

A large percentage of British sailing vessels in the eighteenth century were coasters. 'There are supposed to be about eighteen hundred ships and vessels in the Coal trade and about nine hundred more in what they call the Northern trade', wrote a naval officer in 1774.[6] By far their most important cargo was coal. Indeed the transport of coal dominated the business of coastal shipping for at least 350 years. Between 1670 and 1750, London alone imported more than forty million tons of coal.[7] So completely did coal dominate coastal shipping that the combined trade in all other minerals could not match it in volume. It was as true of the mid eighteenth century as of the mid nineteenth and mid twentieth that the tonnage of coal carried exceeded by far the weight of any other cargo. Not only would many thousands have gone cold in the winter months but for this trade, but also a number of important industries would have been starved of one of their essential raw materials, for large amounts of coal were required in brick-making, glassmaking, brewing, sugar refining, and in the manufacture of salt, lime alum and a wide variety of metals.

Second to coal in importance in the coastal trade was grain. By the late seventeenth century London wharves like Wiggens Key were already handling large quantities of corn from Kent and East Anglia, delivered to the metro-polis by coastal sailing sloops of around forty tons, known as hoys. In the absence of proper quays, the vessels were obliged to moor midstream in the Thames, from which lighters transhipped the cargo to the wharves and warehouses which lined the river around London Bridge. The effect of this time-consuming and labour-intensive procedure was to increase the cost of coastal transport.[8]

While bulk goods were the optimum cargo for coasters, many ships also took passengers; indeed coasters in the days of sail provided a means of transport for passengers to a much greater extent than might be imagined, though its use was generally limited to the months between April and October when the risk of storms was less. Probably the most frequented passenger route was from London to Kentish seaside resorts such as Margate and Ramsgate. According to one source, as many as 18,000 people used these coastal vessels to reach the Kentish resorts in 1792.[9] Meanwhile the east coast route, justly famous as a coal road, also saw a lot of passenger traffic. Smacks (another type of sailing sloop) regularly took passengers from Leith, the port of Edinburgh, on their voyages to London, and it was also common for travellers from the south west of England to use coasters rather than road transport to get to London, as the fare by water was much cheaper. The drawback to coastal transport as a means of passenger conveyance was the same as for cargo: the time of arrival was unpredictable and the journey itself could be extremely unpleasant if a storm was encountered. In 1743, for example, one of the Leith to London sailing packets took twenty days to get as far as Holy Island, off the coast of Northumberland. And Jonathan Swift, wanting to travel to Ireland in 1727, waited five days at Holyhead for a favourable wind and had not been at sea an hour before an adverse wind forced the captain to put back to harbour.[10]

Although the steam engine is most commonly associated with the railways, the coastal *steamboat* actually represents the first use of steam power in transport. In the early nineteenth century the transport of passengers and freight by steamboat grew quickly in British coastal waters and on short sea journeys, such as from Hull to Hamburg or Liverpool to Dublin. These early steamboats were restricted to coastal and short sea trading because their inefficient engines needed such vast quantities of coal to keep them going that the ships were obliged to stay close to the coast and fresh supplies of fuel.[11] Besides coasting work they also performed as tugs, ferries and excursion boats in and around river estuaries. On the Thames the passenger traffic between London and Gravesend grew quickly after the steamboat *Margery* began services in January 1815. By 1842 there were sixteen steamboats on this route, landing and embarking well over a million passengers annually at Gravesend.[12] On Tyneside the Tyne Steam Packet was ferrying passengers from Newcastle to Shields as early as May 1814, although more important in this region was the early use of steam tugs to tow sailing colliers out to sea when the prevailing wind made it impossible to leave harbour with the aid of sail alone.[13] On the Clyde, steamboats linked Glasgow with the suburbs and the holiday resorts in the estuary. For a long time people commuted to Glasgow by steamboat rather than by stage coach, and those seeking recreation on the river banks, or at Rothesay and Dunoon, also took the steamer. On the Mersey the story was the same and ferry services between Liverpool and Runcorn with the *Elizabeth* started in 1815 with similar links to Birkenhead established in 1817.[14]

Between 1820 and the early 1850s, by which time the basic structure of the railway system was in place, British transport was in a state of transition. No one transport mode was obviously superior for any type of cargo or passenger, and a merchant might send his goods to market by a combination of systems according to cost. After 1850 the use of such a diversity of transport forms decreased as the railways were more and more able to carry goods directly to their markets. By this time coastal shipping had largely reverted to its traditional role of moving bulky low-value raw materials and farm produce. In the interregnum in the first half of the century, however, coastal shipping used the new technology of steam to develop a major new business in passenger transport.

Open-sea coastal passenger services – ferry services – were rapidly established around the British Isles. As early as June 1813, the *Rob Roy* provided a twice-weekly summer service between Glasgow and Belfast.[15] Summer services between Glasgow and Liverpool started in the following year. In June 1821 the London and Edinburgh Steam Packet Company began carrying passengers between the two capitals in the four hundred ton *City of Edinburgh* and her sister ship the *James Watt*.[16] Further up the coast the Leith and Aberdeen Steam Yacht Company's vessel *Tourist* began passenger services between Leith and Aberdeen in 1821, calling at intermediate ports.[17] On the south coast the Plymouth, Devonport, Portsmouth and

Falmouth Steam Packet Company began regular summer sailings in 1823, its ships sometimes calling at Torquay and Cowes en route between Plymouth and Portsmouth.[18] By 1825 steamers on the line between London and the southern Irish port of Cork were also calling at Plymouth, Portsmouth and Cowes.[19] All these services were limited to the summer months because none of the steamship companies in the 1820s had enough confidence in their vessels' seaworthiness to maintain services in the winter. What helped to persuade them to establish continuous services was the decision of the Post Office to provide all the year round steam packets for the important Holyhead-Howth (for Dublin) station from the end of May 1821, to maintain similar arrangements for the mail routes between Milford and Dunmore (for Waterford) from April 1824, between Portpatrick and Donaghadee (for Belfast) from May 1825, and between Liverpool and Dublin from August 1826. Whatever the shortcomings of the vessels employed in respect of creature comforts, there is no doubt of the superior regularity and punctuality of the sailings of the Royal Mail steamboats: it was the Post Office which set the standards of steamship operation in the 1820s which other steamship companies sought to follow.[20]

British coastal passenger steamship services achieved their greatest extent and importance in the early 1840s when there were over 1400 route-miles of regular sailings linking ninety ports and harbours.[21] From crowded estuaries, like the lower reaches of the Clyde and Thames, to the infrequent but vital links to the Shetland Islands or the Isles of Scilly, the steamboat had become an essential part of transport in the British Isles. It is impossible to give any precise figure as to the number of people who used this means of travel each year, but by adding together the estimates given by witnesses before parliamentary committees on railway and harbour Bills it is possible to give some indication of the extent to which steamboats were used in the early years of Queen Victoria's reign. Apart from the estuarial services on the Thames and Clyde, which together carried at least a million and a half passengers each year, and the short steam ferry services in the Mersey, the Humber, the Tyne, the Bristol Channel and the Solent, which probably accounted for as many more, steamers on the east coast at various points between Aberdeen and Margate carried about 250,000 persons annually. As late as 1849 only 5792 passengers were booked by the North British Railway from Edinburgh to London in a year when 11,584 persons took the sea route, while on the west coast 53,456 passengers were carried between Glasgow and Liverpool in 1841. On the other hand, coastal traffic around the Cornish peninsula was strongly disadvantaged vis-à-vis overland transport and was quickly eroded by the railways: an estimated 12,000 people sailed between Bristol and Exeter in 1836, the number falling sharply after the opening of the Taunton-Exeter stretch of the Bristol and Exeter Railway in May 1844.[22]

The popularity of passenger steamship services in the second quarter of the nineteenth century is explained by their much greater speed and reliability when compared with the sailing ship, and by their cheapness compared with coach travel. In December 1834, at a time of year when coastal sailing smacks rarely ventured out to sea, the steam packet *Manchester* made the return trip from Liverpool to Glasgow within sixty hours, an achievement for speed and turn-round considered quite remarkable at the time. Passenger fares for the single trip of 240 miles were only £1 5s., or less than 1½d. a mile, compared with 2d. a mile for an outside seat on a coach or twice that amount for an inside seat.[23] Steamboat proprietors were in a position to undercut coach fares because each steamboat was able to carry many times the number of persons that could be accommodated on the most overcrowded stage coach – an economy of scale in transport that was to reappear over a century later with the development of passenger aircraft.

The early history of the passenger steamship services saw keen competition between small concerns anxious to capture a share of an increasingly popular – and profitable – means of transport. From the summer of 1831 the ships of the London and Edinburgh Steam Packet Company were in fierce rivalry with the London, Leith, Edinburgh and Glasgow Shipping Company, which in that year introduced the brand new steamers *Royal William, Royal Adelaide* and *Victoria* to challenge the earlier established *Soho, James Watt* and *United Kingdom* regularly plying the Leith-London station. The usurpers claimed of the *Royal William* that it was 'admitted by all to be unrivalled in the elegance and comfort of her accommodation' and that she had established 'a decided superiority in speed over all the other vessels'. The rival company dismissed this claim in newspaper advertisements, asserting of the *Soho* and *James Watt* that 'the well known character of these vessels supersedes the necessity of any comment as to their speed, safety and comfort'.[24] Competition between steamship companies was accompanied by ruinous rate-cutting, followed by the inevitable truce and consolidation. On the east coast the London and Edinburgh Steam Packet Company was bought up by the General Steam Navigation Company (GSNC) in 1836,[25] while the rivalry between the City of Dublin Steam Packet Company and the St George's Steam Packet Company for the Irish Sea trade ended with a pooling agreement in June 1826.[26]

Steam power was adopted more slowly for cargo than for passenger coastal traffic. There was not the same sense of urgency in the delivery of goods as there was to complete a frequently unpleasant passenger sea voyage. A much greater amount of capital had been invested in cargo vessels before steam, and the men who had spent a lifetime in learning how to man sailing vessels were understandably reluctant to change. The initial investment in building and equipping a steamship was far greater than that for a sailing vessel of comparable size. In the mid nineteenth-century coal trade between Newcastle and London, a new screw-propelled steam collier cost around £10,000, while a second-hand sailing vessel could be bought for £1200; the cost of buying six new sailing collier brigs of 300 tons capacity each was no more than that of one new screw collier suitable for carrying 600 tons of coal.[27]

Once the railway system had been created, however, the inertia against converting coastal cargo transport to steam was overcome. Meanwhile the passenger steam packets were increasingly threatened by the railways, except where geography came to their aid, as in the case of cross-channel or island services. Their attempts to stay competitive with the railways focused on cutting fares. When a rail link was established to Edinburgh in 1846, the GSNC reduced steamship fares between London and Edinburgh for first class cabin passengers from £4 4s. to £3 and for second class cabin passengers from £2 10s. to £1 15s. Three years later there were further reductions to £2 10s. and £1 10s., presumably because the earlier changes had not arrested the passengers' growing preference for rail. By 1885 coastal passenger fares, including the steward's fee in the chief cabin, were down to £2 2s. and in the second class cabin to 16s.[28] The GSNC, which gained its main revenue from the short sea routes on the North Sea, kept the passenger service on the east coast largely as a feeder to its more lucrative north European traffic. Passenger coastal liner services continued until the First World War, and beyond, and provided a source of competition with the railways which helped to keep down rail fares on the east coast and on other routes such as Glasgow-Liverpool.

Steadily, coastal shipping switched – or rather reverted – to a cargo-carrying role, specialising in the bulk goods like coal and grain which had been its staple cargo in the days of sail. Coal was the most important cargo in the late nineteenth century by a wide margin. By the 1880s the single largest coastal trade was the transport of coal from the north east to London and other southern ports. These colliers, which were often large and returned north with water ballast, kept London warm and lit, and supplied large coal consumers like power stations and gas works, brewers and sugar refiners. Coal was also critical on other coastal stations. For south Wales the rapid expansion of steam navigation both increased the demand for the bituminous coal with which the region was so richly endowed and provided the means for its much wider distribution around the Bristol Channel, to Liverpool and the south coast – this, of course, in addition to the booming export trade in Welsh coal. Coastal shipments of coal from Cardiff rose from 171,978 tons in 1833 to 2,644,520 tons in 1911. For London, sea-borne Welsh coal remained uncompetitive with Newcastle coal because of the greater cost of the longer journey round the Cornish peninsula and along the English Channel.[29]

Next to the trade in Tyneside coal to London, grain, livestock and other agricultural produce ranked high as cargo for the typical steam coaster. Wholesale meat salesmen took advantage of steam navigation to bring livestock more speedily from northern Scotland to the markets of Edinburgh and London, avoiding the damaging loss of weight associated with the driving of cattle and sheep 'on the hoof'. The trade in both live and dead meat grew rapidly until the 1850s, when the railways began to take away most of the dead meat business, although the steamships clung to a larger share of the livestock.[30] Cattle dealers and arable farmers in the western part of Scotland also took advantage of the facilities offered by the steamboat. Thanks to the opening of regular services between Annan, Dumfries and Liverpool, cattle and grain could be resold within a few days of purchase and the dealer was in a position to pay cash to the farmer, who in turn acquired a new confidence to sell more of his produce in distant markets.[31] Coastal trade with Ireland was also dominated by livestock and agricultural produce. With the opening of British ports to foreign corn from 1846, and the Irish famine of 1845–47, the cargo ships of the Irish Sea changed from transporting grain to supplying meat and livestock. Whereas in the 1820s, at the dawn of the steam age, about 200,000 head of cattle were shipped from Ireland to England, by the 1860s the number had increased to over a million annually.[32] Steam shipping, with its reliability and speed, made the livestock trade across the Irish Sea a much more attractive proposition to Irish cattle breeders. It also made the trade in Irish eggs profitable for the first time. With the greater certainty of sales, more poultry was reared and trade expanded.[33] Irish entrepreneurs were also pioneers of steam in cross-channel shipping – indeed steam transformed shipping on the Irish Sea. While sailing ships had taken anything up to three weeks to complete the voyage between Dublin and Liverpool, by the 1850s steam vessels were doing the trip in under ten hours and it had become one of the busiest passenger lines in the world. Irish owners built more new large and powerful steamers than any other owners in the British Isles.[34]

For the greater part of the nineteenth century, the collective efforts of the sailors who manned the ships to improve their wages and living standards were generally ineffective. Even on regular short-distance passenger packet boats wages were paid sporadically. The earnings of those who worked the collier brigs out of the port of Sunderland were highly unpredictable.

In 1854 a sliding scale of wages was adopted, varying with the freight charge, per ton of coal, carried to London. When coal was carried for 6s. a ton, able seamen's wages were £3 15s. a voyage; with coal at 12s. a ton, wages were £6 15s. Thus a man's yearly earnings fluctuated according to the state of the weather (and the number of voyages completed) and the state of the coal market. Men employed on the early screw colliers were more fortunate. Though their rate, at £2 15s., was less per voyage than that of the men employed on the sailing vessels, their annual earnings at £80 8s. were double because the steamships could complete thirty round trips a year to the sailing ships' ten.[35] Men employed on steam packets could also count on a more regular rhythm to their working lives. Times of payment as well as the duration of voyages were more predictable; and, because their main function was to carry passengers, their ships were cleaner and more seaworthy. The labour of able seamen and firemen on steamships could, however, be very arduous. After their ship was tied up in harbour the crew of the City of Dublin Steam Packet Company's Prince Arthur were usually employed blacking the funnels, scraping the soot off the masts, cleaning the steam pipes, coating the ship's bottom or lending a hand to the painters. The crew was not even at liberty to do as it pleased on off-duty days. Against the date 26 December 1852 the master of the ship wrote 'Ship's company sent to church'.[36] By contrast, life on board the superseded sailing ships in the second half of the century was much worse. On the collier brigs, which employed a majority of the sailors engaged in the English coasting trade, living conditions were overcrowded and filthy. Under pressure from the steam colliers to cut costs, the owners skimped on maintenance and repairs with the inevitable result that losses among the ships were appalling: no fewer than 675 collier brigs went to the bottom in the winter season of 1865–66 alone.[37]

Throughout the nineteenth century Britain experienced a relentless process of industrialisation and urbanisation that would have been quite impossible without a modern transport system. The national railway network, which was established with almost startling rapidity from the 1840s onwards, has rightly been given pride of place in this system's development. Coastal shipping also played a vital role, however, and this fact has to some degree been overlooked; indeed the paucity of historical research into the subject – in comparison with the railways and even ocean shipping – suggests that it has been neglected.[38] Measured by tonnage entering British ports, coastal shipping was more important than ocean shipping for the entire nineteenth century. In 1841, for example, coastal shipping entries, at over 12,500,000 tons (excluding ballast), were three times the tonnage entering from foreign and colonial trade.[39]

Coastal shipping was also extremely varied – its strength and the secret of its survival. There were coastal liners operating scheduled steamship services between ports, carrying passengers and small cargoes. There were regular cargo coasters specialising in a certain trades, like the steam colliers that brought coal from the Durham coal fields to markets in the south of England. There were coastal tramps which traded around the British coastline and occasionally at continental ports.[40] Lastly, there were the dwindling number of coastal sailing ships which were still able to offer the lowest prices for bulk cargo transport. Coastal shipping grew steadily throughout the century and the railways did not cause it to decline in the way they seem to have affected the canals. By 1900 coastal shipping was really the only transport mode in Britain that remained competitive with the railways for the long-distance transport of bulky cargoes such as coal, grain, iron ore, china clay, bricks and timber, fodder and manure. Notwithstanding its contribution to passenger traffic, this is where coastal shipping's true value lay. How would London have been kept illuminated and warm in winter without the daily arrivals of Newcastle 'sea-coals' in the Thames estuary? How would Londoners have been fed without the steady stream of coasters laden with grain and livestock? How would new dwellings have been built without the bricks and cement which came by the coastal route?

Coastal shipping was vital to London, indeed to the entire coal-based economy of the nineteenth century. Throughout the century, London's predominance over the coastal trade of the British Isles was unchallenged. Although the tonnage of shipping involved and the quantities of merchandise carried both increased up until the First World War, the pattern of the trade did not alter significantly. In 1824, of the 2,230,000 tons of merchandise brought into London by coastal shipping, 84 per cent was coal and 14 per cent grain. In contrast with what it brought in from other British ports, London sent out along Britain's coasts a variety of produce, although foodstuffs, textiles and alcoholic beverages took the lion's share. Except for places within a short radius of the capital, foodstuffs could be supplied more cheaply by sea than by land. Eighty years later, at the beginning of the twentieth century, coal still dominated London's coastal imports; the quantity entering the Thames in 1905 (8,494,234 tons) having more than doubled over the preceding eighty years.[41] At the same time imports of grain from British ports declined sharply in the last quarter of the nineteenth century, so that in 1895 they amounted to 36,588 tons, or little more than 10 per cent of the amount brought in 1825.[42] There was, however, in compensation a remarkable growth in imports of hay to feed London's burgeoning horse population. This fodder for horse trams and hackney cabs was brought up the Thames in special flat-bottomed barges which carried twelve-foot-high haystacks on their decks. In the heyday of this traffic, just before the First World War, hundreds of vessels were employed in this trade stretching from Harwich to the Pool of London. On occasions as many as thirty of these 'stackies', as they were known, could be seen sailing up river. The trade was a profitable one, for there was an assured return cargo of horse manure shipped via such harbours as the appropriately-named Mucking on the Essex shore of the Thames estuary to the farms further up the Essex coast which supplied the hay.[43]

One of coastal shipping's most lasting and significant contributions to Britain's transport infrastructure was the impulse it gave to port and harbour development. As the railway became more universal in the second half of the nineteenth century, it became apparent that, for the coastal cargo trade to survive, ships' efficiency would have to be improved: by the enlargement of their carrying capacity, the adoption of steam power and the quicker turn round of ships in port so that shipping freights and delivery times would remain competitive with the railways. The enlargement and deepening of Britain's harbours required massive investment on the part of railway companies, river commissioners, the government and private investors. Port authorities which failed to meet the challenge provided by the larger steamships and lagged behind others in the improvement of navigation in their district soon fell behind their more enterprising rivals.

Under the Harbours and Passing Tolls Act of 1861, the government authorised the Public Works Loan Commissioners to lend money at low rates of interest to harbour authorities carrying out works of modernisation and improvement. In the following twenty years nearly a million pounds was advanced to supplement local efforts at Aberdeen, Belfast, Falmouth, Greenock and Newhaven, and on Teesside and Tyneside. In the same twenty years over £22,000,000 of private and municipal capital was invested in new harbour works.[44] On Tyneside, Teesside and the Wear the coastal trade in coal provided the impetus for dock and riverside improvements. From the moment the first iron screw collier, the *John Bowes*, entered the Thames in July 1852, the proportion of coal coming from the north east in steamships increased rapidly. But because they cost more to build and run than the sailing brigs they replaced, they could only be kept in service economically if they were able to discharge their cargoes quickly and complete thirty round trips between the north east and London each year, compared with the eight to ten trips managed by the brigs. This was a powerful incentive to the authorities responsible for the ports of the north east and on the Thames to provide modern cranes, deep anchorages and extended berthing space. A significant milestone in the improvement of the shipping facilities on Tyneside was the passing of the River Tyne Improvement Act in 1850, providing for joint control over the river by the Admiralty and the four municipalities of Newcastle, Gateshead, Tynemouth and South Shields through a Tyne Improvement Commission.[45] Within the next twenty years the navigability of the river was transformed through a massive campaign of dredging. The quantity of earth removed from the river bed to widen and deepen the channel of navigation and increase harbour acreage rose from 496,402 tons in 1859 to 5,273,588 tons in 1869.[46] Without these far-reaching improvements, the increase of Tyneside coal shipments from 3,805,633 tons in 1850 to 20,299,955 tons in 1913 would have been impossible.[47]

Further north in Edinburgh new facilities had to be built to handle the growing size of the passenger steam packets. As long as they were under 200 tons, the chain pier built in 1821 at Newhaven served its purpose well; but a decade later the powerful ships coming into service drew more than the maximum six feet of water available at low tide and they were obliged either to await a favourable tide or to anchor out at sea. The Duke of Buccleuch then sponsored the construction of a new pier at Granton for the steam packets. Meanwhile the cargo trade of Leith was developing rapidly and in 1847 the government granted £135,000 for a new dock (the Victoria Dock) which was opened in 1852.[48] The trend to larger vessels, as steam engines grew in size and power, and marine engineering developed, meant that the smaller harbours became inaccessible, and from 1870 steam coasters abandoned many of them to concentrate on the larger ports like London, Bristol and Newcastle-on-Tyne. In southern England piers were constructed at a large number of seaside resorts to cater for the growing steamship traffic – a new form of steamboat tourism. Southend is an example of where it was the building of a pier rather than a railway which gave the initial boost to the town's popularity and its expansion. The first 'New Pier', built opposite the Royal Hotel in 1802, stood in water too shallow to accommodate the steamships which began to call from 1819 onwards. Visitors to Southend in those days needed to possess a stoical patience. When the steamers had sailed far enough inshore for safety they had to wait for small vans, capable of carrying seventeen persons, to cross more than a mile of sand to their rescue. The alternative, much preferred by adventurous young maidens, was to be carried ashore on the backs of sailors. These romantic opportunities ceased in 1830 when steamers started to call at the second 'New Pier'. With the problem of landing resolved (at least for some years), there was a tremendous rise in the number of visitors to Southend from London, some seven thousand people making the sea voyage in 1834.[49]

Coastal steam shipping may also be credited with bringing a certain regularity to transport in Britain, although this task was largely fulfilled by the railways. As we have seen, the Post Office set the standard on the

Irish Sea with regular steam packet sailings in the 1820s. The idea of regularity and predictability of arrival is an essential element of modern transport and was beyond attainment until the arrival of the steam engine. For passengers and light cargoes this regularity was manifest in the fact that by 1900 all the major ports of Britain were connected by coasting lines with scheduled times of departure and arrival. For bulk cargoes, the predictability of delivery meant that a national market could be created: coastal coal and grain helped to eliminate local scarcities and even out regional differences in prices. On the other hand, the very vigour and success of coastal shipping may have contributed to delay in the development of overland road transport, to a degree not experienced by nations without a significant coastline. Long before the arrival of the railways delivered a death blow to long-distance coach traffic, the activities of the steamship companies, particularly on the east coast, were causing distress to coach proprietors on routes to the north. In 1837 the revenue of the East Lothian, Berwickshire and North Durham turnpike trusts, for example, was reported to have declined 'in consequence of the steamboats'.[50] A year later, the stage coach proprietors of the Great North Road petitioned Parliament for exemption from taxes on guards and coachmen, and from stage coach duties, because 'improvements in steam navigation' were causing travellers to the north to prefer the sea route.[51]

The critical factor in the ascendancy of British coastal shipping was the combination of the early and widespread adoption of steamships, with the low cost of founding a coasting enterprise. An important reason for the earlier exploitation of steam power for water transport was the far lower initial capital costs involved in launching a coasting enterprise compared with starting a railway. Coastal shippers did not need to raise large amounts of money at the outset, nor did they find themselves burdened with debt repayment for a long time thereafter.[52] While 'the smallest railway company needed to spend millions to purchase land, carry out civil engineering works, buy and lay ballast, sleepers and iron rails, pay for locomotives, wagons, carriages, goods vans and signalling, and then complete stations, goods yards, and bridges ... a coastal shipping company could start with only one ship and this costing from a couple of thousand pounds for a small wooden sailing ship to a few tens of thousands later in the nineteenth century for a triple expansion, steam engined, steel hulled liner.'[53] It could even be cheaper to establish a steamer service than provide for scheduled stage coach travel over the same distance. The steamboats *Superb* and *Robert Bruce*, which provided the first reliable service between Glasgow and Liverpool, cost together less than £16,000. When the Post Office ordered two of the latest steamships to man the Holyhead station in 1821, the cost came to less than

£20,000. By contrast the capital expended on the Newcastle and Carlisle Railway up to the date of the opening of the line was £950,000.[54]

Because steam power was adopted in the coastal trade before it was applied to ocean-going vessels, the early developments in steam engine construction and marine engineering for steamships, took place with coasters. The first experiments and applications of many successful and familiar techniques were to be found among river, coastal and cross-channel shipping.[55] The *Rainbow*, built for the GSNC in 1837 and still sailing in 1871, is claimed to be the first iron sea-going vessel. Not only was this paddle-steamer the fastest ship afloat in 1837, she also pioneered the use of watertight bulkheads.[56] Initially the demand for steam vessels was so great that there were neither enough qualified shipbuilders nor masters knowledgeable enough about steam engines to ensure safety at sea. The earliest coastal steamboats put to sea without being subject to any government regulation as to the safety of their machinery or the number of passengers they were permitted to carry. It took the destruction of the *Telegraph* steam packet at Norwich on 4 April 1817, and the death of many of its passengers through the explosion of its boilers – the weak link in many early steam engines – to persuade Parliament to appoint a Select Committee on Boiler Pressures later that year. Unfortunately, the committee's recommendations were not adopted and Westminster did not stir again on the subject until the number of shipwrecks had reached alarming proportions in the early 1830s. The sinking of the *Rothesay Castle* off Beaumaris on 17 August 1831, with the loss of over a hundred lives, convinced MPs that a further enquiry into steamboat accidents was necessary.[57] The deliberations of the resulting committee of enquiry were, however, as fruitless as those of its predecessor in 1817. Britain had to wait until the Steam Navigation Act of 1846 before the process of regulating steam boat practice could begin. By the mid 1850s passengers boarding coastal steamers were much better protected against disaster at sea than their predecessors of the 1820s and 1830s had been.[58]

By 1910 almost every major British port had a regular coastal liner service for passengers. Coastal shipping was, however, never a large-scale mover of people like the railways, and its strength lay in holiday excursions, cross-channel services and services to islands. The British coaster was, and remains, essentially a cargo vessel. At the end of the nineteenth century coastal shipping remained competitive with the railways for long-distance freight transport and was almost unbeatable in the transport of bulky cargoes like coal, particularly where the coal field lay near the coast. Until the First World War, coasters continued to carry more freight, and at a higher overall speed, than the railways. Between 1908 and 1912, for example, British coasters were responsible for over twenty billion tonne-miles of freight, while the railways carried between thirteen and fifteen billion tonne-miles.[59] During the First World War, coastal coal shipments declined, partly as a result of labour shortages at the mines themselves, and partly because of the need to transfer shipments inland, away from sea lanes which were vulnerable to attack by German U-boats. In the post-war years strikes in 1921 and 1926 caused further breaks in coal shipments, although they reached 270,000 tons in 1927, the last good year before the Depression.[60] There was some recovery in the inter-war years and the process of concentration amongst the smaller coastal shipping firms, which had been in progress since the beginning of the century, strengthened the industry's structure. The trend towards gradual decline persisted, however, and by 1938 coastal shipping had still not recovered its 1913 level of operations.[61]

3

Road Transport before the Car

In the second half of the eighteenth century the population of England and Wales rose by approximately 50 per cent to over nine million in 1800.[1] By the beginning of the railway age in 1830 it had increased to over fourteen million. The population of Scotland grew at the slower rate of one third, to a total of 1,608,000 in 1800. At the beginning of the nineteenth century the people of Britain included a larger number who were industrially employed, though the majority of the population was still engaged in agricultural pursuits as they had been for centuries previously. The regions of industrial growth included, for example, the West Riding of Yorkshire, where the production of woollen cloth rose by four times over the half century,[2] and the iron-founding and coal-mining areas of South Wales and Northumberland and Durham, whose growing importance was reflected in the volume of coastwise shipments, the cotton-spinning and weaving districts of Lancashire, and the linen and silk producing areas of Scotland.

These changes involved the substantial movement of both people and goods. As a growing number of the people were engaged in manufacturing raw materials into finished goods by hand, animal power, water power or steam power, they created a demand for food, clothing and domestic goods. It has been widely assumed that this growing demand was met through the employment of inland navigation – canals and rivers – and coastal shipping. But these forms of transport had their limitations. The wind could be too light or in the wrong direction. Canal transport was slow and subject to delays in winter frost or summer drought. Before the age of steamships, storms and rough seas delayed the sailings of coastal vessels. Most importantly, many centres of population and industry were not easily accessible by river or canal. In any case road transport was needed to reach canal wharves, and ports for coastal vessels or ships trading overseas.

It should not be forgotten that in the second half of the eighteenth century most people born in England and Wales did not travel far from their place of birth. Even as late as the British census of 1841, all sixty-three men listed as 'labourers' in the Dorset village of Stinsford, the model for Thomas Hardy's *Under the Greenwood Tree* had been born in Dorset. Twenty years later 756 of the 1417 inhabitants of Ringmer, Sussex, were born in the parish and 93 per cent of the remainder were born elsewhere in the same county.[3] It could be argued that Dorset and Sussex were exceptional in their degree of immunity from the forces of change; but Durham and the West Riding were also exceptional for the degree of industrialisation already achieved.

In the second half of the eighteenth century there was a great variety in people's modes of travel, depending on income and social standing. The poor travelled long distances on foot – or 'by shanks's pony' to use the colloquial term. It was common for labourers to walk six miles or more a day getting to and from their work. Samuel Bamford, the radical political reformer and one of the organisers of the Manchester meeting which ended in the so-called 'battle of Peterloo' in 1819, wrote of his experiences in walking to London to surrender his bail. When he tried to obtain food and a bed for the night at wayside inns he was repeatedly told that they did not serve anyone who travelled on foot. Many years later he related in his book *Passages in the Life of a Radical* the tactics he had adopted to overcome the prejudices of the proprietor. He did not at first ask for a bed for the night, but instead took possession of a seat at the table and ordered food and a succession of drinks and paid for them, until, at nightfall he was offered a bed by the innkeeper who was by then convinced of his creditworthiness.[4]

For many decades both before and after the coming of the railway the country carrier with horse-drawn wagon was a primitive form of public transport available for those of small means. According to one source, there could be 'no doubt that an integrated system of London and provincial carrier services did exist in the mid eighteenth century' and that the extent of the carrier services network 'was far more considerable than that which is usually accorded'.[5] In 1868, and in earlier decades, it was typical that in every Dorset village 'eager girls with small corded trunks awaited the carrier's cart to take them on their townward journey' and a life of domestic service.[6] The advantage of travelling by carrier's wagon was that it was cheap. It cost as little as a halfpenny a mile, whereas the outside seat on a coach would cost at least three times, and an inside seat six times as much. The disadvantages were that, when the gradient of the road was steep, passengers were often expected to walk, and the average speed of the wagon was no more than three miles an hour. Furthermore, as often as not, the wagon turned aside from its main route to deliver or collect packages in nearby villages. When anyone wanted to reach his destination more quickly there was, in places, the option of travelling by fly wagon such as was illustrated by the artist Thomas Rowlandson in *Kendal Flying Wagon* (1816), but for this privilege he was charged at the rate of 2d. per mile.

Higher up the scale of comfort and speed were the stage coaches, the first of which appeared in the 1630s. At first these only covered the shorter distances, linking nearby towns, though there were a few routes, as between London and York and London and Exeter, which were served by coaches, in summer months only, in the later 1650s. The London-Exeter trip in 1658 took four days.[7] Even in 1780 many provincial towns had no coach services other than those originating in London. The advantage of stage coach travel included a somewhat faster journey time – the average rate was 6.4 miles per hour – accommodation at coaching inns along the route, and generally advertised times for departure and arrival. The chief deterrent to stage coach travel, from the point of view of the poor, was the cost. On a fast coach, fares for 'inside' travellers were typically 4d. or 5d. a mile, while the charge for 'outside' varied between 2d. and 3d. Another uncertainty was the character of your fellow travellers. You might be fortunate and sit next to a considerate and well-mannered person; or you might be landed alongside a talkative busybody for many hours.

Travel by royal mail coach was, by the end of the eighteenth century, considered superior to that by stage coach. From 1635, when King Charles I decided to open the king's postal delivery service to use by the general public, the royal mail was carried by mounted postboys. By about 1780 this system was outmoded. More and more coaches, travelling faster than the six and a half miles per hour which was the rarely achieved objective of the postboys, took to the road and carried (illegally) an ever-increasing proportion of the nation's mail.

John Palmer, a theatre proprietor of Bath, suffered business losses from the delays caused by the postboys, who took nearly two days to deliver the mail from Bath to London. He proposed that the mail should be carried in the latest designed coaches with an armed guard appointed and paid for by the Post Office. The responsibility of providing the horses and recruiting the coachmen was delegated to contractors at different stages of the journey. At first there was strong opposition to Palmer's plan by the Postmasters General, but William Pitt the Younger, who formed his first ministry in December 1783, was more sympathetic and authorised Palmer's 'Mail Diligence' to run between Bristol and London for a trial period in the following year. On 2 August 1784 the vehicle left the Rummer tavern in Bristol. Travelling via Bath, it arrived at the Swan with Two Necks in Lad Lane, Wood Street, London sixteen hours later, an hour less than the time taken by the stage coach and more than a day quicker than the postboys.[8] In the following year permission was given by the government to extend royal mail coach services to other parts of the kingdom, so that by 1791 twenty-six other routes were served, including those to principal towns and cities in England and Scotland (but not yet Wales).[9]

The royal mail coach was highly esteemed because, in its time, it was the best form of public transport available. With an average speed of nine miles an hour, it was faster than any other form of transport. The times of its services were more regular and dependable than any alternative. Delays at each stage were reduced to the minimum. Approaching an inn the coach postillion sounded his horn, warning the ostler at the inn to have the relay horses at the ready, and barmaids brought drinks to the passengers in the coaches where stops were not of sufficient duration to allow disembarkation. But even at the time of their maximum mileage in about 1834, Royal mail coaches only accounted for some 11 per cent of coach mileage.[10] The reason for the limited extent of their operation was their cost. For the decade of the 1790s they carried only 'inside' passengers, who were charged between 5d. and 6d. per mile. To maintain an average of 9 mph, horses had to be stretched to the full, shortening their lives to about three years, little more than half of those drawing the slower of the stage coaches, and giving an excuse to the contractors that they could not lower fares and stay in business.[11]

In the closing years of the eighteenth century stage coach proprietors increased their competition with the royal mail. Their coaches carried inside passengers at 3d. or 4d. a mile and up to ten outside passengers at 2d. a mile. Their times of departure were in the late afternoon, rather than the less convenient 8 p.m. of the many royal mail coaches. The Post Office tried to counter these challenges by gaining the permission of Parliament for provision for outside passengers in 1803. Royal mail coaches were built, serviced and maintained at the Post Office's Millbank factory in London. The experience gained by successive superintendents of the mail coaches prompted one of their number to recommend John Besant's patent for a pedal-released steering catch to prevent wheels locking when turning at speed, and an improved mail axle which prevented wheels coming off when the coach was in motion. These were adopted by the Post Office. In 1804 a more important innovation was linking the coachman's box with the main body and the rear boot. This single unit could be mounted on horizontal springs. The weight of the coach was reduced and its height from the ground lowered, improving the comfort of the passengers.[12] After 4 November 1830, however, when the Post Office signed a contract with the Liverpool and Manchester Railway for the conveyance of mail by train, the writing was on the wall. This would be how the mails were to be carried in the future. The number of royal mail coaches on the road had reached its apogee and no improvement in the technology of the horse-drawn coach could match the speed of the railway in the later 1830s.[13]

The most secluded and elitist of the different forms of horse-drawn means of transport was that of 'travelling post', in practice confined to the wealthiest section of the community. The family coach, often with a coat of arms emblazoned on the door, was drawn by horses, hired from farmers of horses, who were based at staging posts on the public roads. It was the most expensive means of travel; but it ensured to the individual or family who used it freedom to choose either a speedy or more leisurely journey, and freedom from any chance contact that might be made with 'commoners' on the royal mail. The passage of one such vehicle through a village would be an occasion of note. At Lark Rise 'people rushed to their cottage doors' to see 'a carriage with gentry pass by'.[14]

Parson James Woodforde, Rector of Weston Longville, a country parish in Norfolk, from 1774 to 1803, has left us a description in his diary of how a gentleman of the 'middling sort' travelled from a Norfolk village to visit his nephew at Shepton Mallet in Somerset in June 1784. The first part of the journey, to Norwich, was undertaken by post chaise and occupied an entire afternoon. At seven o'clock that evening (24 June), Woodforde, his niece and her brother boarded the 'inside' of the 'heavy coach' to London with three 'strange' women occupying the three remaining inside seats. Woodforde wrote: 'It was very hot this evening.' They breakfasted at an inn before reaching the Swan with Two Necks in Lad Lane and then going on to the Belle Sauvage at Ludgate Hill, their base for sightseeing in London. At the inn they were 'very much pestered and bit by the buggs in the night'. The journey to Bath by the Balloon Coach took sixteen hours, including a stop for breakfast 'at a place I know not'. Such was the 'comfort' of travel by a better off than average citizen of the late eighteenth century.

The consensus expressed by most economic historians is that road transport of goods was so inefficient that, because of its expense, it was little used by comparison with inland waterways.[15] The cost differential between road and waterway transport has been exaggerated, however, because of a failure to take into account such factors as accessibility to centres of demand, wharf dues and insurance. It is dangerous to generalise about the carriage of goods in the eighteenth and early nineteenth century. Each consignor weighed in the balance the advantages and disadvantages of five possible means of transport (royal mail; stage coach; country carrier; inland waterway; and coastal shipping) and opted for the means that served him or her best.

The records of Peter Stubs, a filemaker of Warrington, reveal that where there was a steady demand for his products it paid to use the canals and rivers proximate to his factories; only in the case of meeting an urgent demand did he choose to dispatch the goods by the quicker, but more expensive, land carriage.[16] It would be hard to find a more flexible approach to the problem of sending goods to market than that of the firm of John Wilson,

linen merchants of Leeds, which for most of its half century of existence
obtained its raw linen from Fifeshire in Scotland to be processed by the
factory in Yorkshire. In times of peace, coastal shipping, the cheapest means
of transport, was adopted; but between 1753 and 1762, and after 1793, England
was at war with France. Shipping and insurance rates became prohibitively
high and road transport retained a positive place in the firm's transport. In
1772, however, the Leeds-Edinburgh route was dominated by a single carrier
who raised charges steeply. The decision was promptly made to switch to
sea transport once more. Another influence on the firm's transport policy
was the value of the cloth in relation to its weight, increasing the proportion
of transport costs to the total cost of production and increasing the
attractiveness of the quicker land transport.[17]

In the case of a need for quick delivery, small parcels could be sent by
either royal mail or stage coaches, but these carryings were minimal compared with the contribution made by the carriers. There was some long
distance horse-drawn carrier trade in England even in the 1760s. Provincial
directories show that, although London was the main centre of conspicuous
consumption at that time, and therefore created the biggest demand for
transport services, provincial centres such as Birmingham, Bristol, Nottingham, Newcastle-on-Tyne and Liverpool saw busy daily activity of carriers'
wagons arriving from and departing to other provincial centres and the
capital. There were, for example, twenty-six services a week to Newcastle-
on-Tyne, forty-four to Southampton and forty-six to Bristol.[18]

Through the chance of a prolonged legal dispute between two of the
partners in the firm of Russell and Co., which took place during the first
two decades of the nineteenth century (and the survival of documentary
evidence of this dispute), we know more about the long-distance carrying
between London and Exeter than is known about any other long distance
carriers.[19] After earlier activity as Andover and Dorset carriers, with a largely
localised trade, the partners entered the London-Exeter trade in the 1750s
and gradually built up an organisation second only to Pickfords in the extent
of their operations.

The success of the firm was partly due to successful dedicated control of
a widely scattered organisation. Stables, warehouses and offices were set up
at centres including Andover, Salisbury, Blandford and Dorchester on the
route of the wagon. Thereby a more direct control of provender costs for
horses (the biggest single running cost of the business), farmers and ostlers
for the management of the horses, could be secured. The economy of large
wagons was exploited, as was the benefit of regularity in operation. 'There
were strong internal reasons for regularity in a flying wagon concern since
a complicated arrangements of teams and stops could not otherwise be

maintained.'[20] Great care was exercised in the selection of horses and their positioning in the teams of eight animals that drew the wagons. A mixture of Kentish shire horses and others reared and pastured in the meadows of Derbyshire was found to be the best, since they had greater strength of bone. This policy paid good dividends. In 1820 the firm's horses were moving twice as much weight as had those employed in 1650. The importance of the long-distance wagon services, and especially Russell's concern, was not that they introduced any outstanding technical revolution but that they demonstrated that it was possible to overcome the barriers of distance. This was a gradual transformation rather than a revolution.

Long-distance goods carriage by road disappeared quickly after the coming of the railways. Henry Gray, a job and post master of Birmingham, questioned on 16 April 1839 by a Commons' Select Committee, testified that on the Great North Road and the Birmingham Road the loss of horse-drawn coaches had been 'very great'. His evidence was corroborated by Edward Sherman, the well-known proprietor of the Bull and Mouth Inn, London. The committee came to the general conclusion that:

> The general decline in the transit on Turnpike Roads in some parts of the country arises, not only from the railways formed, but from steam vessels plying on rivers and as coasting vessels. Whenever mechanical power has substituted for animal power, the result has hitherto been that the labour is performed at a cheaper rate.[21]

The outlook for horse-drawn road traffic was not, however, so gloomy as many contemporaries suggested. The committee also reported that 'nearly all roads or highways leading to stations or termini of steam communications, have increased in their traffic'.[22]

The committee was unsure whether the number of carriers who fed the railway stations and termini exceeded the number of long-distance carriers who were driven off the road by the coming of the railway.[23] The total number of country carriers grew to at least 25,000 by the 1880s. They fulfilled an essential function in the growth of the economy in those areas which were not heavily industrialised (such as the Black Country). Unlike the long-distance carriers who linked towns, they linked market towns with their surrounding villages. Only one sixth of villages had a railway station when the railway network was at its fullest extent. Carriers acted as shopping agents buying for their rural customers 'everything from knitting wool to patent medicines, joints of meat and pounds of tea'. The carrier's cart was the chief means by which parcels were delivered from the railhead to their country destinations.[24] They were the only form of public transport in areas not served by the railway, though in this function they were sometimes replaced by the relatively small capacity horse-drawn bus, as in the bus-cum-carrier's cart which linked Tenterden, Cranbrook and Ashford in Kent in the 1880s. Perhaps their most important activity was in carrying the produce of farms to nearby towns for sale to provision merchants or greengrocers. London provided the largest single example of this kind of activity. Country carriers grew in number and the number of miles they traversed increased throughout the railway age, and indeed into the 1920s when motor trucks began to replace them. They provided a door to door service and learned their customers' requirements quickly. Even in the early years of the twentieth century they were indispensable.

The number of carrier services from market towns was surprisingly large, especially in the south of England, which, even in the later years of the nineteenth century, was catching up with the industrial north in individual prosperity. In many areas the carriers' carts were most frequently seen on market days, generally Wednesdays and Saturdays. Zachary Cripps, R. D. Blackmore's fictional carrier, made his visits to Oxford on those days and 'was in and out with the places and the people, as busy as the rest of them'. At the market he had 'a great host of commissions' to execute for his numerous contacts in the outlying villages. He had dealings with 'farmers, butchers, poulterers, hucksters, chandlers and grocers', and the villagers for whom he traded 'knew that he would spend their money quite as gingerly as his own'.[25] Market day carrier services were also much in evidence in Hampshire. The goods carried were extremely diverse and included wine, silk, cheeses, hops and even patent stoves. As a result of the speeding up in movement of the carriers vans, and the more extensive link between the country areas and the towns, the volume of goods moving in and out of Southampton increased twenty times between the 1770s and the early 1830s.[26] Besides the 'common carriers', with their regular routes and days in service, there were also specialists with their smaller carts or donkeys. There were men and women engaged in newspaper rounds, an occupation that was increasing with the growth in production of local newspapers in the nine-teenth century;[27] pedlars who called from house to house and farm to farm, sharpening scythes and shears; and 'egglers', such as Flora Thompson's grandfather, buying up eggs from farms and cottages and selling them to market traders and shopkeepers.[28]

While humans often moved by 'shanks's pony', animals were frequently driven to market 'on the hoof'. The drovers who brought cattle to Smithfield Market in London reputedly had fun stampeding cattle on the way and the tormented beasts sometimes took refuge in shops and houses (probably the origin of the phrase 'a bull in a china shop').[29]

For the entire period up to about 1896 the horse was one of the most expensive pieces of capital equipment used in British transport. William Horne, of the Golden Cross Inn, Charing Cross, who provided horses for both stage and mail coaches, told a Select Committee of the House of Commons on 25 June 1819 that he bought 150 horses a year 'to keep the stock of 400 in order'. Each animal had a useful life of only three years. Another witness to the same committee, William Waterhouse, said that he could buy horses for £15 'at a distance from London, equal to those that they were obliged to give £30 apiece for, on average, for the work near town'. The fact was, as stated by John Eames, the proprietor of the Angel Inn, St Clements, London, that horses 'did not, on average, last above three years in the fast coaches' operating within a radius of fifty miles from London, whereas horses in more distant parts lasted 'as long again'.[30] The work that could be done by a team of four horses pulling a stage coach or a royal mail coach depended very much on the state of the roads they traversed, the speed they were expected to maintain (for the royal mail it was nine miles per hour), and the seasons of the year. Waterhouse commented that from London for the twenty-seven miles to Redbourn a total of twenty-seven horses had to be employed and in winter six horses, rather than four, were required to work each coach because of the 'excessively bad' state of the roads. Charles Johnson, who in 1819 was surveyor and superintendent of mail coaches, said it was reported to him that the mail coach to Exeter lost fifteen or twenty minutes every night because at Egham the road 'had been covered with gravel, unsifted, eight or nine inches deep from side to side' and that, especially in winter, this reduced the ability of the horses to draw the coach at the required speed.[31] It is clear that the way the road was constructed made a substantial difference to the efficiency of horse-drawn transport.[32]

For a long time the government of England and Wales had intervened in an attempt to improve the condition of the roads. By a law of 1555 once a year every common labourer of town or countryside was to give four days unpaid labour, supervised by parish authorities, for the upkeep of the roads. The number of days of 'statute labour', as it became known, was increased to six in 1563. Those of the better off who could afford it were allowed to pay 'composition' money in lieu of working on the roads. In the case of some larger parishes a surveyor was appointed to supervise the work done; but there was little knowledge of road maintenance techniques. Local justices of the peace fixed also the prices carriers and coaches might charge for the carriage of goods over the areas in their jurisdiction. But this system failed to produce much improvement in the roads. The decision by Parliament in 1663 to allow the justices of Hertfordshire to erect toll gates on part of the Great North Road marked a turning point in road history and a stepping stone towards the emergence of the turnpike trust over the older justices' trusts. An Act of 1706 recognised the control which a group of thirty-two trustees exercised over the road from Fernhill to Stony Stratford. This encouraged other districts to follow their example, so that by 1714 the turnpike trust had completely replaced the justices' trust. The Acts which established such trusts gave the trustees power for a period of twenty-one years to erect toll gates, to charge tolls to the users of the road and to use the revenue thus obtained for the maintenance and repair of the highway. Royal mail coaches were always exempt from the payment of tolls.[33]

Already by 1750 the mileage of road turnpiked in England was 1382, with main routes such as the Great North Road and roads from London to Portsmouth, Dover, Harwich, Bristol, Chester and Birmingham turnpiked. In their book *The Story of the King's Highway* the Webbs were right to note that there was no overall plan for road improvement, but they were misleading in their comment that there were 'scattered cases of turnpike administrators unconnected with each other'.[34] The disadvantages of different maintenance standards and the frequent payment of tolls could be overcome by the merging of trusts. This was done for the county of Breconshire in south-east Wales in 1830, with the result that the county's one full-time surveyor had brought its roads up to a higher standard of maintenance than was the case with roads in surrounding counties. Such an amalgamation had been recommended by select committees of both the House of Commons and the House of Lords, the Commons committee recommending that 'persons should be appointed for the purpose of arranging trusts into unions'.[35] But Parliament and the trusts were slow in implementing these reforms. Agitation from a number of wealthy citizens of the City of London led to an amalgamation of trusts in the built up parts of north London (then small in area) into the Metropolitan Roads Commission in 1826. An Act in 1829 removed tolls from this part of North London.[36] The population of the city, however, grew rapidly in the next three decades and spread into suburbs where there were still toll bars. In 1857 a Toll Reform Association supported by prominent city businessmen and the railway tycoon, Sir Samuel Morton Peto, petitioned Parliament for the removal of the remaining eighty-seven toll gates within a four mile cab radius of Charing Cross. *Punch* in its issue of 16 May 1847, observed:

> It is pretty clear then that no *pater familias*, within an ear shot of Bow Bells can ever drive out for an airing with the Mrs and Misses P. without being stopped by some half dozen licensed highwaymen, each of whom commands him to stand and deliver.[37]

Reform came at last. The Metropolitan Turnpike Act came into operation in 1864 and the last main turnpike gate – that on Mile End Road – was taken down two years later.

Political events in Ireland between 1796 and 1802 affected the development of the road from London to Holyhead, the port which was the most important gateway to Ireland via Howth. A rebellion of the United Irishmen, led by Wolfe Tone, began in 1796. It was to have been backed by a French republican army of 14,000 men, but the thirty-five ships of the invasion fleet were dispersed, and partly wrecked, in Bantry Bay. The expedition was called off. Nevertheless, it had been a serious fright. If it had not been for a persistent east wind the men from the French ships would have landed. Ironically the rising, which aimed to break Ireland's connection with England, led to the passing of the Act of Union (1802) which abolished the separate Irish Parliament and provided for the election of a hundred Irish MPs to the Parliament at Westminster. From then onwards it was a prime consideration of Parliament to speed up the lines of communication with Ireland. A royal mail link was established to Holyhead via Chester in 1808, taking forty hours for the journey. Throughout 1819 the Post Office directed its efforts to reduce the time taken by the royal mail to reach Holyhead.[38] On the recommendation of Thomas Telford, the route was shortened by going through Shrewsbury rather than Chester. By this and other regulations the time taken on the journey was reduced to thirty-six hours. According to a Commons Select Committee which reported on 2 March 1819, the expenditure of tax revenue on improving this link was well worthwhile:

> In proportion as this expenditure of Public Money upon these roads shall contribute to render more productive, by expediting the communication, the industry and capital of those persons who are engaged in the great traffic which is carried on between England and Ireland, it will at the same time, and in the same degree, contribute to secure the repayment of that money to the Public, by increasing the general stock of our national resources of wealth and taxation.[39]

This general principle, that it is worth spending public money on productive investment in the short run to save money in the long run, has frequently been followed in British transport history, with the best-known example being the construction of the motorways from 1959. The difference of the situation between 1819 and 1959 was, however, that there was no alternative transport by land to the London-Holyhead Road. In 1959 there was a rail link between London and Birmingham.

Each of the three leading road engineers of the age, John Metcalfe (1717–1780), Thomas Telford (1757–1834) and John McAdam (1756–1836), made his own contribution to speeding the movement of traffic on roads by improving their method of construction and maintenance. Metcalfe, in his area of operation in the Pennines, where he was responsible for 180 miles of turnpike roads, laid a foundation of ling or heather over which he placed stones and sifted gravel. Telford placed great emphasis on a solid foundation of big stones to be covered with other stones roughly cubic in shape and small enough to pass through a two and a half inch ring.[40] McAdam did not consider it was so important to construct deep foundations as to ensure as nearly as possible an impervious surface of closely compacted small stones covered by sifted gravel.[41]

Under the Highways Act of 1555 public bodies, notably the parish councils, were made responsible for the maintenance of the roads. In the seventeenth and eighteenth centuries turnpike trusts maintained a small proportion of the road network, the greater mileage still remaining in the care of local authorities. The turnpike roads were unpopular both with the labouring classes, who thought they mainly benefited the well-to-do, and who rioted for the removal of the toll bars right up to the time of the Rebecca riots in parts of Wales in 1843, and with the commercial classes, who campaigned for freedom of access to markets.[42] In 1888, under the Local Government Act, county councils were made responsible for roads within their boundaries. Much later Parliament decided that some roads were of such outstanding importance that they should be financed by central government. The Trunk Roads Act of 1936 authorised this change and helped to reinforce the consensus that the road infrastructure should be paid for from general taxation. The owners of road motor vehicles got into the habit of thinking that the costs of running a motor vehicle were the costs incurred 'at the point of use'. This attitude caused no great problem when there were a few hundred thousand vehicles on Britain's roads in the years following the First World War, but it had become a major public issue by the late 1990s when 24,000,000 vehicles were licensed.

The delivery of letters and parcels by the Post Office also contributed to the improvement of communications and transport services before the coming of the motor car. It has often been assumed that, following the introduction in 1840 of the penny post by Sir Rowland Hill, Secretary to the Post Office, a delivery was ensured to every address in the kingdom. This was not the case. The policy of the government was stated in a Treasury minute of 13 August 1841. It was held to be obvious that the post could not be extended to every place in the kingdom. 'Any attempt of the kind' would certainly 'entail an enormous expense on the Post Office', and this could only be met by new legislation. Whether there was or was not to be 'any delivery of letters, as well as the extent of such delivery' was to depend on the number of letters, and the density of the population in the neighbourhood of each post office. Although in the years after 1840 the Post Office opened new posts

(621 serving 1942 villages between 5 June 1843 and 5 January 1845), it was not until 1871 that the Postmaster General announced his hope 'that the time is not distant, when a free delivery, i.e. no extra charge on the penny post, at least two or three times a week, will be provided for every house in the country, however remote'. It was not, however, until Queen Victoria's Diamond Jubilee in 1897 that it was announced that a regular delivery would be given to every house in the kingdom. This welcome announcement was made possible by 'the extended use of bicycles which were now used in some thousands of posts'.[43]

The 'some thousands' of Post Office bicycles used by postmen in the 1890s and later were a visual demonstration that a new form of personal road transport was now available. The Cyclists' Touring Club was founded in 1878 and cycle ownership and riding increased until the cycle boom of 1896. The advent of the 'Safety' bicycle and pneumatic tyres increased the popularity of this means of travel and membership of the CTC reached a peak of 60,000 in 1899.[44] This membership mainly comprised cycling club enthusiasts; there were also thousands more who used bikes to get to and from work, or to visit the countryside with a friend.*

There is no means of telling how many bicycles were on the roads at the century's end as no registration of ownership was or is required, but two facts may be noted: ownership of bicycles decreased in twentieth-century Britain, and technical innovation and increased sophistication in the design and technology of the vehicle contributed ideas for the improvement in design of the early motor cars.

---

* In 1906, in order to have their engagement photograph taken, Philip Bagwell's mother and father cycled from Tenterden (in Kent) to Hastings (in Sussex) and back.

4

The Growth of the Railways

The initial impetus for the development of railways came from the growth of the coal and copper mining industries. Total output of coal in Britain grew by four times between 1750 and 1815. The most important region of coal production was the north east, where output increased from 1955 to 5,395,000 tons.[1] Copper ore sold at public ticketings in Devon and Cornwall – the principal region of copper production – rose from 9400 tons in 1750 to 78,500 tons in 1815.[2] To meet the rising demand for their products both of these extractive industries needed more efficient means of transport, to get the mined minerals to inland waterways or ports, than the pack horses commonly in use before the Industrial Revolution.

Before steam power was applied to the movement of wagons there were improvements to the track. At some date between October 1603 and October 1604 the first wooden rails were laid down at Wollaton to Nottinghamshire by Huntington Beaumont, lessee of coal pits from Sir Percival Willoughby, a substantial landowner of the district.[3] It was, however, on Tyneside that wooden rails were to be seen in the greatest abundance: it was estimated that some 20,000 horses were employed drawing wagons, or wains, there in 1696.[4] Although wooden rails were a great improvement, they needed replacement at least once in three years, and good, hard timber was in short supply. The improvements in the iron industry in the later part of the eighteenth century, and particularly the patenting of the reverbatory furnace in 1766 and the puddling process in 1784, increased the availability and lowered the cost of cast iron, which could be used to protect the wooden rails in their most vulnerable places. By the early years of the nineteenth century wrought iron rails had entirely replaced wooden ones.

The mechanical genius who made the greatest contribution to the development of the steam locomotive engine was Richard Trevithick, a Cornishman who, as manager of a copper mine near Penzance, had become familiar in his early years with the use of steam power to pump water from the workings. In 1800 he devised a steam-driven road carriage which he tested at Camborne. Three years later he and his cousin drove another steam carriage at a speed of eight miles an hour up Tottenham Court Road in London, breaking down a garden fence at the end of the run.[5] These were the first high-pressure steam locomotives, but problems remained to be solved before a commercially viable steam railway was possible: stronger wrought iron rails were needed to bear the weight of the mineral wagons and, if locomotives were to outpace horse-drawn wagons, they needed more power but less weight in relation to the weight of the trains they hauled.

These were the difficulties which had to be overcome by the Quaker families who largely financed the Stockton and Darlington Railway, which obtained its Act of Parliament in 1821 and was opened for traffic on 27 September 1825. The territories served by their railway were a proving ground on which were tried out alternative means of transport. The company's corporate seal depicted a horse drawing four wagons on rails.[6] This is less surprising when it is recalled that, up to the year 1821, there were twenty-one Acts of incorporation for horse-drawn tramways. The historian of the company describes the original objective of its founders as being to establish 'a coal line serving a small number of landfall collieries in the south west of Durham with the shipment of minerals, such as limestone, and the carriage of passengers very much as afterthoughts'.[7]

It was not beyond the bounds of possibility that a canal might have been constructed to do the work of carrying coal from the mines to the staiths on the River Tees. In 1818 Christopher Tennant of Stockton sponsored a scheme for a canal from the coal fields to the Tees at an estimated cost of £205,283; but this was dismissed as too expensive by Edward Pease, who with his family owned a bank, collieries and port facilities in the region, and could afford to wait until steam locomotive power was improved.

In the thirty years after the opening of the Stockton and Darlington Railway British civil and mechanical engineers led the world. George Stephenson (1781–1848) developed both the steam-blast pipe and the tubular boiler. His son, Robert Stephenson (1803–1839) founded the first purpose-built locomotive works at Newcastle-on-Tyne in 1823, where he built a succession of innovatively designed locomotives. His appointment as chief engineer of the London and Birmingham Railway in 1838 marked his pre-eminence. Joseph Locke (1805–1860) was a business organiser as well as a skilled builder of tunnels both in Britain and in France, Spain and Holland. Without the energies and abilities of these dedicated pioneers the growth of British railways from localised concerns to a national network would not have been possible.

In the early months of the operations of the Stockton and Darlington Railway company traction was effected partly through the use of horses, partly by stationery engines and locomotives. To augment its revenue its lines were leased to horse-drawn passenger coaches, in appearance like road coaches but running on the company's rails; but it was the company's rule that mineral wagons had precedence over passenger carriages. In 1827 the management committee of the company instructed Timothy Hackworth, its superintendent engineer – successor to George Stephenson – to construct a locomotive that would 'exceed the efficiency of horses'. The *Royal George*, with its direct drive from cylinders to wheels, the most powerful engine of the day, met this objective outstandingly. In 1828 it conveyed 22,422 tonnes of coal over twenty miles at a cost of a farthing per ton mile, or including all repairs and maintenance and interest on sunk capital at 10 per cent £466, when the cost of the same work performed by horses was £998, a difference of £532 or 53.3 per cent in favour of the engine.[8]

One consequence of the success of *The Royal George*, and the more frequent haulage that it provided, was that it became operationally difficult to lease the line from time to time for the conveyance of other proprietors' passenger coaches. The company became the sole provider of transport services on its rails in 1833, although the use of horse-drawn wagons on some of its branch lines continued until 1854.[9]

The great achievement of the Stockton and Darlington company's management and staff was to demonstrate that steam railways could be a reliable and cost-effective form of transport. It was also the most profitable British railway before 1860, delivering a mean annual dividend of 9.5 per cent in the latter half of the 1850s.[10] It was a green light for future railway investors.

Economic and commercial activity had been increasing rapidly in Lancashire in the same years as coal mining was expanding in Durham and North Yorkshire – the area served by the Stockton and Darlington Railway. The population of Manchester increased from about 20,000 in 1760 to 163,188 in 1824. Over the same time the population of Liverpool grew from 25,000 to 135,000, and the customs receipts of the port rose by at least eight times.[11] In the prospectus of the Liverpool and Manchester Railway Company, issued in 1824, the promoters complained about the high charges of the Mersey and Irwell Navigation and the Bridgewater Canal for carrying goods between the two cities. Service was also slow. In 1829, therefore, to determine whether locomotive traction was best for the carriage of passengers and freight on their line, the directors of the Liverpool and Manchester Railway offered a prize of £500 to the designers of a locomotive which did not exceed six tons in weight, but which proved able to pull a load of at least three times its weight, at a speed of no less than ten miles per hour. At the Rainhill Trials in 1829, Robert Stephenson's *Rocket*, which had the decisive advantage in steam generation through its multi-tubular boiler, attained a speed of thirty miles per hour, completely outclassing all other competitors. The *Rocket*'s triumph marked the beginning of the Steam Age. Man at last could travel faster than the speed of a galloping horse. Unlike the Stockton and Darlington Railway, the Liverpool and Manchester was therefore operated, from its inception, entirely by steam-powered locomotives. Furthermore, it was managed and run solely by the company, which made all the arrangements for carriage of both goods and passengers.

From the opening of the Liverpool and Manchester line railway passenger traffic expanded rapidly. Within a few weeks the company ran its first excursion train, taking a Manchester Sunday school party of 1500 to Liverpool. In the summer of 1831 it carried tens of thousands of people to the Newton races.[12] Nationally, the number of passenger journeys made by railway rose from 27,763,602 in 1844 to 288,632,921 in 1870, or by more than ten times.[13]

What had contributed to this impressive increase in the amount of railway passenger travel was the decision of the railway companies to give those who travelled by train a cost advantage over those who made the journey by road. On the Leeds and York Railway the fare initially charged for the thirty-one mile journey of eighty minutes was 3s. 6d., compared with the 3s. charged for a four hour journey on the outside seat of a coach. But it was not long before the directors of the railway decided to reduce the fare to 2s. 6d., giving the passengers by railway the advantage both of time and cost.[14]

By contrast with their engineering achievements, financially railway companies were not well managed. The capital market in the first half of the nineteenth century was in a primitive state of development for industrial and public utility concerns. Railway shares were sold through advertisements in newspapers or printed leaflets. The flotation of new companies fluctuated from uncertainty to wild speculative growth. There were two railway manias in the first half of the nineteenth century. From 1835–37 Acts were passed for fifty new lines and 1600 miles of track. Many of these projects were ill-conceived. Bankruptcies occurred, frightening off new investments. Between 1838 and 1839 schemes for only ninety-two miles of line went ahead. The mania of the years 1835–37 was small fry compared with that of 1844–47, sparked off by good harvests, resulting in a favourable balance of trade and cheap money. In the one year, 1846, 4540 miles of line were sanctioned, equal to the total mileage built since 1820. In an environment of a rapidly expanding press, and the minimum legislative interference, conditions were favourable for wild speculation and skulduggery. George Hudson, one-time mayor of York and with over a thousand miles of track under his control, was known as the 'Railway King'. But his fortune was made through paying shareholders dividends out of capital stock. Once doubts were engendered, a precipitate slump occurred and Hudson, from being fêted everywhere, was obliged to live most of the rest of his life abroad to escape the clutches of his creditors. Nevertheless, a great many miles of railway had been built, however wastefully, and the railway map of 1850 showed something like a national network for the first time.

In the 1830s when Railway Bills proliferated and the mileage of the network increased rapidly 'the mind of the public [was] that competition, which was so powerful a regulation in most commercial affairs, would also suffice to regulate railways'.[15] Both parliamentary and public opinion then changed rapidly. When a select committee of the Commons heard evidence in 1839 the opinion of some of the witnesses was that the interests of the railway companies could 'never be at variance' with the interests of the public. In its second report the committee was less sure. It pointed out that:

> A main objective which the directors of a company must have in view is to obtain a good return for the capital expended, while it is the primary interest of the public that the intercourse should be regularly maintained, with the greatest safety, speed and economy.[16]

Despite the concerns expressed by the select committee, Parliament was broadly content to follow *laissez-faire* policies in the period 1840–42. The provisions of Lord Seymour's Act 1840 and a supplementary measure in 1842 were limited to questions of the safety of the travelling public and to the appointment of a Railway Department of the Board of Trade.

The events of 1844–45 changed the mind of W. E. Gladstone to favour an interventionist policy. 2816 miles of new line were sanctioned in the one year 1845, a total about equal to the entire mileage sanctioned from 1821–44 and more than twice the number approved in the first railway mania of 1836.[17] George Hudson's activities aroused fears of monopoly control and persuaded Gladstone to appoint a Parliamentary Select Committee which he chaired. Justifying the appointment of the committee to the Commons on 5 February 1844, Gladstone warned: 'By the Bills which it was proposed to pass during the present season, it was intended to increase railway communication by nearly one half, and the House therefore was in duty called upon to give attention to this subject.' The Railway Bill, which broadly followed the report of the select committee, besides compelling the companies to provide for daily third class travel at least once a day, gave government the right, under certain conditions, to acquire all new lines built after 1844, twenty-one years later. Some of the more radical members of Peel's party in the Commons urged Gladstone to include all railway companies – those whose rails were laid down between 1821 and 1844 as well as those proposed in the draft Bill to be included. But the President of the Board of Trade and his premier had not envisaged the intense pressure exerted by the recently awakened railway interest against any increase of government control over the companies' activities. In the 1830s the number of railway directors in Parliament was small – in 1837 there were only seven in the Commons – but by 1847 it had risen to eighty.[18]

In the face of Gladstone's determination to exert a stricter control over railway promotions, the railway companies, ably led by the legal firm of Burke and Venables, mobilised their opposition. On 1 July 1844 a deputation consisting of representatives of nineteen of them, headed by George Hudson, saw Peel, Gladstone and Lord Granville Somerset. Two days later in the House of Commons Gladstone berated the parliamentary agents of the railway companies who 'knew how to get up an opposition' in the Commons. He complained about the 'gross misstatements' made about his Bill. Nevertheless the government was badly shaken, and, after Hudson met Gladstone on 17 July, substantial concessions were made to the railway interest. Of the original Bill's forty-eight clauses half were abandoned and others modified.[19] The Bill became law as the Railways Act 1844.

Meanwhile railway company promotions continued at breakneck speed. A number of the new lines proposed duplicated existing railway links and had little prospect of financial stability. Other lines, started when money was cheap, could not be completed when it was dear. The result was the passing of the Railway Abandonment Act of 1850, which allowed the Railway Commissioners, on the request of two thirds of the shareholders, to issue a warrant for the abandonment of part or the whole of the works previously authorised. By this means, two thousand miles of line projected during the railway boom of 1845–47 were abandoned.

William Galt, who in 1844 compared British railway policy with that of Britain's European neighbours, declared that the waste associated with the railway mania could have been avoided, as the example of Belgian railways manifested. There the construction and operation of the main lines linking principal cities such as Antwerp and Bruges, and those linking Belgian cities with neighbouring states, were built and operated by the state. After about 1850, branch lines were provided by private companies, only to be bought up by the state in the 1870s. Galt pointed out that the average cost of construction for the lines of seventy-one railways in England was £32,360 per mile. The average cost of a similar mile of railways in Belgium was £17,120. It was also a fact that average fares on the Belgian lines were half those charged in England. Of course the English companies could claim that gradients in England were steeper than were most of those on the other side of the Channel.[20]

Neither the government at Westminster nor the railway companies in the next two decades were in a mood to draw any positive lessons from the

Belgian example. The companies were preoccupied with expanding their networks and with absorbing smaller branch lines within their spheres of influence; the government was content with expanding its revenues from passenger duty, left luggage offices, and other small charges, to take seriously the option of public ownership available from 1865–66.

The appointment of a Royal Commission on Railways in 1865 marked the end of an era. In its report in 1867, however, its members came to the general conclusion that it was:

> inexpedient ... to subvert the policy which has hitherto been adopted of leaving the construction and management of the railways to free enterprise of the people under such conditions as parliament may think fit to impose for the general welfare of the public.[21]

The government, nevertheless, came under increasing pressure from traders, chambers of commerce and, after 1872, the railway unions, towards checking the arbitrariness of the companies to its customers and its employees.

The railway companies were slow in making provision for the accommodation of the poorer classes of the nation. When C. A. Saunders, the Secretary of the Great Western Railway, was asked in 1839 what provision his company made for the conveyance of third class passengers, he answered that they might send carriages 'of an inferior description at very low speed ... and at a very low price and that it might only be done at night'.[22] Even in 1844 there were still some companies which made no provision for third class travel. When the House of Commons debated the question on 5 February that year, R. Wallace, the MP for Greenock, argued that any government legislation on railways should be based on the principle 'that the poorer classes of the country always had, and always ought to have, an equal right to equal accommodation on the public roads ... with the richer classes of people'.

On the previous Monday he had arrived at Lancaster by mail coach from Scotland and was taken to the railway station at which he heard several persons enquiring for the second class train to London.

> 'Oh', was the answer, given at the booking office, 'there's no second class here.'
> 'Well then', said the applicants, 'we'll go by the third class.'
> 'Third class', cried the clerk, 'we've never heard of such a thing here.'
> 'But we've not got money enough to go by first class', said the poor fellows, honest, sober, steady cotton-jackets. That was their affair they must get on as best they can, then ... Now this was a monstrous case.[23]

It was such instances that persuaded Gladstone, the President of the Board of Trade, to include, in his Regulation of Railways Bill of 1844,[24] the requirement that all railway companies should provide one cheap train each way, daily, at a charge not exceeding one penny a mile, on the entire length of its rails. The speed of this train was to be not less than twelve miles per hour, including stops at every station. The carriages were to be covered and protected from the weather. Children under three years of age were to be carried free, and those between three and twelve at half fare. The passenger tax on these third class fares was to be abolished.

Parliament in 1844 considered it necessary to secure the interests of poorer travellers, but in 1872 a joint Select Committee of the Lords and Commons considered the necessity had passed since, by then, the railway companies realised that without the revenue gained from third class fares their earnings would be insufficient to meet their costs.[25] In 1844 one third of railway journeys were made by third class passengers; by 1870 it was two thirds. In 1844 one eighth of passenger revenue came from third class passengers; in 1870 the proportion had risen to nearly one half. This was the revolution in passenger travel wrought by the railways.

Railways are natural monopolies. The track of a road for horse-drawn or motorised vehicles is free to any vehicle owner who has paid the required vehicle and driver taxes; in contrast, railways run on a permanent way only available to one user at a time. As we have seen, the Stockton and Darlington Railway Company allowed other vehicles than its own to use its track. It was soon realised, however, that this policy was unworkable. In 1833 the directors ruled that the company should be the sole provider of transport services on its own rails.

The prevailing view of economists in the 1830s was that a policy of free competition was the best guarantee of business efficiency and social welfare. In 1839, when hundreds of Birmingham traders petitioned the House of Commons against the monopolistic practices of the London and Birmingham Railway, they expected MPs would mete out some form of punishment to the offending railway. Instead, a Select Committee on Railways was appointed, heard witnesses and reported in the same year that

> the safety of the public also requires that upon every railway there should be one system of management ... On this account it is necessary that the company should possess a complete control ... although they should thereby acquire an entire monopoly.

Parliament failed to do anything to control the monopoly partly because there were clear advantages of economies from large-scale operation and partly because the railway interest was already influential. Successive governments dithered.

Amalgamation being neither supported as a necessity or opposed as an evil, the railway companies resorted to such devices as pooling of earnings, working agreements and joint workings as stepping stones to outright amalgamation. The result was that by 1914 around a thousand railway companies had disappeared, chiefly by amalgamation. The number of survivors had shrunk to 247 in 1875 and 120 by the time the 1921 Railways Act was passed. The fourteen companies which before 1914 had called themselves 'Great' completely dominated the track mileages as well as the capital assets and revenue.[26]

Throughout the nineteenth century no alternative means of passenger travel could seriously challenge the railways. It was a different situation with freight transport, where canals and coastal shipping were successful competitors for business. In the contemporary environment of *laissez-faire* the railway companies were perfectly free to amalgamate with canals and then, if they chose, subsequently transfer traffic from waterway to rail. They could buy up parts of a canal network and prevent the canal company from quoting through rates. The railway companies had strong reasons for doing so. As authors of a royal commission report expressed it: 'On railways they are carriers as well as owners of the road, and earn profit in both capacities. On canals they carry, if at all, only in competition with other large owners.'[27] Thus by 1866 one third of the four thousand mile canal network had been amalgamated with railway companies. By then public alarm at the further growth of railway monopoly led to legislative checks on the absorption of the canals. The Regulation of Railways Act (1873) and the Railway and Canal Traffic Act (1888) prevented further control of railways over canals except under very careful safeguards; but the relentlessness of the pressure of competition from the railways had greatly reduced the role of canal transport by 1914.[28]

The most important check on the railway companies' domination of freight traffic was coastal shipping. C. H. Parkes, a parliamentary agent for shipping companies for 'about thirty years', told a select committee that sea competition affected rates charged for goods at three fifths of the railway stations in Britain.[29] The select committee of 1872 noted that:

> If, by sea competition, the charge for carrying coal from Newcastle to London [was] reduced, that reduction [would] rule for the charge for carrying coal from any other place to London. Consequently, the competition of sea carriage is an important element in determining railway rates for goods.[30]

The best way of comparing the amount of work done by canals, railways and coastal shipping in the carriage of freight is by measuring ton mileage: the quantity carried multiplied by the mileage covered. In Britain in 1910 the ton mileage of freight carried by coastal shipping was 59 per cent to the railways' 39 per cent and the canals' 2 per cent. The reason why coasters outclassed the railways in freight movement was that the average haul of cargo by sea was 296.7 miles compared with the railways' 40.0 miles.[31] Coastal shipping was the cheaper medium because it offered economies of scale.

The circumstances of the early carriage of minerals by rail also affected the competitiveness of rail freight for many decades. Most collieries were small concerns with their own ideas as to the most suitable capacity for their wagons, and their individual eccentricities about the right positioning of brakes, coupling appliances and destination notices. When larger rail companies merged with smaller ones their rolling stock therefore comprised a bewildering variety of company-built and colliery-built vehicles. As late as 1948, when the railways were nationalised, the new publicly-owned industry inherited 1,279,543 wagons, the majority of which had belonged to the four main line companies – the Great Western, Southern, London and North Eastern, and the London Midland and Scottish – which were in operation between 1923 and 1939, but a substantial minority of 544,000 had belonged to private companies, mostly collieries. Few modern refinements were present throughout the wagon fleet, with the privately owned wagons the least up to date. 'Automatic brakes and screw couplings were fitted to very few vehicles so that the number of fully fitted freight trains was pitifully small.'[32]

The absence of standardisation of appliances on British railway wagons slowed down the speed of goods trains and therefore added to the railway companies' costs of operation. This was a matter of serious interest to the Board of Trade, concerned about the export prices of goods. It was also a matter of great concern to the Amalgamated Society of Railway Servants, whose shunter members suffered the highest fatal casualty rate of any railway employees. These parties exerted pressure, on both the railway companies and successive governments, to establish new regulations and legislation designed to save the lives of railwaymen involved in the movement of goods traffic and to speed the movement of goods trains.

In the nineteenth century most railway accidents were caused by defective brakes, faulty engine boilers, inadequate signalling and the difficulty of reconciling the claims of railway shareholders with the need to spend money on securing the safety of operations. They were not primarily caused by the 'neglect of servants', as was claimed by George Findlay, the General Manager of the London and North Western Railway, when answering a question put to him by the members of the Royal Commission on Railway Accidents in 1877. Reform came through the enquiries which followed horrendous accidents, especially after 1840, following the reports of inspectors appointed by the Board of Trade. Thus, following a derailment on the Great Western

Railway at Sonning on Christmas Eve 1841, when third class passengers were thrown out of trucks attached to a goods train and eight of them were killed, all railway companies were asked to inform the Board of Trade of what arrangements they had for conveyance of third class passengers.[33] Improvements in third class accommodation and terms of travel were included by Gladstone in his Railways Act of 1844.

Brakes on the early passenger trains were hand-operated by a brakesman. Experiments were conducted by both the railway companies and the Board of Trade to devise a 'continuous' brake, one that would apply to the whole passenger train and not just the carriage nearest the engine. The search was also for an automatic brake designed on the 'fail safe' principle. Continuous brakes were of two kinds, vacuum and air. With the vacuum brake, the pressure of the atmosphere acted against a partial vacuum.[34] Air brakes used compression. But improvement was painfully slow until 1889. In June of that year a terrible accident occurred at Armagh on the Great Northern Railway of Ireland. Most of the passengers on a crowded train, with no continuous brakes, were hurtled down an incline, and either killed or seriously injured. In this case the government acted promptly. Within twelve weeks of the accident the Regulation of Railways Act was passed compelling companies to introduce block signalling – based on the division of the track into sections and allowing only one train at a time in each track in each direction – and continuous and automatic brakes which had to be approved by Board of Trade inspectors.[35]

Throughout the nineteenth century the government was reluctant to interfere with freight movement on the railways. In 1914 there were some 600,000 privately owned coal wagons, mostly of eight or ten tons capacity and with variable, but inadequate, braking and shunting arrangements. There were few major accidents involving freight trains; but there was a steady slaughter in the shunting yards. Most goods wagons were 'loose coupled': the chain fixed at the end of one wagon had to be attached to the hook on the neighbouring wagon by a shunter standing on the buffers and hand signalling the driver, a practice known as 'fly shunting'. (But it was every bit as dangerous for the shunter to be between the buffers.) In 1882 twelve shunters were killed on duty on British railways. Through the cooperation of the North Eastern Railway Company their trade union staged an exhibition of automatic and other coupling devices, improved brakes and improved lighting for goods yards. Four years later, most railway companies having failed to respond to their demands for automatic coupling and either side brakes on wagons, they staged another exhibition at Nine Elms goods yards on the London and South Western Railway between 29–31 March. Rather than agreeing with the union on immediate negotiations, the railway companies persuaded their union representatives to agree to the appointment of a Royal Commission to explore the possibilities.[36]

A Royal Commission on Accidents to Railway Servants met in 1900, and the Railway Employment (Prevention of Accidents) Act was passed, obliging the companies to fit automatic couplers on all new wagons. One consequence of this measure was that fatal casualties amongst shunting staff dropped from one in every 156 employees in 1894 to one in 444 in 1913. By the 1920s working or travelling on the railway was much safer than it had been twenty years earlier.[37]

In the meantime the Board of Trade sent one of its senior railway inspectors, Francis Hopwood, to examine the extent of the use of automatic couplings on railways in the United States. In his report to the Secretary of the Board of Trade on 20 December 1898 he stated that the American Railroad Association had been successful 'in standardisation of coupling equipment'. He found the association 'less pressed with financial questions' than was the Railway Companies' Association in Britain. The Master Car Builders' Association, a body with a strong professional outlook, had devised an automatic coupling system which was widely, if not universally, adopted by American railroads. The result was that the companies had 'saved large sums of money'. The Federal Government came to the support of the American Railroad Association through the Safety Appliances Act of 2 March 1893. The result was that in 1897 there were 2119 fewer men killed and 4994 fewer injured in coupling and uncoupling cars than there had been in 1893.

Though Hopgood lamented that the Railway Companies Association of Britain 'lacked the moral force, to say nothing of the initiative, which characterised its sister body across the Atlantic', a 'coupler had to be found' and he did not see how this could be done without legislative assistance. The UK Patent Office had 'about 550' patents for automatic couplers, so that the onus rested 'very heavily' on the railway companies to state why it was 'impossible – to discover a coupler which will couple automatically'.[38]

In 1900 the government was convinced that legislation could play a part in reducing casualties both of passengers and railway workers when the Railways (Prevention of Accidents) Act was passed that year. But the problem was complicated through the circumstances of the early growth of railway freight traffic and it was not until after the Second World War that substantial modernisation took place.

Apart from the obstacle of antiquated freight train appliances delaying the speeding up of trains, there were what has been called an unfortunate legacy of multiple ownership of assets in railway services manifested in the right of colliery owners to own their own trucks.[39] Throughout the first hundred years of operation of railways in Britain, freight traffic was carried in predominantly small wagons of ten, or even eight, tons capacity. Since the overwhelming majority of these were colliery wagons, they generally returned as 'empties' to their owners after customer demands had been met; this was the retail character of much of British railways freight traffic.[40]

There can be no doubt that the impressive growth of passenger traffic, and the substantial (though less impressive) growth of freight traffic made a significant contribution to the wealth and well-being of the nation. It has been estimated that, comparing the situation as it was in 1870 with a railway system in operation with what it would have been without railways, a diversion of resources to the older forms of transport costing about 6 per cent of the national income would have been necessary to make up the deficiency.[41]

Economic efficiency and social welfare were undoubtedly improved by the speedier communication directly or indirectly brought about by the railways. Thomas Edmondson, a Quaker employed from 1836 as both booking clerk and stationmaster at the small station at Milton (later called Brampton) on the Newcastle and Carlisle Railway, was appalled at the inadequacy of the ticket issuing and collecting system. It was left entirely to the integrity of the station clerks to account correctly for monies paid to them. With plenty of spare time on his hands, Edmondson replaced paper tickets with cardboard ones and invented machines for printing, numbering and date-stamping the tickets. It was not long before his ticket issuing system was adopted not only at the large majority of British railway stations but also at a large number abroad. It was so aptly suited to its purpose that it was only withdrawn from use in March 1984.[42] Edmondson's system greatly helped the development of both goods and passenger services where more than one company's lines were used. It was a vital instrument in the hands of the Railway Clearing House, founded in 1842, in its task of settling the accounts of the railway companies with each other. The Railway Clearing House's rules and regulations from 1867 onwards helped to standardise signals, while its classification of goods, although not agreed with the companies until 1882, eventually contributed to the speedier movement of goods other than bulky freight.[43]

When the horse-drawn Irish mails opened for business via Chester and Holyhead in 1808, the guard of the mail coach was instructed to carry with him a watch bearing Greenwich time and to inform each postmaster at coaching inns along the route of the correct or standard time. After its opening in 1830 the Liverpool and Manchester Railway adopted Greenwich time, but there was resistance in the west country and Wales until, on 2 November 1852, the Dean of Exeter ordered that the time of the cathedral clock should be advanced by fourteen minutes to conform to Greenwich time. The erection of a public clock soon became a fashionable civic gesture so that citizens could observe the correct railway time, from the 1850s onwards.[44] The conduct of business became more exactly timed than ever before.

W. F. Cooke and Charles Whetstone, having both experimented with the electric telegraph in the 1830s, took out a joint patent for its use in 1837 and persuaded the London and Birmingham to accept telegraph wires by its line between Euston and Camden Town. The Great Western Railway followed in 1839 by allowing an experiment between Paddington and Hanwell.[45] By the 1850s three large telegraph companies were competing – as Parliament considered, rather wastefully – so that by 1868 a Bill, empowering the Post Office to acquire the private companies and establish the first nationalised industry, passed into law.

The telegram, a cheaper means of communication than the early telephones, rapidly increased in popularity. The number of telegrams despatched in Britain increased from 9,000,000 in 1870–71 to over 84,000,000 in 1900–1. In photographs of Post Office staff the uniformed telegraph boys are seated cross-legged on the ground in front of their senior colleagues. Their grimmest months of duty were during the First World War when their appearance in the neighbourhood was dreaded, as residents were all too well aware that they brought news of death of loved ones in battle.

Before the days of the telephone, locomotive superintendents often had no means of discovering why a train was late in arriving. Edward Bury, superintendent of locomotive power of the London and Birmingham Railway, admitted that while his men were 'very much improved' in reliability, there were times when they were inexplicably delayed. In those circumstances, he said, 'we send a look out engine to find what has happened'.[46] But after Alexander Graham Bell had patented the telephone in 1875, Edison the carbon transmitter in 1877 and Hughes the microphone in 1878, the technology was available for further improvements in communication on the railway and elsewhere. It was first used on the Great Northern Line between King's Cross and Finchley in October 1879, but thereafter its further adoption was sluggish.[47] A clutch of small telephone companies were set up throughout Britain and Postmaster General Fawcett declared in 1882 that there would be 'free competition amongst private companies and ... of private companies against the Post Office'. The free for all which followed was chaotic and the Asquith Liberal Government had little opposition to its proposal under the Telephone Transfer Bill of 1911 selling the National Telephone Company (which had absorbed numerous smaller concerns) out to state ownership.[48]

These developments spurred the railway companies into action. A Railway

Companies Association had been formed in 1858; but it did not gain the allegiance of all the companies and disappeared in 1861. By the summer of 1867 the companies were more aware of the need to work together. On 26 June that year representatives of the leading companies met in the Midland Railway offices in Great George Street, near Parliament Square, and established the United Railway Companies Committee, which shortly afterwards changed its name to the Railway Companies Association, an organisation which continued in existence until railway nationalisation in 1948.[49]

Meanwhile the amalgamation movement on the railways continued apace. Developments in the second half of the nineteenth century were characterised by one authority as comprising 'Bursts of competition which created excessively high costs alternating with the formation of local or regional monopolies that charged the public inordinately high prices'.[50] Between 1846 and 1872 four large groupings or 'systems' had emerged. The first of these, the London and North Western, was formed in 1846 by the amalgamation of the London and Birmingham, Grand Junction and others, covering 379 route miles. In the next quarter century it extended further into the midlands and north west so that route mileage had grown to 1507 by 1872. The second company was the Great Western. Built for the 110 miles between Bristol, Bath and London from 1838 to 1841, it had a network of 1387 miles in 1870. The most compact of the four great companies was the North Eastern which between 1854 and 1870 grew to a wealthy regional monopoly of 1281 miles.[51] The fourth company, the London and South Western, originated as the London and Southampton (seventy-seven miles) in 1840. By 1872 it owned 862 miles of line. These formal consolidations into large regional empires were supplemented by pooling arrangements, pricing agreements and understandings. Free competition, so ardently advocated in public by George Hudson and his friends in the 1840s, had virtually ceased to exist.

The growth of concentration of ownership in ever fewer companies is shown by the fact that whereas in 1846 seventy companies controlled 66 per cent of the total railway mileage, in 1872 sixteen companies controlled 85 per cent and in 1907 thirteen companies controlled 88 per cent.[52] Captain (later Sir Henry) Tyler, chief railway inspector at the Board of Trade, came to the conclusion as early as 1872 that:

> monopolies must either be managed by the state in the interests of the general public, or must be managed by the directors of the monopolising companies in the interests of their shareholders, with such advantages to the general public as they may consider it expedient to afford.[53]

The first impression one gains of the performance of these monopolised railways is favourable. Nominal fares halved between 1870 and 1914 and freight rates fell by as much as a quarter, the number of train journeys rose three times and the ton miles of goods carried rose by four fifths. But British railways were no longer on the frontiers of best practice. Train speeds were increasing, encouraged by the races to Scotland in 1888 and 1895 using the East Coast and West Coast routes. Those who travelled by ferry and rail to France in the 1890s found, however, that, on coming home, the journey from Paris to Calais of three hours fifteen minutes was quicker by more than half an hour than the journey, of comparable distance, from King's Cross to Leeds. In the twelve largest British railway companies the rate of technical innovation between 1900 and 1912 was as low as 0.3 per cent per annum.[54]

This reform added to the companies' costs of operation. Since their foundation the principal freight carried by the railways was coal. In 1880 they carried 63.1 per cent of all coal moved. In the next two decades, however, more powerful and bigger capacity colliers made possible a reduction of shipping freights. The railway companies responded to this loss of revenue by increasing their charges. Protests from the chambers of commerce followed and Parliament eventually responded by passing the Railway Rates and Charges Order of 1891, fixing maximum rates for the different types of freight. In the following months the railway companies promptly raised their charges to the maximum allowed by law. There was a sharp dichotomy between – in most cases – the large railway and its small-scale business clients whose hostility to monopoly was intensified.

Ever since its foundation in 1872, the Amalgamated Society of Railway Servants had advocated legislation to limit the hours of work of their members. The Victorian artist Felix Moscheles (1833–1917) showed sympathy for their cause in his painting *The Signalman* which showed his subject's tired eyes and his arms leaning on one of his signal levers. Moscheles's work had been prompted by a Board of Trade report of an accident in 1892 which included the comment that 'At the time of the accident the signalman had ... been on duty thirteen consecutive hours'. The sympathy for overworked railwaymen aroused, in part, by this painting, made easier the passage of the Railway Regulation Act (1893), which gave the Board of Trade the power to impose some limitation on the excessive hours of labour worked by employees of the railways.

All the above items of legislation resulted in some increase in railway operating costs. The companies also added to their costs by such innovations as a twenty-four hour delivery service for goods, increased comforts for passengers, and cheaper, or free, warehousing costs. Although the stocks of the principal railways yielded returns approaching those of government bonds in their assured relatively high interest rates, some of the smaller, more remote railways, such as the Cambrian lines, failed to pay interest on their ordinary shares.[55] The decline in the profitability of the railways before 1912 has by some been attributed to poor management, by others to extravagant capital expenditure, and by yet others to circumstances beyond the railways' control.[56] The most serious criticism is that they failed to invest sufficiently in modernisation. As a result, following the heavy use to which the railways were put between 1914–18, they were ill-equipped to meet the challenge of motor transport in the inter-war years.

5

British Railways, 1914–45

On 4 August 1914 Britain declared war on Germany. Ten days later the 12,000 strong First British Army was established in northern France, complete with equipment.[1] This seemingly sudden outbreak of war was a shock to the public in towns and villages throughout the land. Was the mobilisation which followed a brilliant triumph of improvisation, or had it been carefully planned months in advance?

Under the Regulation of the Forces Act (1871), passed under the shadow of the Franco-Prussian War, it was provided that, in the event of the outbreak of war, the direction of all railway traffic movements passed from the individual railway companies' general managers to the War Department. Thus from 4 August 1914 'the railways of Great Britain were to be regarded as constituting for all practical purposes ... a national system in so far as they permitted of rolling stock passing from the lines of one company on to those of any other'.[2]

The railways remained under private ownership, but the government would decide how they were to be used. Although news of the war came suddenly to the British public, the companies' general managers had received earlier warnings. During the Agadir Crisis in Morocco in 1911, when war between Great Britain and Germany seemed a distinct possibility, the South Eastern and Chatham Railways' lines to the Channel Ports were quietly patrolled.[3]

The general managers of the main line railways also met to detail plans for the eventuality of mobilisation. They formed a Railway Executive Committee from among themselves to oversee the arrangements. Thus when the real crisis came, on 4 August 1914, everything worked like clockwork and Lord Kitchener could claim, as Commander-in-Chief of the British forces, that 'mobilisation took place without any hitch whatsoever'.[4]

Soon after war was declared the government promised compensation to the railway companies of an annual net revenue of £44,000,000, equal to that of 1913, the most profitable pre-war year. In discussions in the next two years between the Railway Executive Committee and the government this amount was increased to £60,000,000 to cover arrears of maintenance, the rise in costs of wages and materials, and payments for interest on capital.[5] After the war emergency was over, William Graham MP claimed that, when the terms of compensation were agreed, there was 'a complete absence of bargaining power on the government's side, since there was an almost complete dependence on the railway executive' for the successful prosecution of the war.[6]

Once the initial mobilisation of troops and material had been completed, rail passenger traffic flourished in the first summer of the war. It was optimistically assumed that 'the boys would be home for Christmas', so that the opportunity should be seized to take a holiday by the sea. On Saturday 22 August 1914 full excursion and cheap ticket arrangements were announced by the London and South Western Railway. The number of excursion trains from London Bridge and Victoria terminals to the coastal resorts had to be doubled. Although a number of branch line stations nationwide were closed and no special excursion trains were run in 1915, there was an increase in passenger traffic, so that in 1916 its volume, measured in train miles, exceeded that of 1913, hitherto a record year. There were signs, however, that with the reduction in staff numbers through volunteering for the armed forces, economies were having to be made. In April 1915 the London and North Western Railway announced that restaurant car services, the epitome of Edwardian luxury travel, were being withdrawn. Cold luncheon baskets were offered in lieu.[7]

Following the disasters of the battle of the Somme in 1916, the government realised that more drastic economies would have to be introduced to make possible an increase in the supply of railway equipment for the Western Front. Sir Alexander Kaye-Butterworth, who had served on the board of the GWR and was general manager of the NER, was asked to investigate what could be done. In his report, published on 2 December 1916, he recommended that passenger trains should be considerably curtailed, to liberate equipment for France: there should be a reduction in the number of Sunday trains and of trains bringing members of the forces home on leave. Collection and delivery services from railway stations should cease.

Passenger fares remained unaltered for nearly two and a half years after the declaration of war, while the general level of prices doubled between 1913 and 1917.[8] Rail travel was a relatively cheap bargain. To rectify this situation, and to discourage frivolous rail travel, fares were raised by 50 per cent from 1 January 1917.[9]

The economies made in the movement of freight were more impressive than those introduced for the passenger traffic. These were achieved by the more efficient use of locomotives and rolling stock. In February 1915 Sir Walter Runciman, the President of the Board of Trade, arranged with the Railway Executive Committee for the transfer of wagons from companies with surpluses to others, particularly the LSWR and NER, where there were shortages. This was followed in January 1916 by an agreement between the Great Eastern, Great Central and the Great Northern Railways for the pooling of their wagons. By January 1917 the REC instituted a general wagon pool and in April of that year imposed time limits on the companies for the loading and unloading of wagons. Through the common user schemes the empty running of wagons was reduced from 60 per cent in October 1913 to 20 per cent six years later. To reduce wastes which existed in the distribution of coal and coke – the largest component of railway freight traffic – the Board of Trade introduced the Controller of Coal Mines Order of July 1917 which established twenty coal zones within which coal was to be distributed locally. This was expected to save the movement of 700,000,000 tons annually.[10]

With the more economical use of railway equipment, the War Department pressed the REC to make railway workshop space, especially in the workshops towns of the largest companies, such as Derby, Crewe, Swindon and Doncaster, available for the manufacture of war equipment. The co-ordination of railway workshop activity to meet the needs of the army and navy was the responsibility of the Railway War Production sub-committee of the REC. By December 1914 twelve howitzers had been produced in Swindon and eleven in Derby, and numerous contracts in these and other workshops were carried out for the navy. By the end of the war the works of thirty-two companies (out of a total of 120) were involved in war production of all kinds from shells to small arms ammunition and components of heavier weapons.[11]

Since 184,000 railwaymen enrolled in the armed forces, the remaining 400,000 or so were required to work longer hours in arduous conditions. They were supplemented by the employment of 55,942 women, including four thousand women who were already engaged as clerks, ticket collectors and station advice bureaux workers before the war. The main occupations of the wartime women recruits were engine and carriage cleaning, and acting as guards, ticket collectors and porters. An additional 25,000 women were employed in the Woolwich Arsenal and similar factories making components of weapons of war. Women's wages at the time were never more than two-thirds of men's, the companies arguing that their productivity was approximately that proportion of men's. There were no protests by the women since, at that time, the dominant view was that the man was the breadwinner and should therefore earn more than his spouse.

In sum, because the railways had to carry large volumes of government traffic with fewer locomotives and units of rolling stock, and did so more economically, unified government control proved a great advantage to the nation.

Long before the guns were silenced through the signing of the Armistice on 11 November 1918, members of the Cabinet, the Board of Trade and the General Managers of the leading railway companies had been debating what should be the peacetime policy for railway transport in Britain.

In the late summer of 1918, before the war had ended, the government appointed a Select Committee on Transport to hear reports from railway company managers and others on how the passenger and freight services had fared since 1914, and to consider their views on the future organisation of the railways. The most important witness interviewed by the committee was Sir Herbert Walker, who before he was chairman of the REC had been general manager of the London and South Western Railway. He explained the steps that had had to be taken after seven hundred locomotives had been sent by the companies in the REC to northern France, Egypt, Mesopotamia and Salonica. He said that the 50 per cent increase in passenger fares which had been imposed to discourage rail travel in Great Britain had been ineffective because, with full employment and high wages, more passengers were carried than 'they had ever had to carry before'.[12] Freight traffic was at a record level since, apart from the movement of ammunition and weapons of war, Durham coal was carried to London by rail, rather than coastal vessels, because of the incursions of enemy submarines and destroyers.[13] For peacetime he favoured a unified system of working with a national pooling of wagons. When asked what he thought of the government policy, before 1914, of encouraging competition on the railways, he replied that 'unfortunately, we have had to suffer from it'. When asked whether he could contemplate a position where railways would return to the old system, he said, 'That would mean ruination to the railway companies'.[14] Sir Francis Dent, general manager of the South Eastern and Chatham Railway, was not perturbed by the ending of the old competitive regime. He said: 'I think on the average the public would not suffer if competition had been eliminated. There would always be comparisons with other countries.'[15] Frank Potter, general manager of the GWR, questioned by Sir Frederick Hall, a member of the select committee, conceded that under unified control 'there would be a very large saving' of account keeping and administration.[16] The select committee published its report on 14 November 1918. It concluded that:

> From a purely technical point of view it appears ... to be desirable that there should be a unification of ownership, not merely unification of management, of the main railway systems, because while unification of management would undoubtedly be a great improvement on pre-war conditions and would assist materially to secure more efficient organisation and management, it would not, without modification of ownership, permit of the use of the assets of the combined system to the best advantage.[17]

From the time of his appointment as Prime Minister on 5 December 1916, David Lloyd George was on the look out for a strong-minded and active man to sort out the transport confusion behind the Western Front. Sir Eric Geddes (1875–1937) proved to be the answer. He had had a varied early career, lumbering in the southern states of the USA, working on the Baltimore and Ohio Railway, and the Rohkind and the Kumson Railway in India, before joining the North Eastern Railway in England in 1904. There he had had a rapid rise to positions of responsibility, becoming Deputy General Manager in 1911 and Traffic Superintendent in 1912. Following 'the great shell scandal' after the failure of the spring offensive on the Western Front in 1915, Lloyd George established the Ministry of Munitions. When he interviewed Geddes and asked him whether he had any knowledge of munitions, Geddes replied that he did not but 'he had a faculty for getting things done'.[18] Thereupon he was appointed Deputy Director General of Munitions Supply and then, in quick succession, Director General of Transportation on the staff of the Commander-in-Chief of the British Army in France, Director General of Military Railways and Inspector General of All Theatres of War (1917) and a member of the Board of the Admiralty. He was elected MP for Cambridge and was a member of the Cabinet from 1919–21.

On his arrival in France Geddes noted:

> The troops were fagged out because of lack of transport. The railheads were ten to fifteen miles back. The roads were blocked and the ammunition and guns were piling up in England. The transport network was so heavily sectionised that responsible officers had a narrow focus on problems which enabled them to make slight adjustments, but not to tackle the larger problems.[19]

Geddes filled the gap between the railheads and the front by building light railways, unifying the direction of supplies to eliminate delays. More importantly, in the longer term, he saw similarities with the transport system at home, with the 120 separate railway companies and almost antiquated freight movements (compared with the USA). In a letter to Lloyd George, of 18 November 1918, he wrote 'the experience of war should be harnessed in the government's search for economic recovery. I am impressed more and more, as I think it over, with the importance of dealing with the transportation problem'.[20] Geddes's plan was to establish a Ministry of Ways and Communications with ownership and control of roads, railways, light railways, canals, ports, air transport and electricity supply.

On 26 February, a Bill to establish a Ministry of Ways and Communications was introduced in the Commons by Edward Shortt, the Home Secretary, and Albert Stanley, the President of the Board of Trade. Its Clause

4 gave the minister power to own and control for the state, road and rail transport, light railways, canals and inland waterways, trams, ports and harbours, air transport and electric power. Shortt said that these means of communication were so essential to the community that they ought to be under one central control.[21] There was widespread opposition to the Bill, principally from Sir William Joynson-Hicks MP, who claimed that it would bring into being the most powerful ministry that had ever existed. He therefore advocated the creation of a separate department for roads.[22] Nevertheless, the second reading was carried. After an amendment accepted from the Lords to change the title to the 'Ministry of Transport', it eventually became law after it had received an unprecedented mauling from Opposition MPs, making it a very different animal to that which appeared in the first drafting.

Between the first and third readings a General Election was held on 14 December 1918, little more than a month after the armistice had been signed. Most of the newspapers stressed the need of the economy to be freed from 'excessive' government controls. Pro-Coalition candidates were elected by large majorities in an atmosphere of euphoria after victory. There was a record number of 174 MPs who were businessmen, many of whom 'had done well out of the war'.

The detailed discussion of the Bill for a Ministry of Transport came before the Cabinet on 19 February 1919, where it was first agreed that its clauses giving the ministry power to own shipping and ports should be removed. Then the clauses giving the ministry 'power to convey passengers and goods by air' were deleted. Responsibility for tramways was also deleted after R. Munro, the Secretary of State for Scotland, warned that Glasgow corporation would 'raise the strongest opposition' to any curtailment of its powers over transport services.[23] Finally, Austen Chamberlain, the Chancellor of the Exchequer, questioned 'whether it was right that the Bill should provide for the purchase of railways by the state'. Lloyd George only salvaged this part of the Bill by urging that it was necessary to keep it as a conciliatory gesture to the labour movement. 'If the government could say that they had in mind a proposal to make the railways state property it would be much easier to deal with the menacing industrial trouble.'

Meanwhile the Bill was subject to attack from other quarters. The parliamentary council advised that it conferred 'such autocratic powers' on the new minister that it would be difficult to get it through Parliament. It was undoubtedly an aspect of the Bill which reflected Geddes's experience as transport dictator on the Western Front, rather than any understanding of long-cherished parliamentary traditions.[24] On 10 March 1919 a deputation from the Federation of British Industries brought Geddes a resolution

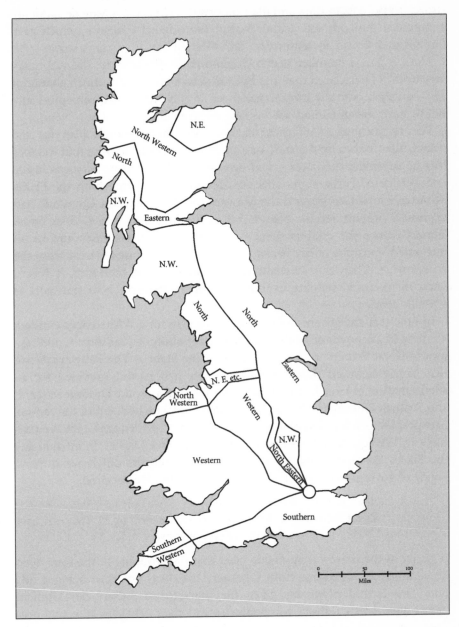

Map 2. Railway Grouping in 1921.

of unanimous opposition to any plans for railway nationalisation.[25] In committee meanwhile, Edward Shortt, the Home Secretary, yielded to strong pressure from rank and file Conservative MPs. On 6 May he suddenly announced the complete withdrawal of the original Clause 4, which gave the minister power to nationalise the different forms of transport.[26]

Thus, a senior member of the Commons, Sir F. Flannery, did not exaggerate when he declared that 'the Bill had sustained about as much alteration as ... anyone, even the most experienced in this House, can remember any Bill to have sustained and yet to have survived'.[27]

The significance of all these changes was that Geddes's plan for the ownership – either by the state or a private monopoly, and he told the CBI that he preferred the latter – had been wrecked by private interests inside and outside of Parliament. This was despite the fact that both the Prime Minister, Lloyd George, and the Minister for War, Winston Churchill, had expressed support for his plan.[28] But as the biographer of Geddes noted 'almost before the establishment of his department, Geddes's aim of an integrated transport policy became a casualty of the state's retreat from the economy'.[29] When the Railways Act followed in 1921 therefore, it was 'a quest for financial stability in industry, not the perception of transport as a public service'.[30]

In June 1920 the government produced its plan for a White Paper entitled: 'Outline of Proposals as to the Future Organisation of Transport Undertakings in Great Britain and their Relation to the State'.[31] The Railways Act of 1921 largely followed these proposals. In its first part it provided for an amalgamation of 120 companies into four large groups: the London Midland and Scottish Railway (LMS), which would control 60 per cent of the railway network; the London and North Eastern Railway (LNER); the Great Western Railway (GWR); and the Southern Railway (SR) (see Map 2). In introducing the Bill to the Commons, Sir Eric Geddes stressed the difference in basic policy of government from the pre-1914 principles. He declared:

> They had said, 'the more competition the better. If we only have two instead of one, they will cut each other's throats, and we shall benefit by it'. That may have been sound theory forty years ago. You cannot afford it today.[32]

A glance at the railway map makes clear that the grouping of the four main line companies, operative from 1 January 1923, was far from being a tidy one. This is understandable given the character of railway development before 1914, when railway companies spread their tentacles into any area they considered had prospects of profitable operation, irrespective of the niceties of geographical regions. In the railway map of 1923 the LMS had lines running to the south coast at Southampton, the east coast at Scarborough and the west coast at Liverpool. The SR and the GWR shared territory in Devon, and the LMS and LNER overlapped in Central Scotland.[33] After 1923 there was therefore still competition for custom in both passengers and freight. According to one authority 'perhaps one half of the receipts of the consolidated systems were exposed to competition possibilities'.[34] Of the eighty-four towns and cities with a population of over 50,000, sixty-four were served by more than one company before the 1923 grouping, fifty were still served by more than one company after it.[35]

So how successful were the changes introduced by the Transport Act of 1921? The result for freight transport was disappointing. In none of the inter-war years did the volume reach that of 1913. Even in the best year, 1937, the volume of merchandise goods carried was only 74 per cent of the 1913 level; and even though the record of heavy freight, predominantly coal and iron and steel, stood up better, it was still only 83 per cent of what had been achieved before the war. The number of passenger journeys in 1928 was similar to that of 1913. The revenue position of the companies was also disappointing. Freight receipts declined from £13,000,000 in 1922 to £10,200,00 in 1938. Over the same span of time passenger receipts fell from £83,000,000 to £59,000,000. Even allowing for a fall in the retail price index of one third, it was not very encouraging news to the railway companies' shareholders.

Among the causes of these depressing performances was the failure to establish a more rational system of railway rates and charges. In the pre-war years there was a widespread practice of allowing special discount rates for the transport of freight, in anticipation of retaining customer loyalty. In the hope of curbing this practice and creating a comprehensive system, a Railway Rates Tribunal was established under the 1921 Railways Act. But it proved difficult to achieve a simple nationwide scale of charges. In the search for covering all eventualities, much longer lists, filling huge ledgers, were compiled. This was unfortunate, as motor van competition was increasing. In the areas of keenest competition the railways' goods managers would have welcomed the opportunity of offering more flexible rates. After the war, army trucks were being sold at knockdown prices and demobilised soldiers could use their post-war gratuities to buy them. Then they could look up the scales of local collection and delivery charges posted in stations or goods depots and offer to carry merchandise at marginally lower prices than the railway company charged. In the 1920s the railways loss of custom for merchandise – generally short-distance – transport was more severe than for minerals and other heavy freight. In the 1930s the railways suffered more severely on the heavy freight side of their business – due to the great depression – than they did on the merchandise side.[36]

The *GWR Magazine* in its review of the year 1924 commented that 'the standard of freight working was well maintained, the miles per hour averaging between six and seven'.[37] This statement reveals the backward state of railway freight movement technology. The biggest obstacle to the more economical movement of freight was the survival of the ten ton wagon as characteristic when twenty ton capacity ones would have brought substantial savings in labour and time of delivery; but only 5 per cent of the wagon stock was of the larger capacity in 1939. Britain was far behind her main industrial rivals, as Table 2 reveals:

Table 2

Wagon and Train Loads in Tons in 1930

Country	Average Wagon Capacity	Average Load per Wagon	Average Train Load
Britain	11.3	5.64	130
Germany	16.0	7.7	290
USA	42.2	26.9	804

Source: K. G. Fenelon, *Railway Economics* (1932), p. 170.

A further influence holding back the railways from the greater development of their freight business was a certain complacency on some boards of directors, most notably on the LMS board, regarding the impact of road competition. The assumption throughout the company was that business would continue coming to them as before. The recently created Ministry of Transport did not attempt to disillusion management of their easy-going outlook.[38] It assumed that competition would be 'peripheral'. The government had established a Road Board on 18 February 1918. When its chairman, Sir Evan Jones, was interviewed by the Select Committee on Transport he said:

> So far as the development of a through or trunk service is concerned, I cannot conceive the possibility of development in this direction where railway or water development is available. Neither can motor transport compete in restricted areas with horse transport ... The special sphere of road transport will be in local distribution and as a feeder accessory to trunk systems.[39]

Ever since 1913 the railway companies were under a legal obligation to compile ton-mile statistics of their operations as well as passenger mile statistics. The statistics were gathered but were not published or used. They could have been a useful guide to operational policy.

At the outbreak of the Second World War in 1939 Great Britain had only two thousand route miles of electrified railways out of a total route mileage of 52,248.[40] The largest component of the electrified mileage was in the Southern Railway, where the Southern Electric boosted commuter services in the south east and holiday traffic to the south coast resorts. On the company's attractively produced posters, 'Sunny South Sam' urged passengers to 'take the plunge'. But with the important exception of SR, and some short lines in the Manchester area and on Tyneside, Great Britain's record was not impressive when compared with other European countries as Table 3 reveals:

Table 3

Percentage of Electrified Track in 1938

Belgium	0.9
Denmark	1.6
Hungary	3.3
Germany	5.0
Britain	5.3
France	7.8
Norway	9.2
Holland	15.1
Italy	28.2
Sweden	42.4
Switzerland	73.8

Source: *Modern Transport,* 12 August 1939.

While the number of private cars in Britain rose from 315,000 in 1922 to over two million in August 1939, the level of passenger fares on the main line railways was of considerable importance. Since it 'was often the case that passengers on the same train, travelling between the same places, were booked at half a dozen or more different fares',[41] it is necessary to treat with caution the assessment that some British passenger fares for a 186 mile journey were more expensive than they were for comparable distances in continental Europe.[42]

Passengers on through routes on British trains were not, in general, carried to their destinations any more speedily than they had been in 1913. The exceptions were the speeds on certain selected crack trains on the GWR, which brought the average speeds on that line in 1928 to 3.18 per cent above the pre-war level and the speeds on the SR, where electrification had improved average performance to 0.65 per cent above the level of 1913.

Speeds on both the LMS – at 2.86 per cent lower – and the LNER, at 1.12 per cent lower, served to bring the national average level of speed down to one per cent below that of 1913.[43] The fastest scheduled run in Great Britain in 1939, 71.9 miles per hour, on the London to York route, was fortieth in the world's list of fast trains.[44]

Meanwhile, the price of private motor cars fell by a third between 1923 and 1929, as did the cost of motoring. Petrol was cheap until the railway companies persuaded the Exchequer to tax it in 1928. Not surprisingly, those who could afford to buy a car decided to travel to Brighton, Eastbourne, Bournemouth, or elsewhere, in their 'baby' Austin or Vauxhall 8s, rather than going along with Sunny South Sam by rail. There were at the same time increasing opportunities for the less well off to travel by charabanc (later transformed, in terms of comfort, into the coach).

There were notable differences between each of the big four companies in how they coped with the rapidly changing circumstances of the inter-war years. The LNER had to contend with coastwise shipping competition more than did the other three. In this area post-war overcapacity produced some remarkably cheap rates, so that the coastal carriage of coal, which had been diverted to rail in the emergency of the war, was now fully restored, to the detriment of the rail company's finances. The 'senior railway', as the LNER was often called, also suffered from the economic depression of the early 1930s. In 1932 the volume of its mineral traffic was half that of 1924. The industrial relations on the railways of the north east had been good ever since the establishment of a conciliation scheme was established on the NER in 1909, but the cost of granting the eight hour day, forty-eight hour week, and the more comprehensive Central and National Wages Boards during the immediate post-war years, was an additional, though justified, burden on the company. (There was a pay cut of 2½ per cent in 1931 not fully restored until 1937.)[45] The LNER, more than the other three companies of the big four, stressed the importance of training. The craftsmanship in producing streamlined locomotives such as the *Flying Scotsman* and the *Mallard* (the locomotive which broke the world speed record for steam) was magnificent.

The LMS improved its productivity very little in its twenty-five year history. It pursued a gradual policy of replacing forty-five foot rails by sixty foot ones and containerisation of its merchandise traffic was brought in more rapidly than it was in the other companies. In respect of electrification of rail services, however, it was the most backward of the four. In his report of 1931 on the economic and other aspects of the electrification of the railway systems of Britain, Lord Weir reported that the circumstances were very favourable and that a return of 6.7 per cent on capital invested would be possible. But Lord Stamp, Chairman of the LMS, in his address to the company's shareholders in 1935 said:

> There does not appear to be any likelihood of any large scale outlay in the immediate future. We have a statutory obligation to show annually to the Railway Rates Tribunal that our affairs have been conducted with efficiency and economy, quite apart from the Board's obligation to you in this respect; and any new outlay for electrification or anything else must comply with that test.[46]

The company also preferred to use horse-drawn vehicles for collection from and delivery to stations. It handed over six thousand horses to the Railway Executive in 1948 when the Transport Act of 1947 came into operation.

The GWR was the second largest supplier of railway services in Britain before 1914 and the pre-war company was the dominant partner in the newly formed organisation of 1923.[47] The exception was the importance of the dock and coal lines of South Wales. The inter-war company concentrated on improving the dock services, but these were unprofitable until 1932.[48] As was the case with the LNER, it suffered severely from the falling demand for coal, iron and steel in the great depression of the early 1930s. In 1932 it was only able to pay its ordinary shareholders dividends by taking £1,700,000 from reserves and by selling some of its investments. Through its splendid 'Castle Class' locomotives, such as the *Caerphilly Castle* and the *Pendennis Castle*, it achieved greater speeds with less consumption of coal than did the LNER 'Pacifics'.[49] Less glamorous was the closure of seventeen branch lines on 22 September 1930 and the slow rate of improvement in signalling and freight trains.

The Southern Railway was the most successful, both in its finances and in its modernisation, of the big four companies. This was in part due to the fact that it was in a more prosperous region of the country than were the other three, and in part due to its good fortune in having the very able and imaginative Sir Herbert Walker as general manager until 1937. Walker saw the potential of railway electrification more clearly than his contemporaries. After extensive developments in the commuter areas of Kent, Surrey and Hants which were very profitable, he gained authorisation for electrification of the main lines to Portsmouth, Brighton, Hastings and other south coast towns. He was well known for his 'clock face', or regular interval, timetabling of trains.[50]

In the early 1920s neither the railway companies nor the government was unduly worried about the competition between privately-owned motor cars and the railways for passenger traffic; but motor coach competition was a different matter. During the railway strike of September and October 1919 the firm of Elliot Brothers of Bournemouth started an experimental weekend return service to London. This was extended until it was soon a twice daily one. Thereafter there was a 25 per cent expansion of the number of motor buses and coaches on British roads between 1920 and 1925.[51] One obvious response of the railways was to seek authorisation of Parliament to run their own bus and coach services. Their appeal to do so was rejected in 1922, but granted in 1928 when it was evident that the railways' passenger revenues were suffering from the competition. In the same year Baldwin's government appointed a Royal Commission under Sir Arthur Boscawen to consider the problems raised by the growth of road transport. Through the chaotic state of road signs and driving regulations, the number of those killed on the roads each year rose rapidly from 4856 in 1926 to nearly 6700 in 1929. Under Herbert Morrison's Road Traffic Act of 1930 all public service vehicles had to be licensed by the appropriate area traffic commissioner. The Road Service Licence, which every operator was obliged to have, was the means by which entry into road passenger service was regulated. The speed limit of twenty miles per hour, which had been in operation since 1903, was abolished; but compulsory third-party insurance was introduced.

Under the Road and Rail Traffic Act of 1933 the licensing system was extended to include all road freight vehicles. The Act also introduced a speed limit of thirty mph, except for commercial vehicles which were restricted to twenty mph. Some relaxation of the railway freight rates was allowed by permitting the use of 'agreed charges' under which the companies could do a package deal with a trader to carry the whole of his traffic at a flat rate per ton anywhere in Great Britain. Business firms could be granted 'C' licences to carry their own goods in their own vehicles.[52] At the time of the passing of the Act it was thought that this would only involve short-distance collection and delivery, but by the later 1930s there was a rapid growth of freight and merchandise collections and deliveries over long distances.

This was the last straw for the railway companies, who turned from a policy of negotiation and acceptance of the law to a vigorous campaign for radical changes. In November 1938, after discussions between the general managers, Sir R. L. Wedgwood of the LNER gained approval for his suggestion that they should call it a 'Square Deal' campaign. One of the arguments used was that 'motor vehicles were not required to bear in full either the capital or current cost of building or maintaining their "tracks"'.[53]

Coaches could unload their passengers at the kerbside and private motor cars could be parked in the street outside their owners' homes without paying local rates; but railways in 1928 paid 20 per cent of their net revenue in rates.[54] The situation had not changed ten years later. The statutory obligations of the railways, drafted in many cases before 1914, were based on the assumption that railways were a monopoly. This was no longer the case in the 1930s and the restrictions on the companies should therefore be removed. The negotiations following the publicity of the Square Deal campaign resulted in the report of the Transport Advisory Council (a body set up under the Road and Traffic Act of 1933), which recommended the removal of the legislation regarding classification, standard charges, exceptional rates and the railways' obligation to carry. The government accepted these recommendations but made no time to implement them by legislation before war broke out on 3 September 1939.[55]

In 1939 the railway companies seemed better prepared for the eventuality of war than were their predecessors before 1914. In September 1938, nearly a year before the declaration of war on Hitler's Germany, the Ministry of Transport appointed a Railway Executive Committee (REC) under the chairmanship of Sir Ralph Wedgwood, general manager of the LNER, the general managers of the other three companies and Frank Pick of the London Passenger Transport Board. An underground headquarters for the REC was prepared in London in the disused station of Wood Street on the Piccadilly Line between the Green Park and Hyde Park Corner stations.[56] The government appreciated, more keenly than did the cabinets of 1914–1918, the need to exercise control over all the principal forms of transport, and to that end set up a Coastal Shipping War Control Committee in 1938. At the same time it required the Regional Transport Committees (for road transport) to adjust their districts to coincide with railway districts for the better integration of services.

When war was declared, previously prepared plans for the evacuation of children, the sick and the elderly were put into effect. Congestion at the London and other main provincial termini was avoided by nominating 'designation' stations, such as Ealing Broadway, Bowes Park and Watford as assembly points. Over 600,000 persons were carried to the reception areas from London and a further 700,000 from other cities.[57] Wagon and locomotive pools were established, but the confidence in their ability to meet all demands expressed by the companies before the war was undermined when, as a result of traffic being moved from the east coast routes to the west, shortages of both were revealed. On 20 March 1940 the REC reported to the Ministry of Transport that, through delays in arrival of freight trains, the ICI had been obliged to collect and deliver its freight by road. The companies did their utmost to reduce empty running of wagons and to squeeze more freight into vehicles of all capacities. At Doncaster the staff at the plant works was instructed to plate up twelve ton wagons so they could carry thirteen tons.[58]

In Britain the number of railway-owned wagons decreased from 644,789 in 1938 to 593,177 in 1946. The number of passenger coaches fell from 40,793 in 1938 to 35,697 in the same period.[59] Nevertheless, with this reduced capacity the net ton miles of freight traffic grew from 16,266 net ton miles in 1938 to 22,023 in 1945, while passenger miles travelled increased from approximately 19,000,000 in 1938 to approximately 29,000,000 in 1945.

Conditions for passengers worsened during the war. The average number of persons carried per vehicle rose and locomotives – often reconditioned from the scrap heap – had more carriages to pull. The average passenger train load doubled. Air raid warnings and black outs made for uncertainties and accidents. Box-like lamp shades in carriages focused a low voltage light direct to the lap of the person trying to read. Railway posters and newspaper advertisements carried the message: 'Is your journey really necessary?'

The Dunkirk evacuation revealed the British gift for improvisation in an emergency; hundreds of 'little ships' rescued thousands of troops from Dunkirk's beaches. From the English Channel ports the REC's Operation Dynamo provided a pool of 186 trains to deal with the emergency. Nearly 4800 special trains were provided for the D-Day landings.

The financial arrangements under which the railways were operated by the companies for the government were defined in two Railway Control Agreements which guaranteed the railways, as a 'floor,' their net revenues of 1935, 1936 and 1937 with any excess above this figure shared fifty-fifty with the government. But the assets handed over to the Railway Executive under the Transport Act of 1947 were in a depleted and run-down state. By September 1947 124,000 wagons or 16.6 per cent of the stock were either under or awaiting repair, and 12,000 coaches, or about 21.5 per cent of the stock, were over thirty-five years old.[60]

6

Motor Transport

Once the practicability of steam-powered locomotion on rails had been demonstrated by Timothy Hackworth, and George and Robert Stephenson, it was only to be expected that the question would be asked why there could not be steam locomotion on the king's highway?

The motor vehicle evolved over decades and a multiplicity of adaptations: from the hobby horse, to the bicycle, tricycle and motor cycle, to the light motor car. Indeed, 'the cycle, propelled by human energy, not the carriage drawn by a horse, was the important precursor and indeed prerequisite of the motor vehicle'.[1]

Throughout the railway age horse-drawn transport continued to increase. In the second half of the nineteenth century the number of horses on British roads increased from one and a quarter million to three and a quarter million. There was a strong incentive for anyone who could devise a mechanical replacement for horse transport over short distances between towns and villages. In fact the challenge was met by French, German and British inventors. In the 1860s the Frenchman Pierre Michaux fitted a crank and a pedal to the front wheel of a scooter. British inventors further improved the bicycle in the 1870s and 1880s, especially with the patenting of the safety bicycle in 1886, manufactured by firms such as Singer, Rover and Lodge. Such improvements as the light tubular frame, ball bearings, chain drive and pneumatic tyres further increased the acceptability of this mode of transport. The manufacturers' policy of standardising parts and introducing regular changes of model at the beginning of the spring season also became the policy in the motor car industry.[2]

From the stage of the bicycle there were three main possibilities of development. First, steam tractors and steam bicycles; secondly, motorised bicycles; thirdly, motor cars. Steam tractors had been used for heavy work on farms before the invention of the safety bicycle; but their invasion of the public roads was unpopular. The *Engineer*, though favouring their use in agriculture, found them 'utterly hideous, astoundingly noisy and to the last degree offensive in the matter of smoke'.[3] Despite these disadvantages, some gas works and breweries used them, and Thomas Aveling, a Kent manufacturer, told a parliamentary committee in 1873 that he had built 800 of them.[4]

By the end of 1903 the number of steam vehicles on British roads was estimated to be about a thousand, and Fodens, Thornycroft and Leyland had joined Aveling among the main producers. Horse-drawn vehicles were more expensive to use than steam-propelled ones because horses required costly acreages of hayfields for their feed.

In the meantime the production and use of motor cycles (with tricycles and quadricycles) had grown apace, though from a slow start. The first motorised cycle did not appear until 1869. This was essentially a Pierre Michaux machine which was popular in France, its country of origin. It was known in Britain as the 'Boneshaker' and was the first successful mechanically driven machine. Within its simple frame a particularly neat Perraux single-cylinder steam engine unit was installed, which drove the rear wheel by means of pulleys and a flexible belt. A leading authority on the history of the motor cycle claims that it was important historically as the prototype of motor cycle designs which appeared subsequently.[5]

Motor cycling thrived in Britain from 1919 to 1929. In 1924 the number of motor cycles on British roads exceeded the number of cars. In 1929 the number of motor cycles registered reached an all time high of 790,000. This part of the industry had benefited particularly during the First World War and its immediate aftermath. The engineering industry of the Midlands developed precision manufacture of shells, small arms and engine parts for army cycles and lorries in a big way. A special issue of *Motor Cycle* in 1934 celebrated 'the ascendancy of the British motor cycle industry over all international rivals'. It was ahead of all others in design and workmanship. In the fifteen yeas before the outbreak of the Second World War there was a concentration of motor bicycle firms from 120 to 32 and standardised production increased sharply. In 1929 a mere 103 foreign motor cycles entered Britain. In the 1930s, however, the industry declined as the Model T Ford, the Austin Seven ('Baby Austin') and other small cars were reduced in price through larger orders.[6]

Using a motor cycle in the early days presented a decided challenge, which was one of the reasons why the 'young bloods' of the 1920s chose it as a means of transport. Starting the engine required vigour and patience. A regular columnist of the journal *Motor Cycle* described the process:

> The first essential was to pedal the machine off on a stand until it felt hot and free and willing. No 'stand' was provided; but 'steps' were available on either side of the back wheel. At long last the engine would fire. There would be no hearty roar, such as salutes the ears of a modern rider a few seconds after he has tickled the float chamber. The initial explosion would be a singleton – as card players say – and it would sound like a maiden's sigh. Still, it converted your growing despair into ardent hope. You increased the revs of your ankling. In

perhaps half a minute, you would wring a genuinely audible puff from the engine. Faster and faster flew your legs and anon a 'tutta-tutta' would begin, and with further peddling would swell into quite a regular noise.[7]

It is true that to start a motor car in those days required repeated turning of the starting handle and tickling of the choke were required, but this was a decidedly quicker operation than starting a motor cycle.

The growth of motorised transport in Britain was at first heavily dependent on the technological inventiveness of Germans and the commercial imagination of the French in putting these discoveries to practical transport uses. At the Paris Exposition in 1867 a gold medal was presented to the German firm of Otto and Langer for producing an internal combustion engine. In the seventeen years following the award of the medal, fifty of these engines were sold worldwide, totalling 200,000 horsepower. In the meantime a fellow German, Gottlieb Daimler, and his associate conducted experiments at Connstadt into a high-speed petrol-driven engine and in 1886 a four-wheel petrol-driven carriage was to be seen in the streets of Stuttgart. Yet another German, Karl Benz, produced a prototype three-wheeler which could attain a speed of ten miles per hour and was almost certainly the first ever motor car sold commercially. The patents for these engines eventually passed into the hands of a Frenchman, Edouard Levassor. Although an Englishman, Edward Butler, the son of a west country farmer, made what was the first petrol-driven car produced in England, further progress was impeded by the terms of the Locomotive Act of 1861, which gave the Board of Trade power to ban the use of any locomotive traction engine which was found 'to cause excessive wear and tear on the road surface'. A further Locomotive Act of 1865 imposed a speed limit of four miles per hour on all mechanically propelled vehicles on roads and obliged each owner to send a man with a red flag to walk sixty yards in front of the vehicle to warn pedestrians of its approach.[8] The Act was amended in 1876 to reduce the distance of the man from the vehicle to twenty yards. These Acts were repealed in 1896.

The early British contribution to the development of motor transport was primarily entrepreneurial and commercial. The two most prominent innovators in this context were Sir David Salomans, who founded the Self-Propelled Traffic Association – the first of the motoring associations – in 1895, and H. J. Lawson, who bought up many patents for car engines and established the Automobile Club (later the Royal Automobile Club) in 1897.

There was considerable hesitation from British investors in the 1890s about which type of machine would best meet the requirement of farmers (looking for a suitable means of conveying hay to horses), professional people or members of high society. The road races which took place in France, Germany, Spain and Britain helped them to make up their minds. Pierre

Gifford, a Frenchman, arranged the Paris-Rouen run of 1895 in which 102 vehicles of all kinds, including some driven by steam, took part. All the petrol-driven cars finished the race. The correspondent of the English journal the *Engineer*, who witnessed the race, reported of the petrol-driven vehicles that 'they can go as fast as any ordinary cyclist cares to travel'.[9]

In June of the following year, 1896, a more ambitious race from Paris to Bordeaux and back, a total of 732 miles, was organised. Emile Levassor, who came in first, completed the course in a running time of forty-eight hours forty-eight minutes. He had a mechanic with him, but he supervised his own machine constantly. To have achieved an average speed of fifteen miles per hour 'was an astonishing achievement that caught the world's imagination ... it was for motor vehicles what the Rainhill Trials had been for railways'.[10] These happenings persuaded car enthusiasts in England such as F. R. Simms and Edward Montagu (Lord Montagu of Beaulieu) to arrange events, including the London to Brighton and back race, later in 1896, and the more ambitious 'thousand mile' run from London to Edinburgh and back in 1900. In all these contests, both on the European Continent and in Britain, petrol-driven cars proved the most reliable. They were decisive events for the motor industry in Britain and abroad.

One of the pioneers of British motor car manufacture was Herbert Austin. Born at Little Missenden, Buckinghamshire, in November 1866, he emigrated to Australia where he served an apprenticeship in engineering in Melbourne, before returning to England to serve as a director of the Wolseley Sheep Shearing Company and then managing director of the Wolseley Tool and Motor Car Company. From this base he produced, first, a motorised three wheeler, then, in 1898, an improved three wheeler in which he drove the 250 miles to Rhyl and back in June 1898. In 1900 he began making cars on his own account at Longbridge, Birmingham. The famous Austin Seven appeared in 1922, and was soon in quantity production. Another pioneer, William Morris (later the first Viscount Nuffield), was an Oxfordshire man without much formal education but with an understanding that it was necessary to reduce costs and prices if the objective was to increase sales. With his Morris Minor car he reduced the price of the vehicle so that it was brought within the means of a skilled artisan or a better-paid clerk. At the other end of the car market, the Rolls company, formed in 1902, was soon producing its high-quality limousines.

Early motorists of late Victorian and Edwardian days were often viewed with serious misgivings and even loathing. The machines were noisy and highly obtrusive. Many of the first motorists came from the aristocracy. Lord Montagu of Beaulieu recalled that when he went on his first car journey from London to Windsor in 1897 in a Panhard:

The people by the roadside were not only interested but alarmed ... some people rushed into their homes, most horses cocked up their ears and in some cases attempted to bolt. Public attention in fact, was divided between curiosity and cursing ... Hotel keepers generally regarded us as people not to be admitted ... One irate proprietor said he was not going to have any of those contraptions near his place, for they might blow up at any time.[11]

The arrogant behaviour of some motorists led a group of MPs to press the government to rush through Parliament, late in the session in August 1903, a Motor Car Bill which became law on 1 January 1904. In the Second Reading debate in the Commons on 4 August 1903 a strong feeling was expressed by some members that 'road hogs' (to use the current term) should receive steeper punishment for reckless driving than the £10 fine generally given. Sir Brampton Gurdon said that fines were 'quite useless' and that 'it is necessary that we should be able to inflict the penalty of imprisonment ... I would almost consent in some cases to the punishment of flogging'.[12] The speaker had the support of Walter Long, the President of the Board of Trade, who conceded 'it is not only the security of life and limb that has to be dealt with, but also the extraordinary discomfort suffered by people who live on the roads which motors largely frequent'.[13]

Consequently, the Act's first clause declared it an offence for any person to drive a car on the public highway 'recklessly or negligently'. The Act also required all motor vehicles to be registered with a County or County Borough Council and for them to display a number plate on the front and rear of the motor body; the driver of a vehicle must have an annually renewable driving licence for which the charge would be 5s.; a court of law could suspend or withdraw the licence and a motorist had the duty to stop and help the police and others dealing with the incident Since it was generally agreed that the speed limit which existed before the Roads Act was passed – four miles an hour – was widely ignored and useless, a new limit of twenty miles per hour was introduced.

Critics of the 1903 Motor Car Act were not satisfied, however, that it had provided sufficiently stiff penalties for those driving recklessly on the roads. In 1905 the government therefore set up a royal commission under the chairmanship of Lord Selby to inquire into the working of the Motor Car Acts of 1896 and 1903, comparing the use of motor cars in Britain with those of other European states, finding out whether any amendments were necessary and whether any, and what, additional changes should be imposed in respect of motor cars.

The evidence heard from witnesses to the members of the commission made it clear that many influential people were dissatisfied with the working of the 1903 Motor Car Act. Miss Evelyn Everett-Green who lived close to the main road between Guildford and Dorking, one of the best-known novelists of her day and authoress of over a hundred books, had owned a car for the one year of 1897 and kept it in the stable with her horses, before she gave it up as too dangerous. Drivers of cars would go 'at any speed they chose', the dust stirred up by cars passing her house at speed meant that 'all her flowers were spoiled, and our health was injured'. She could not use the house 'from the vibration, the noise and the smell' and 'had to build a study' away from the road, further down the garden. She was sorry for her neighbours and afraid for the lives of the children, as 'the cars come at such an awful rate'. Under questioning, she agreed that 'if the main roads were made dustless, it would be a great boon to the public', but she did not believe they could be.[14]

Dr H. E. Porter, who was the first medical man in Britain to use a motor and was at the time of the royal commission in practice at 6 Grosvenor Street, London, had a very different story to tell. He gave numerous cases of his having saved lives through having a car. Called out to a patient with angina, if he had to turn out horses and a man, the patient might possibly have died through the delay. In the event, with a motor car it meant 'the turn of a handle and I was off'. G. B. Lockwood, a surgeon at St Bartholomew's Hospital, London, was emphatic 'I could not possibly go back to horses', he said.[15]

Another witness who was dissatisfied with the working of the Motor Car Act was James Boyce of the Cyclists' Touring Club. He pointed out the inadequacy of road sign warning notices and their variation as between different counties, and observed that cars in the £150 to £180 range caused more smell than did the expensive limousines. He favoured a lower speed limit than twenty miles per hour.

Two witnesses before the commission who could be said to represent vested interests were the Hon. Arthur Stanley MP, chairman of the Automobile Club of Great Britain and Ireland (1897), shortly afterwards renamed the Royal Automobile Club (RAC), and William Rees Jeffreys, secretary of the Motor Union. The RAC recruited mainly the better off motorists while the Motor Union's members were less aristocratic. Both organisations were opposed to any general speed limit. Stanley maintained that the existence of a 20 mph limit caused the police to set up speed traps on open roads away from towns and villages. This 'encouraged inconsiderate motorists to drive at a speed, which is undoubtedly high, through the villages'.[16] He dubbed the government driving test as 'no test at all'. It should be left to the trade to deal with. Significantly, he told the chairman, Viscount Selby, that, before the hearings, the chief motoring organisations of all kinds had 'met together' to agree how they might assist the royal commission. It could be said, therefore, that the 'motoring interest' was established in the autumn of 1905. By contrast, cyclists, pedestrians, and representatives of local authorities, such as H. Hampton-Copnall, the Clerk of the Nottinghamshire County Council who wanted more government funding of roads, had not met together to devise a common approach to road transport policies. Thus the road lobby had a head start in influencing Whitehall opinion which it kept for many years.[17]

The most influential witness interviewed was William Rees Jeffreys. His organisation had more than three times the number of members as Arthur Stanley's and he spoke with authority and was treated deferentially by the chairman. He stressed that the car was 'taking its place with the horse-drawn carriage in the daily life of the people'. He criticised the prevalent belief that 'the motor car is used mainly for purely pleasure touring. We get the picture of rich men rushing round the country causing dust and annoyance for which there is practically no compensation'. If they realised that 'the typical automobilist is the doctor using his car for his professional work, the businessman and the country gentleman using it to and from the station, I am inclined to think their attitude would be very largely modified'. Regarding the complaint that drivers created excessive noise through the repeated sounding of their car horns, he found 'a practical difficulty from the automobilist's point of view'. If an accident happened 'it was at once alleged on the other side that the driver did not sound his horn, and that is practically fatal to the case of the motor driver in a county court action'. He admitted the dust problem, but pointed to 'numerous experiments with tars' and regretted that there was 'no machinery for centralising the results'. He recommended the creation of a small highway department of experts at the Local Government Board 'to collect together the experience of road construction and especially dustless road construction'.[18]

The report of the royal commission was drafted in the period of the Conservative government of A. J. Balfour but published following the victory of the Liberal Party in the general election of 12 January to 7 February 1906. It recommended the abolition of the general speed limit for light cars and the introduction of the annual registration of motor vehicles. The money motorists paid in tax for this registration would go to local authorities via the government, which would give grants for the improvement of existing roads and the construction of new ones. These proposals were shelved, however, pending the new administration's adoption of its welfare programme, particularly the introduction of old age pensions. Nevertheless, David Lloyd George, who was appointed Chancellor of the Exchequer under Herbert Asquith on 12 April 1908, was very concerned about the state of

Britain's roads and the high death toll that occurred on them. In his budget speech of 29 April 1909, he said:

> This problem is urgent ... Any man who takes the trouble to consider the damage which is done to the roads of this country by men who do not contribute ... to the upkeep of the roads they help so effectively to tear up ... the consequence of the rapid increase in the expense of road maintenance, the damage done ... to the amenities of rural life by the dust clouds which follow in the wake of these vehicles, above all the appalling list of casualities to innocent pedestrians, especially to children, must come to the conclusion that this is a question which demands immediate notice at the hands of central government.[19]

The Lloyd George budget increased one of the taxes on motorists and introduced a new tax. The licence duty of motor cars was raised from a uniform four guineas to a variable one, from two guineas for cars of less than six and a half horsepower to ten guineas for cars of up to forty horsepower, and forty guineas of large cars of above sixty horsepower. The new tax was on petrol levied at three pence a gallon. The Chancellor assured the Commons that the whole of the new money so raised would go to the improvement of the roads. The administration of these monies would be through the Central Road Board in Whitehall, to be established in 1910.[20] This was an important innovation. Since the departure of the Romans from Britain in 410 AD central government had had no responsibility for the main roads. Under the 1555 Highways Act the maintenance of roads had become the responsibility of local parishes employing unpaid labour under the direction of unpaid surveyors. As we have seen, the users of the numerous turnpike trusts contributed to the upkeep of such roads (a very small proportion of all the highways of the kingdom) by the payment of tolls. Under the Local Government Acts of 1888 and 1889, however, responsibility for the main roads had been transferred to county boroughs and county councils. Lloyd George's establishment of the Road Board was an important turning point: the government had accepted the principle that it had some responsibility for the maintenance of the nation's roads.

The resolution of the problem of the dust thrown up by cars on roads came through improvements in the technology of road construction and maintenance rather than the reduction of government imposed speed limits. Agitation for more energetic research on improvement of road surfaces came from cyclists through their membership of the Road Improvement Association founded in 1886, and through their largest organisation, the Cyclists' Touring Club, which had a membership of 60,499 in 1899. Asphalt slabs were first laid on a London carriageway in 1869 and the use of limestone slag as a road-building material followed soon after. In 1901 Parnell

Hooley patented his 'black top', later known as 'tarmac', for the firm top-surface of roads in 1901.[21] The foundation of Tarmac Ltd in 1903 was timely. The number of motor vehicles (apart from buses) licensed rose rapidly from 35,000 (23,000 private cars and 12,000 goods vans) in 1906 to 214,000 in 1914.[22]

The nature of the early car market in Britain encouraged individualistic methods of production and delayed the introduction of standardisation and mass production. It was said that automobilism as a sport was mainly for rich men. Like Toad of Toad Hall, the younger gentry who predominated as early owners of the new means of transport were possessed by the new craze and were mesmerised 'by the magnificent motor car, immense, breath-snatching ... with an interior of plate-glass and morocco'.[23] Such customers wanted high-powered cars made to their own specifications.[24] Manufacturers complied with their wishes. The firm of Napier, for example, through its selling agent S. F. Edge Ltd., quoted 'a price for the frame and all the driving mechanism ... but without any body'. The superstructure was constructed according to the particular requirements of the purchasers – a continuation of the practice of coaching days. Also, although James Whitworth had introduced a system of standardisation of screw threads as long ago as 1841, there was very little standardisation of spare parts for cars. Henry Ford, in Detroit, had the advantage over his British contemporaries that there were already standardised components available when he began the production of his famous Model T.

Although at the lower end of the market the three firms of Morris, Austin and Singer produced 40 per cent of the output, they were the exception in that they survived and expanded to become household names in the 1920s. The turnover of firms in the industry was rapid as Table 4 indicates:

Table 4

Number of Firms Making Motor Cars in Britain to 1914

Date	Number Founded	Existing in 1914	Failed pre-1900	Failed 1901–5	Failed 1906–10	Failed 1911–14	Total Number of Firms at End of Period
To 1900	59	21	6	18	12	2	53
1901–5	221	22	–	59	112	28	197
1906–10	49	24	–	–	13	12	109
1911–14	64	46	–	–	–	18	113
Total	393	113	6	77	137	60	

Source: S. B. Saul, 'The Motor Industry in Britain to 1914', *Business History*, 5 (December 1962), p. 22.

The circumstances of the First World War had mixed effects on the motor car industry in Britain. Personal travel and civilian business activity were curtailed in the later stages of the war, but car firms such as Daimler benefited through large-scale army orders for tanks, staff cars and ambulances. Possibly the greatest boost to transport was given through the training given in driving to thousands of servicemen.

An important influence on the long-term future of motor transport was the character of the department set up under the Ministry of Transport Act of 1919. Sir Eric Geddes, the first Minister of Transport, had wanted a ministry with comprehensive powers over all forms of transport so that the minister could exercise a balanced control over all modes of land, sea and air transport. The motor lobby, however, was concerned that the new ministry would be a predominantly railway lobby – after all, the minister and his secretary had been leading executives of the North Eastern Railway Company. After extended discussions, a compromise was reached. There was to be a department within the ministry. Section 2 (4) of the Act read: 'there shall be attached to the Ministry a separate department charged with dealing in the ordinary course of departmental business with road construction improvement, maintenance and development'. Section 22 (1) of the Act further curtailed the minister's comprehensive powers over the nation's transport thus:

> for the purpose of giving advice and assistance to the Minister with respect to and safeguarding any interests affected by the exercise of the powers, and performance of his duties under this Act in relation to roads, bridges ... and traffic thereon, a committee (hereafter referred to as the Roads Committee) shall be appointed. (2) The Roads Committee shall consist of not less than eleven members, of whom five shall be representative of highway authorities and five shall be representative of the users of horse and mechanical road traffic, appointed after consultation with the interests concerned, and one shall be a representative of labour appointed after consultation with the interests concerned.

The creation of a separate Roads Department was a victory for the road lobby. In addition, 'the consequence of this struggle for independence was that each department within the Ministry acted in a totally uncoordinated fashion so far as policy developments in other modes of transport were concerned.' [25] In the years that followed, road building and motor transport experienced an ever-growing importance by comparison with the railways. The proportion of the staff employed in the ministry concerned with road transport, as compared with those dealing with railway matters, increased sharply, so that in the second half of the twentieth century they outnumbered them by four to one.

In the decade which followed the establishment of the Ministry of Transport in 1919 there was growing disquiet in both business and political circles over the shortcomings of post-war transport policy. There was growing alarm at the rise in the number of road deaths. The number killed in road accidents rose sharply from 4856 in 1926 to nearly 6700 in 1929. The rise was widely attributed to the increase in the number of heavy lorries on roads in built-up areas. At a meeting of the Manchester Chamber of Commerce held early in February 1928, the view was expressed that 'too much of the heavy transport was being diverted to the roads, that the roads were gradually being made impassable and that an enquiry should be made into the whole question'.[26] In fact, a few weeks earlier Wilfred Ashley, the Minister of Transport, had suggested, in a memorandum to the Cabinet that there was a strong case for the appointment of a royal commission to consider the coordination of all forms of transport.[27]

Later in 1928 the government appointed a royal commission under Sir Arthur Boscawen

> to take into consideration the problems arising out of the growth of road traffic and, with a view to securing the employment of the available means of transport in Great Britain (including transport by sea and by ferries) to the greatest public advantage, to consider and report what measures, if any, should be adopted for their better regulation and control, and, so far as it is desirable in the public interest, to promote their coordinated working and development.[28]

The commission sat for thirty days hearing evidence from fifty-six witnesses and often challenging the views expressed. Sir Arthur Stanley spoke to a memorandum submitted by a conference of motor organisations. He claimed that transport coordination could best be achieved when left to the stimulus of 'normal economic and commercial' forces and believed that 'no good purpose' was served by the existence of a general speed limit. The introduction of compulsory driving tests was 'not in the public interest'.[29] Stenson Cooke of the AA agreed with Sir Arthur Stanley in his opposition to speed limits but offered positive suggestions about road widths and building lines with the object of preventing ribbon development. He deplored the chaos of road signs resulting from each county or county borough having its own policy, and favoured the enforcement of national standards.[30]

The general secretaries of the three principal railway unions were agreed that the transport situation in Britain was chaotic and that the Minister of Transport should be 'restored to the position he was intended to occupy at the time of the ministry's inception'. Proper coordination between the railway service and other means of transport could only come through the ministry itself.[31] Charlie Cramp, the Industrial General Secretary of the

National Union of Railwaymen (NUR), favoured a coordinated transport system where goods were taken to main freight centres by rail and then small quantities taken by road short distances, for instance London to Birmingham by rail, then on to Wolverhampton by road.[32] John Bromley of the Associated Society of Locomotive Engineers and Firemen (ASLEF) favoured traffic-free zones in the great cities. John Cliff, the Assistant General Secretary of the Transport and General Workers Union, maintained that competition was 'wasteful and inefficient'. In the 'thickly populated' bus routes there was oversupply of services while 'the sparsely populated areas were ill-served'.[33]

The final report of the Royal Commission on Transport appeared in 1931.[34] It declared the law on the speed limit was 'obsolete' and that probably not one driver in a thousand observed the general speed limit of twenty miles per hour. Many bus companies had issued timetables, sometimes with the approval of the licensing authority, under which their vehicles are scheduled to travel at greater speeds. The commission did not accept the argument of L. S. Shrapnell-Smith, a leader of the road interest, that, since there were more traffic 'units' operating on the roads than on the railways, road transport was safer.[35] Its report noted that in 1928 6127 persons were killed and 104,487 were injured on British roads. Although it conceded that 'the benefits conferred on the country by mechanical transport [were] indisputable; 6000 deaths in one year, with the prospect of a greater death toll in each succeeding year [was] a very heavy price to pay'.[36] While the drivers of private cars and commercial vehicles were the worst offenders, public service vehicle drivers were commended. 'Great care was exercised by the drivers of omnibuses in London.' In its view 'road hogs, as they have been properly called [had] not been dealt with severely enough'. It recommended for the safety of pedestrians (paragraph 1) that 'special crossing places should be arranged, clearly marked with notices – *Please cross here*'. (This idea was followed up by Leslie Hore-Belisha, as Minister of Transport, in 1935.)

Following the creation of the second Labour government after the general election of 1929, Herbert Morrison, the new Minister of Transport, was keen to bring his Road Traffic Bill before the Commons, as he knew that Lord Cecil of Chelwood had introduced a Road Regulation Bill in the Lords the previous July and that it had received popular support. He did not wish the Conservatives in Parliament to steal Labour's thunder. Morrison's Bill was given priority and became law as the Road Traffic Act of 1930. This included the complete overhaul of the system of licensing public service vehicles. All the previously existing arrangements were abolished. The country was divided into thirteen traffic areas – eleven for England and Wales and two for Scotland, with a full-time paid Area Traffic Commissioner in charge of each. It was provided that each public service vehicle operator was required to hold three licences. The public service vehicle licence was required for the vehicle and was issued subject to an approval by an inspection by a qualified motor engineer. The drivers' and conductors' licences were issued on condition of the operator paying adequate wages and not employing drivers more than five and a half hours continuously, or eleven in a day. Compulsory third party insurance was to be introduced. Under section 48 of the Act it was laid down that all traffic signs were to be of the 'prescribed size, colour and type', thus ending the confusion arising from conflicting practices – hitherto a frequent cause of accidents.

The most controversial part of the Bill was the provision for the abolition of the speed limit of 20 mph. Dr A. Salter, Mr E. Scrymteor and other MPs spoke very strongly against it, so that four years later in 1934, when 7343 persons were killed on Britain's roads, Parliament responded with the passing of the Road Traffic Act in 1934, reintroducing a speed limit of thirty miles per hour in built-up areas. Compulsory driving tests were introduced for the first time and penalties for breaking the law were increased.

It was not until 1933 that Parliament extended the system of licensing and control to road hauliers. The existence of many small haulage firms had deterred ministers from taking action, but pressure from the three main railway unions persuaded P. J. Pybus to agree to ask Sir Arthur Salter, one time director of the economic and finance section of the League of Nations, to chair a conference of road and rail representatives to examine the claim that road hauliers did not pay in taxes the full cost of the damage they did to the roads, and to consider what changes in regulations should apply to goods transport by road and rail, 'in view of modern economic developments'. The Road and Rail Traffic Act of 1933 largely followed the recommendations of the Salter Conference in its belief that it was 'not in the national interest to encourage further diversions of heavy goods traffic from the railways to the roads'. To establish more effective control over roads goods haulage, it provided that no person was permitted to carry goods commercially except under licence. Regular road hauliers required a public carrier's or 'A' licence; those who used their vehicles partly for their own business and partly to carry for others required a limited carrier's or 'B' licence, and those whose vehicles were used exclusively for their own business required a private carrier's or 'C' licence. The Traffic Commissioners who issued the licences could control the number of carriers in business through the fact that the licence franchises were of limited duration: two years for an 'A' licence, one year for a 'B' licence and three years for the 'C' variety. These new controls brought some satisfaction to the owners of larger businesses and to the railway companies, both of whose traffic was being undermined by the sniping of the small concerns whose owners (and their employees) worked longer hours. The court of the licensing authority could intervene to try to ensure better working conditions for those employed in the industry. It was expected that the implementation of the Act would ensure consolidation of ownership in the industry. This did not happen. When the ministry assessed the nation's resources just before the Second World War, it found that even the 350 largest firms could muster only 30,000 vehicles, an average of under thirty vehicles per firm.[37]

It also seems to be the case that the average distance goods were carried by road remained relatively low over the period from the Railways Act of 1921 to the late 1950s.[38] The average delivery rose only from 22.2 miles in 1952 to 23.8 miles in 1958, while the comparable railway freight deliveries fell only slightly from 73.5 miles to 70.6 miles. Although the volume of road freight carried did not exceed that carried on the railways until 1954, the value of the road freight moved amounted to 67.2 per cent of the combined road and rail total in 1953. This was due to the fact that the railways carried the high volume, relatively low value freights – coal and iron and steel – whereas the roads took the shorter distance higher value freights.

Following the success of the right-wing coalition candidates in the general election of 14 December 1919, the government launched a determined campaign to reduce industrial costs by cutting wages. One result was the national railway strike of 29 September to 5 October 1919. This provided an opportunity for the cabinet to test its previously arranged plans to organise the distribution of foodstuffs and other essential goods by road. Military transport and food rationing helped the government at that time. Wage cuts were no remedy for the coal and railway industries in urgent need of new investment, and the railway workers' solidarity with the miners was fully understandable. When the General Strike came, on 3 May 1926, the government had to depend on private owners of trucks voluntarily lending them to the Ministry of Transport during the emergency. Over the nine days of the strike 'the emergency organisation of transport by road was tested (through the arrangements made by fifteen transport committees), and was found adequate to the essential needs of communal life'.[39] It had been demonstrated that motor transport as well as coastal shipping could transport essential freight long distances as well as the shorter distances hitherto considered the main function of road transport.

The development of the British motor car industry between the wars was aided by the decision of government to retain the McKenna duties of 33.3 per cent on car imports, first imposed in 1915, after the war. It was hoped that these would provide a shield behind which the industry would consolidate into fewer, larger businesses which would be better able in time to stand up to foreign competition; but the rate of consolidation was slower than had been anticipated. Morris Motors, however, which had developed mass production, based on Taylorism (payment by results) for the manufacturer of armaments during the war, switched to standardisation and mass production of its Morris Minor and Morris Oxford in the 1920s. Its output of 55,582 in 1928 greatly exceeded Ford's output of 33,371.[40] Meanwhile the relative importance of the motor cycle industry declined in the inter-war period.

Whereas in 1924 there were slightly more motor cycles than cars licensed – 496,000 to 474,000 – in 1938 there were more than four times as many cars as there were motor cycles – 1,944,000 to 462,000.[41] This was partly due to the Exchequer's failure to reduce the duty on motor cycles of under 200 ccs and the consequent boost of sales of small cars, such as the Morris Minor and the Austin Seven. It was also the case that driving or riding on the pillion of a motor cycle was the most dangerous form of transport before the Second World War. In Britain in 1928 a half of fatal accident victims were motor cycle drivers or their pillion passengers. Drivers and passengers got more protection from the body work of a car.[42]

In the same way as the steam-powered tricycle can be seen as the precursor of the light-weight motor car, so the stage coach, running on a fixed route at regular time intervals, can be recognised as the forerunner of the horse-drawn omnibus. At least a quarter of a century before the opening of the Stockton and Darlington Railway on 27 September 1825, horse-drawn bus services were operating on some British roads.

In 1775 Matthew Pickford, the son of the founder of the famous carrying firm, went into partnership with the proprietors of several inns on the road from Manchester to London to provide a coach service between the two cities, and from 1781–80 was linked with coach proprietors serving eight other towns and cities throughout the kingdom.[43] The famous London coachmaster, Edward Sherman, who operated the Beehive coach from London to Manchester in 1790, provided his customers with spring cushioned seats and an interior lamp for the overnight journey. In 1790 a horse-drawn bus ran regular services between Manchester and Rochdale.[44]

Before the motor age there were numerous examples of horse-drawn bus services linking railway stations with nearby towns and villages – examples of transport integration. White's *Suffolk Gazette* of 1855 lists various coaches that linked Saxmundham and Woodbridge to Ipswich 'to meet the railway trains from London, etc'.[45] The Great Exhibition in London in 1851 prompted the promotion of many coach services to join main line railway stations with termini in the capital.

When motor buses gradually replaced the horse-drawn variety in the first decade of the twentieth century, the larger railway companies began to provide their own bus services to link their more distant termini with outlying towns and villages. Frank Potter, the General Manager of the Great Western Railway, told the Commons Select Committee of Transport that his company ran no less than thirty-three such services, of which ten were in Cornwall, five were in Devon, while there were two each in Carmarthen, Gloucester and Monmouth. The earliest established of these links was between Penzance and Land's End, opened in April 1904 but it only survived a month. Doubts about the value of these experiments were expressed both in the railway company boards and among members of the public who argued that a priority of the railway companies should be to improve their railway services rather than dabble with other forms of transport.[46]

The number of buses on the roads of Britain rose from 35,000 in 1914 to 46,000 in 1928, the year in which the Royal Commission on Transport had been appointed.[47] With the exception of the London General Omnibus Company, formed in 1859, very few bus proprietors owned more than a small number – most frequently one or two – buses. At the beginning of the 1930s there were over 6000 operators. As late as 1937 there were still 1850 operators who owned only one bus each. In the late 1920s Mr Barnes ran a single-decker bus from Ventnor railway station in the Isle of Wight to the villages of Whitwell and Niton four to six miles inland. The single adult fare was 4d. to Whitwell, with children carried at half fare.*

When Herbert Morrison became Minister of Transport in the second Labour government, on 7 June 1929, one of his main concerns was to increase the efficiency of bus services throughout the country. There was an intensively competitive situation with 'pirate' buses 'cutting in' on established companies' vehicles, cutting fares or timing their services to reach bus stops two or three minutes ahead of established rivals and only running their services during morning and evening rush hours. The bankruptcy rate was high. One of the stated objects of the Royal Commission on Transport appointed by Herbert Morrison's predecessor, the Conservative William Ashley, was to promote 'the coordinated working and development of the different means of transport'.

John Cliff, the Assistant General Secretary of the Transport and General Workers' Union, and Richard Horsley, who represented the London and Provincial Omnibus Owners' Association, both pressed the royal commission to establish a limited number, say, eleven or thirteen, public service vehicle licensing authorities in large regions throughout the country. This

---

* As Philip Bagwell returned from school six times a week his father bargained with the proprietor to take him for 6d. a week, and on Saturdays at lunchtime Philip handed Mr Barnes a sixpenny piece. He (Mr Barnes) did have some more renumerative passengers.

proposal was embodied in the terms of the Road Traffic Act 1930. Responsibility for such licensing was in the hands of 1330 authorities from small boroughs, such as Sandwich in Kent, with two thousand inhabitants, to much larger conurbations with six figure populations. Their licensing policies varied greatly.[48] They were regulated by the Town Police Clauses Act of 1847 and 1889 which were no longer appropriate to the situation. There was widespread agreement both among the operators of larger bus undertakings and the travelling public that uncontrolled competition and a great diversity of ownership was not in the public interest.[49]

The Road Traffic Act of 1930 has been described as 'in many ways ... a major reform in a field where it was urgently needed'. But the high hopes that were held as to amalgamation of smaller firms into larger ones were slow in realisation. The proportion of acquisitions in the ten years between 1929 and 1939, compared with the ten years earlier, showed that consolidation was taking place but not as rapidly as had been expected. Thus Ribble Motor Services added sixty companies to its organisation in the latter decade, or 78 per cent of its pre-Second World War acquisitions, and Crossville Motor Services bought out seventy companies or 80 per cent of those companies it had acquired since its foundation. The really big changes in the consolidation process came in the war years, when hundreds of concerns were unable to continue independently.[50]

7

Urban Transport

The history of urban transport is more or less confined to the last two hundred years, during which time Britain was transformed from a land with a predominantly rural population into a nation of city dwellers. Urban transport is central to the history of urbanisation since life in cities, particularly modern cities, is structured around constant movement, and effective transport is the key to making this mobility possible. One of the distinguishing features of urban life is an increase in the distance between where people live and where they work. Up until the Victorian period most Britons walked to work. As towns grew in size so the distance between home and place of employment increased until it was too far to accomplish on foot; one of urban transport's fundamental aims was therefore to carry people to and from work, in modern parlance commuting. But urban transport consists of more than transport *within* towns and cities, it also means transport *into* and *out of* them. Transport, as has been pointed out by numerous historians, was crucial to determining how and where many towns developed.[1] Most of Britain's major urban centres grew in consequence of some advantage in communications and transport. Typically, many of Britain's older cities are ports or situated on navigable rivers, for example London, Bristol, Liverpool, Glasgow and Newcastle. More modern forms of transport also created towns, as the connection between the railways and centres like Crewe, Doncaster and Swindon illustrates. Railway stations became focal points in nineteenth-century city life, like churches or pubs, meeting places and points of departure for people leaving for a new job, a holiday or a war. Goods and produce also needed transport to reach urban markets. Food, fuel and building material had to brought in from the countryside, if not on the hoof, then by cart or railway wagon, canal barge, coastal ship or river lighter. Waste products, both human and animal, had to travel in the opposite direction: there was a lively trade in manure from the cities back to the countryside for fertiliser.

The urban setting was the area where local and provincial authorities dealt with transport systems. City or town councils operated or supervised transport undertaking, even if they did not actually own them. This tier of government at the municipal level often distinguished itself from the central government in London by the course and implementation of its transport policy. Bus and tram services, for example, could be supported out of local rates. The idea of many forms of public transport originates in British towns and cities, where we interpret public to mean collective as opposed to individual travel. In the two centuries since 1800 urban travel has evolved from primarily individual travel modes – the cabs and carriages of the well-to-do – through the collective travel modes of bus, train and tram, back to individual travel in the late twentieth century with the motor car.

In the early nineteenth century the commonest way of getting about a town or city was walking. Until about 1850 most cities in Britain remained walking cities which were small enough to be crossed on foot in under an hour.[2] The vast majority of people walked to work. In London at the beginning of the Victorian era, clerks and workers of similar status formed a large part of the great army of pedestrians who twice a day set out on the march to and from their place of work.[3] Every day, around 100,000 people crossed the River Thames by walking across London Bridge, and another 75,000 over Blackfriars Bridge.[4] City walking was a necessary rather than a pleasurable experience. The main roads of cities were full of people and animals, with the occasional cart or carriage sandwiched between them. They had little provision for pedestrians and were usually covered in horse dung, while the side streets leading off them were dank, ill-lit and sometimes dangerous for a stranger.

In London, which was by far the largest city in Britain, the main horse-drawn vehicle was the four-wheeled Hackney carriage. They had first appeared in the seventeenth century and could be hired by anyone, although the government had tried to control their number. In addition to horse-drawn carriages there were sedan chairs, which were especially favoured by women. London was at this time much wider from east to west than from north to south and an additional means of transport were the river craft on the River Thames which afforded considerable lateral movement across the city. But if a traveller wanted to reach a destination some distance from the river, and did not want to walk, the only other means of transport was horse-drawn. In 1831 Greater London had a population of around 1,900,000 which travelled, when it made up its mind – in sedan chairs, costers' barrows, gigs, buggies, phaetons, wagonettes, hackney carriages and various shandry-dans. The horse-drawn vehicles were iron-tyred, the streets were cobbled, and the din was nerve-shattering.[5] In 1834 Joseph Hansom patented a two-wheeled cab and the Hansom cab remained closely identified with London's transport for the rest of the nineteenth century. The Hansom, immortalised as Sherlock Holmes's favourite conveyance, was something of a revolution in horse-drawn vehicles. Unlike the four-wheeled Hackney carriages, it needed only one horse and had only two very large wheels. Hansoms were more stable that other carriages as the single axle passed beneath the passenger's seat while the driver stood behind and above. By 1896 there were 7586 Hansoms in London and a further 3449 four-wheel Hackney carriages.[6]

Hansom cabs were the forerunners of the modern taxi and thus an essential part of urban transport, providing an individual service equivalent to private carriage or car. They were, however, an expensive mode of transport and the fares were beyond the means of all but the professional and upper classes. From the beginning of the twentieth century they were replaced with remarkable speed by motor-driven taxis as Table 5 makes clear. Long before then, however, an alternative horse-drawn transport mode had already appeared on city streets – the omnibus.

Table 5

Licensed Cabs in London, 1900–35

	Horse-Drawn Hansoms (Two Wheel)	Clarences (Four Wheel)	Motor
1900	7531	3721	–
1905	6996	3935	19
1910	2003	2721	6397
1915	120	842	5832
1918	43	484	3821
1924	14	266	8043
1931	4	47	8152
1935	3	19	8181

Source: D. L. Munby, *Inland Transport Statistics, Great Britain, 1900–1970, Railways*, i, *Public Road Passenger Transport, London's Transport* (Oxford, 1978), pp. 565–67.

The first horse-drawn omnibus in Britain appeared in 1829 in London. They were slow and quite expensive for most workers, although cheaper than cabs or stage coaches, and they provided the first instance of public transport that made it possible for workmen to live more than walking distance from their work. The London service, between Marylebone and Bank, was started by George Shillibeer, who brought the idea from Paris. His vehicle was drawn by three horses and carried eighteen passengers – about the same as the path-breaking Douglas DC–3 airliner, one hundred years later. Shillibeer himself did not last long in the bus business and his successors fought over routes in London while their operations were illegal;

drivers often chained themselves to their seats, but frequently were they arrested. The Stage Carriage Act legalised and regulated the trade in 1832, as well as licensing omnibuses and their drivers. In the 1840s there were several competing bus companies in London. By 1854, of the nearly quarter of a million people who entered the City of London every day, 80 per cent did so on foot, the remainder being divided between horse-drawn bus, Thames steamboat and trains.[7] Buses in the 1850s averaged about five miles per hour and could carry twenty-two persons, twelve seated inside and ten on the top deck on a longitudinal knifeboard arrangement. Handrails were provided to prevent people falling off, although it took some time before 'decency boards' were provided to shield female passengers' legs from the gaze of people at road level. Getting up to a bus's top deck required some physical agility, as it was necessary to negotiate one's way up three or four iron steps fixed to the back of the bus, an ascent made more complicated if the conductor signalled the driver to start before the ascent was completed. This manoeuvre was almost impossible for ladies in crinolines and women usually rode inside until the iron steps were replaced by a spiral staircase at the rear of the bus. At the other end, two seats were provided on either side of the driver, positions which required even more agility to reach, but which were nonetheless highly prized by younger passengers because of the drivers' great reputation for jokes and witty repartee.[8]

Bus transport remained something of a rogue business until the 1850s. There were no standard fares and special events like the 1851 Great Exhibition at the Crystal Palace gave bus operators a golden opportunity to fleece customers from out of town. In 1856, however, London busmen were shocked to discover that a French concern – the Compagnie Générale des Omnibus de Londres – was encroaching on their territory and buying up individual operators. In 1858 the French name was changed to the London General Omnibus Co. Ltd, by which stage the company owned around six hundred buses. The 'General' quickly dominated London's bus transport operations and by 1859 was carrying 39,000,000 riders per year at an average fare of 3¾d. The services were of particular importance in connecting the main London railway termini, which were being erected at this stage; after passengers arrived at Paddington or Victoria, they travelled on to destinations in the centre of London on a horse-drawn omnibus.[9] The General's horse-drawn operations peaked in 1905 with 1418 vehicles a day and a passenger journey total of 217,000,000 at an average fare of ⅓d. The company's only serious competitor was the London Road Car Company, which started services in 1880 and which was working an average of 464 horse omnibuses daily by 1904. In 1903 it carried over 73,000,000 passengers.[10]

Horse-drawn buses dominated London traffic during the mid nineteenth century, causing severe congestion. After the reports of a royal commission (1844–51) and a select committee (1854–55) on congestion in London, a Metropolitan Board of Works created new streets to cope with the traffic, including Victoria Street, Shaftesbury Avenue, Charing Cross Road and the Victoria Embankment. London County Council in 1888 set out rules of the road, such as keeping to the left in traffic. The streets the buses went down were filthy, particularly after rain had turned the usual carpet of horse manure into a vile mud. Crossing the street to get on a bus inevitably meant getting splashed: shoeblacks and crossing-sweepers did a good trade throughout the Victorian era. Buses had the awkward habit of stopping in the middle of street; it was only after the 1867 Metropolitan Street Act that they were obliged to set down and pick up passengers on the left-hand side. [11]

One of the early impediments to bus operations in London were the tolls on bridges and on roads controlled by turnpike trusts. Many of the main roads leading into and out of London were turnpikes. Buses, along with all other passenger and goods vehicles, had to pay to go through their gates.[12] Likewise many of the bridges over the Thames were controlled by companies which farmed them for profit. Only London, Blackfriars and Westminster bridges were toll free; at Waterloo and Lambeth bridges 2d. per horse was the usual toll for using the crossing. The effect of tolls on London transport was to discourage or divert traffic and in 1855 the Select Committee on Metropolitan Communications recommended their removal.[13] Toll revenue was important, however, in providing for the upkeep of the bridges, which became increasingly costly as the heavy wear caused by omnibus traffic grew worse. When the tolls were removed on turnpikes (1864–65) and bridges (1878–80) there was a sudden and substantial increase in London traffic; thanks to the removal of tolls on Waterloo Bridge in 1878, for example, vehicular traffic rose from 3774 to 6657 per day within four weeks.[14]

By the 1860s transport congestion in London had become a matter of national concern as the capital was the main transport hub for the entire country. The need for better urban transport, in addition to the horse-drawn buses and cabs, was overwhelming. Jams were so bad in London that *The Times* reported in 1863 that 'the slightest addition to the ordinary traffic of the city would make the streets impassable'.[15]

Hitherto there had been no mechanically-driven transport in cities, other than the mainline surface railways and they had been concerned primarily with the movement of people and goods over long distances. Surface railways were important for transporting goods and people *into* and *out of* cities, but far less use for moving people around *within* them. They did little to develop suburbs outside London, or in cities such as Glasgow, Manchester,

Birmingham and Liverpool.[16] The railway companies nevertheless had a major impact on the urban landscape because of the enormous construction work that was required to erect their city-centre terminals. These required the demolition of whole stretches of existing buildings as their lines were extended across the city, obliterating slums and creating new ones. They created in their path embankments, bridges, viaducts and, at their ends, grand stations which competed with cathedrals for the domination of city skylines.

The steam engine's first transport application in cities was in fact not on railways but in steamships. London, where the earliest means of transport had been river craft on the Thames, was indeed where the steam engine was first put to work. In 1825 the first steamboats were seen on the Thames and in 1837 these craft were plying regularly between the London and Westminster bridges, carrying up to 120 passengers.[17] They continued to ply between points on the river until the 1880s; interestingly, a century later, Londoners got a new private 'Riverbus' service between Chelsea and Greenwich. The river could, however, only offer a limited solution to London's transport needs.

What might be described as the first suburban railway was opened in London in 1836 by the London & Greenwich Railway (LGR). It had been started in 1834, only four years after the Liverpool & Manchester line, and its chief novelty was that it was carried for much of its length towards Deptford on a viaduct, the arches of which were intended to be houses. Parliament decided that the rival London & Croydon Railway would be allowed to use the LGR's track for the first two miles from its London Bridge terminal when the new company opened in 1839, paying the LGR a toll for its use. In 1837 a second line, in a north-westerly direction, was opened by the London & Birmingham Railway from Euston, although this was little encouragement to suburban traffic since its trains only stopped at Harrow before they headed off towards the west midlands. By 1845 five mainline railways were serving London and by 1860 four additional radial routes had been added with a north London branch line serving the docks.[18] Still, in the mid 1850s no more than 10,000 people commuted into London by rail, compared to nearly a quarter of million by horse-drawn bus or on foot.[19] Beyond London it was a different picture: suburban or local surface railways were carrying large numbers of workers to and from their places of employ-ment by the middle of the nineteenth century. In Newcastle upon Tyne, for example, the Newcastle & North Shields Railway was already carrying over a million passengers between the ship-building towns along the northern bank of the Tyne by 1846.[20]

A burst of railway construction fever hit London in the 1860s. In 1864 alone there were 259 projects for over 300 miles of new railway in the metropolis.[21] In addition main line termini such as Victoria (1860), Black-friars Bridge (1864) and Cannon Street (1866) were completed. By the 1880s all the mainline companies had suburban 'stopping' trains running out of their termini. At the end of 1875, for example, the Great Eastern Railway had twenty-two suburban stops out of its new terminus at Liverpool Street.[22] Central London, however, had not been penetrated by the mainline com-panies. The opposition to their building termini in the City of London had been too great and in 1846 the Royal Commission on Metropolitan Railway Termini had halted their progress at the periphery (a similar situation arose in Paris). This meant that passengers had to change at the rail termini to horse-drawn buses, trams or cabs to get across the central district to their final destinations, or to reach another railway terminus from which to proceed out of London again in another direction.[23] This 'rail-free zone' was eventually bound in 1884 by what became the London Underground Circle Line. But, before this, the central district was bridged by what was, in retrospect, the first truly urban transport system in London – the Metro-politan Railway. This was an underground railway, sunk in a cut and then covered, along the line of the Euston and Marylebone Roads, It was built by the Great Western Railway (GWR), initially to the broad gauge, with 'blowholes' in the street to release the smoke from the locomotives below, and was opened in 1863 between Farringdon and the GWR's terminus at Paddington. The Metropolitan Railway was built remarkably quickly, con-sidering that the engineers had to drive through an labyrinth of water and gas pipes, and sewers, for the first time in London's history. In 1862 they even had the misfortune to hit the Fleet Ditch sewer, which burst, flooding the workings and causing extensive damage in Farringdon Street. The success of the Metropolitan prompted the building of other inner London rail links. In 1868 the first section of the Metropolitan District Railway, known as the 'District' was opened between High Street, Kensington and Gloucester Road, and the following year the East London Railway, having acquired Marc Brunel's Thames Tunnel, converted it to a railway tunnel.[24]

These sub-surface lines were costly to construct because they had to cut through ground riddled with pipes and sewers, as well as having to avoid disturbing the foundations of adjacent buildings; for this reason they usually followed the course of roads. The locomotives which hauled the trains were, of course, steam engines and the tunnels were soon blackened with soot and smoke. 'Travelling on the Metropolitan was uncomfortable,' wrote Arthur Elton.

The tunnels were filled with sulphurous smoke. The carriages were lighted by oil lamps which smelled, dripped and flickered. Gas, held in long rubber bags on the tops of carriages, was not much of an improvement, and passengers who wanted to read often stuck candles on to the sides of the compartments.[25]

The only through surface railway which actually crossed central London – and the only north-south link across the city until the coming of the Tube – was the London, Chatham & Dover Railway's line, connecting King's Cross via Farringdon and Holborn to the river crossing at Blackfriars. It was built in 1866, running through Snow Hill tunnel under Smithfield and Holborn Viaduct, and emerging near the Old Bailey onto a viaduct which carried it to Blackfriars. It crossed Ludgate Hill on a bridge which was heartily disliked by Londoners for spoiling the view of St Paul's Cathedral, a sight which is immortalised in Gustav Doré's famous engraving. This railway carried passengers across London until it was closed in 1916 as uneconomical. In the 1970s British Rail decide to reopen it for passengers and used it to run trains between Brighton and Gatwick Airport to the south of London, and Bedford and Luton in the north; services were resumed in 1988. Ironically the City of London Corporation, which had vehemently opposed railways entering their territory in the 1840s, now welcomed the building of a new station on the line at Ludgate Hill.

Driving the 'cut-and-cover' underground railways through central London in the third quarter of the nineteenth century was costly and caused highly disruptive road works on the surface. The Inner Circle, the last London underground to be built by this method, was not completed until 1884 and was inordinately expensive: it cost £1,000,000 per mile to construct the final segment, compared with only £320,000 per mile on the Paris Metro (1900) or £360,000 on the New York Subway (1904).[26] Not surprisingly, engineers cast around for an alternative method of building underground railways and found the solution in deep-level tunnels – the Tube.

Tube railways became possible in the 1890s thanks to advances in tunnel boring technology and the invention of efficient electric traction. The steam engine was never a very suitable form of tractive power for urban transport and, in deep and unventilated tunnels, it was both impractical and dangerous. Electric traction made tube railways possible and was probably the single most important factor in the growth of underground railway systems.

The first Tube in London was constructed by the City & South London Railway from King William Street in the City, under the Thames, to Stockwell in South London. Today it is part of London Underground's Northern Line. Tunnelling relied on the use of an iron cylindrical cutting shield, the advantages of which over earlier methods had been shown when the engineer Peter Barlow sunk the midstream piers for Lambeth Bridge over the Thames in 1862. Instead of lining the tunnel with brickwork, which was a time-consuming and hazardous business, the new technique used cast iron segments which were simply bolted into place immediately behind the cutting shield. The shield itself had been perfected by Barlow's student, James H. Greathead. With the Greathead shield, boring proceeded through the London clay, well below the level of sewers and the building foundations which had plagued the construction of the Inner Circle, at the rate of eighty feet per week. By the summer of 1887 work on the tunnel was completed and the City & South London Railway line was opened in 1890. It was an immediate success with Londoners and so many people tried to use it that *Punch* christened it the 'sardine-box railway': 'It was so packed with people that getting in or out was a regular scrimmage. We entirely endorse the railway company's advertisement in that it is the warmest line in London.'[27] The next London Tube railway to be built was the Central London Railway (London Underground's Central Line), the first section of which ran in a straight east-west line from Bank to Shepherds Bush and was opened in 1900. An important feature was a depression in the tunnel between each station, helping a train to gather speed as it left a station and descended the dip and brake ready for the next station as it ascended the other side. The Central London Railway, which was even more popular than the City & South London when it opened, began operations using electric locomotives to pull the train, but these proved too heavy and in 1903 multiple-traction units were installed.[28] In the next few years before the First World War, the Bakerloo line opened between Baker Street and Kennington Road, and the Piccadilly line between Hammersmith and Finsbury Park.

By 1900 London already possessed the most extensive underground railway network in the world, larger than either Paris or New York. Unlike those two cities, however, it had been built without any municipal planning or even participation, and without direction by a single authority. Compared to the municipally-run New York Subway, the London Underground was expensive and inefficient. While the Subway was planned from the outset to be a high-capacity and high-speed system, with double tracks to allow express operations, the London network developed piecemeal under a typically British *laissez-faire* regime. The result was that in 1908, the American system was moving cars and passengers on average three times as efficiently as the London Underground.[29] The Tube builders were continuously short of capital, which led to corners being cut at both the planning and execution stages; the City & South London, for example, was bored with the smallest possible diameter tunnel (as anyone will know who has ridden the modern Northern Line) and this severely restricted its capacity from the outset. So short of finance and capital were the Underground schemes in progress in 1905 that they could only be completed when there was an influx of American capital from former Chicago cable-car operators.[30] It was another American, the financier Charles T. Yerkes, who, having already organised the District Line for the purpose of electrifying it, took a broader interest in the London underground railway system and brought about the merger of the independent Tube companies in the years before the First World War. Further interest from private capitalists now waned and after 1910 London did not get another Tube line for the next half century. In the inter-war years the Underground experienced its heyday. Under the leadership of Frank Pick, it used attractive and effective consumer advertising to extend the market for public transport to all segments of the metropolitan population. Its message was simple and consistent: travel on the Tube was fast and convenient, both within the centre and as a means of getting to and from the suburbs. And, unlike the trams, it was socially acceptable for use by prosperous businessmen and suburban housewives to travel to town on the Tube from Richmond or Wimbledon, Ealing or Edgware.[31]

After the Second World War, during which the Tube had its 'finest hour' providing shelter against bombs for thousands of Londoners, there were plans for major rail improvements and extensions in London. Unfortunately, the break-up of the British Transport Commission in 1953 signalled the abandonment of government support for transport coordination which had included a scheme to integrate London Transport with the newly-nationalised British Railways. This would have brought much-needed rationalisation to the labyrinthine network of railway track in London. Dependent on an seemingly hostile Treasury for capital funds, the Underground had to 'make do and mend' until the 1960s, when the long overdue Victoria Line was built. A second new Tube line, the Jubilee Line, was added, after much debate and in conjunction with the redevelopment of the London Docklands area, thirty years later.

The Tube did little to adapt to the changing shape and character of London in the second half of the twentieth century. As the docks declined and tourism became increasingly important to London from the 1960s, a greater emphasis on west London might have been expected; yet it took until 1978 for the Piccadilly Line to reach Heathrow Airport. Even then there was no provision for an additional express track. Foreign tourists had to reckon with a hour's journey from central London to the airport, with the train stopping every two or three minutes along the line. Meanwhile the comparative lack of east-west Tube lines meant that the Central Line was severely overloaded and south-east London remained poorly served by the Tube, at

1 The Neath Aqueduct on the Tennant Canal, *c.* 1811. The canals supplemented existing river waterways.

2 St Helen's Canal, 1840, with a railway viaduct in the background.

3 Robert Fulton's plan for a canal boat lift, 1796. Most canal technology was less innovative.

4 A coastal collier after unloading at a power station. (*National Maritime Museum*)

5 SS *Waverley* at Sandown Pier, 1999. The last remaining working coastal paddle-steamer. (*Philip Bagwell*)

6 A packhorse.

7 The Kendal 'Flying Waggon' travelled at less than walking pace, 1816.

8 The yard of Bull and Mouth, a hub of London's stage transport.

9 The tollgate at Hyde Park Corner, 1798, with stage wagon and diligence.

10 The royal mail picking up bags without stopping.

11 Whiteley's viaduct on the Manchester to Leeds Railway, 1845, by A. F. Tait.

12 Digging near Camden Town, 1839, by J. C. Bourne.

13 The Christmas excursion train – first class, 1859.

14 The Christmas excursion train – second class, 1859.

Shawswater

MAKE SMART Dress Fabrics

Cycling, Golfing, Fishing, Shooting, and "Every-Day" Costumes.

THE DRESS GOODS FOR THE SEASON.

These high-class fabrics neither cockle nor shrink. They are unaffected by weather or climatic influences of any kind, and their colours are guaranteed fast dyed. While always retaining a most stylish appearance, they will stand any amount of wear and tear and, in choiceness of design, are absolutely unrivalled. LADIES should send to us for Patterns, which are sent on approval Post Free to any address. We have an immense variety in the newest styles, and cut pieces to any length required. The Shawswater Dress Fabrics are also most suitable for Gentlemen and Children's wear.

FLEMING, REID & CO., THE WORSTED MILLS,
SPINNERS & MANUFACTURERS. Greenock, N.B.

15 Bicycling made women independently mobile for the first time.

least until this deficiency was partly relieved by the Jubilee Line. The Tube undoubtedly suffered from the general run-down and underinvestment in London's public transport. Some innovations, such as one-person train operation and automatic ticket machines, have cut labour costs, but many Tube stations remain old and crowded, while the maze of tunnels leads the unwary traveller in every direction between platform and street level. These are historical problems, of course, but they are also a result of long-term financial neglect.[32]

One of the weaknesses of the London Underground railway system was its lack of coordination with other urban transport modes, particularly one which grew up at the same time as the Tube and with which it shared a common locomotive source – the electric tram.

Trams predate electric traction by at least two decades. Horse-drawn street cars first appeared in the United States and it was an American engineer, George F. Train, who introduced them to Britain, opening a tramway in 1861 in London from Marble Arch to Notting Hill Gate. The idea did not take hold at the time, and the track was subsequently lifted, but in the late 1860s tram lines were laid in Liverpool, Glasgow and Edinburgh. In 1870 London got its first regular horse-drawn tram service when the Metropolitan Street Tramway Company began running between Brixton and Kennington. The advantage of the horse-drawn tram over the horse-drawn omnibus lay in the much smoother movement, over the poorly-surfaced and ill-maintained streets of Britain's cities, that could be gained by a carriage running on rails. Initially tram rails were flat plates, with an outer flange rising half an inch above the level of the road. This proved unsatisfactory as people tripped over them and the trams were continually being derailed, so the safer alternative was adopted of sinking the track into the road surface, a slot replacing the flange as the means by which the trams were kept on the rails. Trams were much easier for horses to pull, and were therefore faster and could carry more passengers; this made them cheaper than buses and opened the transport market to people who had previously walked.

Trams were the first urban transport mode genuinely available to the working class and were thus a step towards universal urban transport. Moreover, the fact that they required track embedded in city streets meant that private tram companies needed to cooperate much more fully with local authorities than was the case with the horse-drawn bus enterprises, and thus the link between public transport and government was established. After the Tramway Act of 1870 this relationship was strengthened. In order to prevent tram companies achieving monopoly powers, like the gas and water utilities, the Act provided for the acquisition of tramway undertakings by local authorities after a suitable interval of private ownership. It abolished the obligation to obtain a Private Member's Bill for each tram line, which had been the case with railway construction. This may have led to under-investment by the private tramway operators, who knew they would have to sell to local authorities after ten or twenty years operation, but it also brought about a much greater degree of planning of tram networks in Britain's cities. In Manchester, a star-shaped housing pattern emerged as residential building followed radial tramlines extending from the city centre.[33] In Glasgow a pioneering local authority built its own tram track, after an unsatisfactory experience with a private operating company, and ran tram services with great success.

It was electrification which allowed tram transport to reach its full poten-tial. Hitherto horse-drawn trams had been slow (with a maximum speed of about 4 mph) and hardly economic. Tram horses were expensive to feed, they could only be worked for about five hours per day and they had an average life of only four years. A British tram operator, moreover, could expect to need up to ten horses for each tram.[34] Steam engines and under-ground cables had been tried as alternatives to horse power,[35] but trams did not come into their own until electric traction was used. Indeed the practical electric traction which was developed in the 1880s represents a breakthrough in transport technology almost the equivalent of the steam engine sixty years before: it permitted effective tram systems in cities, as well as non-polluting underground railways like the Central London Railway. The credit for the invention, as always, belongs to no single person, but the American electrical engineer Frank J. Sprague deserves primary recognition. It was Sprague who had demonstrated in Richmond, Virginia, in 1888 that electric street cars could work and that a single overhead wire could transmit enough current to power several trams simultaneously.[36] By the early twentieth century most of America's electric street cars were using Sprague's patents. In Britain, his 'Richmond System' was first adopted in Leeds in 1891.[37] Sprague's system meant cluttering up the urban scene with a profusion of overhead wires and supporting poles, and by the turn of the century the streets of most British cities had acquired the aerial latticework of tram wires to be seen on photographs from the period. In the United States the electrification of street cars seems to have proceeded without undue regard for aesthetic values – overhead wires protruded everywhere, but in Britain many people objected that the wires were ruining the appearance of their towns. Sprague's system prevailed, however, because the alternatives were surface contact arrangements involving live rails or conduits which were either inefficient or a safety hazard.[38]

Electric trams brought about a small social revolution in urban travel between 1895 and 1914. Because fares were so much cheaper than horse-drawn buses or cabs, they attracted a section of the community hitherto little catered for by public transport, in other words, the working class.[39] Trams became the workers' means of transport. According to an observer in the *Cornhill Magazine*,

> the working man is rarely seen on the upholstered cushions [of London omni-buses]; he feels himself uncomfortable and *de trop*. The tramcar is his familiar vehicle and he can ensconce himself there in his mortar-splashed clothes without restraint.[40]

On the other hand, the City of London reacted to trams much as it had to the railways: it shunned them and would not permit tramways through its territory. It did not like the overhead wiring and thought 'that trams catered for *an undesirable class of person*'.[41]

Tram companies which began as private undertakings in the 1890s were to a remarkable degree taken over or absorbed by municipal authorities in the next twenty years. Of a total capital invested in British tramways in 1890, £10,800,000 was in private companies and only £2,900,000 in municipalities. In 1910 the figures were very different: £24,500,000 from private companies and £51,100,000 from local authorities.[42] In London the County Council acquired a host of small tram companies, and some larger ones like the North Metropolitan.[43] Elsewhere in Britain the city authorities moved with greater determination to bring tram undertakings under their control and organise them not just as a public transport service but as an instrument of urban planning. Glasgow was particularly pioneering and the city cor-poration there 'saw electrifying and extending the tram system as a way of moving people out of Glasgow's slums into better housing at the edge of the city. Previously transport costs ruled out such options for ordinary working-class people. By the 1920s Glasgow's trams were hailed as the cheapest and most frequent tram system in the world'.[44]

By the First World War public transport in British cities was substantially cheaper than it had been at the beginning of the Victorian period. A large part of the credit can be given to the application of electric power to trams and underground railways. Trams, however, were not to last, unlike trains and buses. By the 1930s they were already being viewed with disfavour by many, although not all, local authorities as motor transport began its irrepressible rise to dominance. They were an inflexible obstacle to traffic flow and a hazard to a new generation of motorists negotiating their way around Britain's city streets. Even such a robust supporter of public trans-port as Herbert Morrison, the Labour Minister of Transport from 1929 to 1931, referred to trams in a disparaging way in his *Socialisation and Transport*, with a nudge and a wink to motorists: 'It will perhaps be interesting', he wrote by way of describing the history of tram companies, 'to many motorists who curse tramways to know who started the trouble and when!' [45]

Trams disappeared from British city streets in the 1950s. After a hiatus of thirty years, however, they have reappeared in modern form, now known as *light railways*. Light rail is a compromise between trams and a more capital-intensive urban transit system like the London Tube. It consists of trains of two or three cars length, running on tracks either at street level, or in tunnels, or on elevated stretches – often on former railway embankments or viaducts. In London the Docklands Light Railway (DLR), was inaugurated in 1987, using five miles of disused railway permanent way elevated on reconditioned brick arches which had been built in 1872. As part of the Docklands rejuvenation programme, it was regarded by the developers as an essential transport link to the City of London. In a sense it was a return of the tram to London, although the DLR trains are fully automated. Elsewhere in Britain light rail systems have been highly successful in upgrading urban transport networks since the 1980s. While on the DLR and the Tyne & Wear Metro segregated track is used, in Croydon (Tramlink), Manchester (Metrolink) and Sheffield (Supertram) street running is featured in the manner of the original trams. In Newcastle the pioneer Tyne & Wear Metro, which was opened in 1980, is a forty mile system using thirty miles of underused rail track, with new stations added between the older ones. The Metro, conceived by the local Passenger Transport Authority and Executive in 1971, is intended to be not just a light rail transit system but part of a integrated transport network for the whole Tyneside region. One of the advantages of light rail is that it has been shown to attract passengers who prefer not to travel by buses; with dedicated rights of way they are faster than buses and predictable in their timetable in the manner of an efficiently run rail service. Of perhaps greater importance, light rail attracts car owners: for example in 1994, 10 per cent of the Manchester Metrolink passengers were former car users.[46]

The internal combustion engine has had a dramatic effect on all modes of transport and its impact on cities and urban transport has been immense. It has powered omnibuses, lorries and cars, but also motorcycles and, in the form of large diesel engines, railway locomotives.

Buses were the first urban transport mode to feel the effects of motorisation and motor buses began appearing in British cities in the first years of the twentieth century. In London a petrol-driven motor bus service began between Kennington and Oxford Circus in 1899. The London Road Car Company started motorising its fleet in 1902, and the London General Omnibus Company – the General – which at this time had a fleet of over

1400 horse-drawn buses, followed two years later. By 1914 the thousands of horses which had thronged the streets of London for much of the nineteenth century were much reduced in number. One consequence of this – greatly welcomed by Londoners at the time – was an alleviation of the horse manure problem. The startling speed with which the horse-drawn omnibus was replaced with the motor bus in London is clear from the figures in Table 6. A contemporary witness, Edwin Pratt, observed wryly that the time was not far off 'when the horse is likely to be found only at the Zoological Gardens, as a curious survival of a bygone age in traction'.[47]

Table 6

Licensed Road Vehicles in London, 1900–33

	Buses			Trams and Trolleybuses	
	Stage Horse	Motor	Charabanc or Coach	Horse	Electric
1900	3681	4	–	1473	10
1905	3484	241	–	786	1124
1910	1103	1200	–	120	2411
1915	36	2761	–	2	2725
1920	–	3365	165	–	2740
1925	–	5478	250	–	2738
1930	–	5953	1762	–	2711

Source: D. L. Munby, *Inland Transport Statistics, Great Britain, 1900–1970*, i, *Railways, Public Road Passenger Transport* (Oxford, 1978), pp. 562–63.

In 1911 the General withdrew its last horse bus from service. The previous year it had introduced the 'B' class – London's first standard motor bus – which carried thirty-four passengers (sixteen inside, eighteen outside) and was powered by a thirty horse power engine. After the war in 1919, an improved model, the 'K', was introduced which seated forty-six passengers. In 1920 fixed stopping places for buses were introduced. Hitherto buses had stopped, like taxis, anywhere they were hailed by a passenger, a custom which had worked well enough when buses were moving a horse's walking pace, but which was now impractical and dangerous. Throughout the 1920s the General advanced the pace of development in motor buses: in 1925 it introduced the first buses with a covered top deck and in 1927 came the 'LT' – a six-wheeled bus with pneumatic tyres and seating for sixty passengers. As a point of interest, the double-decker bus seems to have been a British invention which has hardly ever been copied in other countries. The reason seems to have been a preference for sitting amongst British bus passengers; elsewhere there is a greater acceptance of standing travel, or 'strap-hanging', for short journeys at peak times. In 1924 a strike by tram operators prompted bus workers to strike in sympathy and part of the settlement of that dispute, incorporated in the London Traffic Act of that year, gave the new Ministry of Transport the right to limit the number of London's bus companies.[48] As a result the General got a virtual monopoly and at the end of 1925 this famous London bus operator and its associated companies owned 4373 buses, while the independent bus companies owned a mere 601.[49]

Until the 1930s London's transport services were privately run and distinct from those of other English and Scottish cities in not being under municipal control. In 1933, however, the London Passenger Transport Board (LPTB) was created and London Transport's bus, tram and tube services (although *not* those of the four mainline rail companies) were unified and brought under common administration. London's buses now had their heyday, as did all of London's public transport. With the LPTB at its head, London Transport was fused into a single organisation for the whole of London's transport customers and as such it became the largest passenger-carrying business in the world.[50] Buses now began to replace trams in Britain, starting with the smaller centres, although some cities like Leeds and Glasgow held on to their trams for very much longer and continued to invest in them. According to their critics, trams added to the congestion on urban roads and held up the progress of motor vehicles. Then there was the old argument about the unsightliness of overhead wires. The tram's supporters, not surprisingly, reversed the claim to say that cars and buses held up the progress of trams. It was a reflection of the basic conflict between public and private transport which always reached an acute form in the urban setting; however, since buses and particularly cars were in the ascendant, it was taken for granted that it was the trams which had to give way.

After the Second World War, and particularly in the 1950s, public transport usage in Britain began a process of accelerating decline (Table 7). First the trams and then more gradually buses retired before the invasion of private motor vehicles in towns and cities. Interim solutions like the trolley bus, which aimed to combine the electrically-driven economy of the tram with the flexibility of the bus, were not able to arrest this decline. The problem for urban bus services, once the last trams had been retired in the 1950s, was that the bus is highly vulnerable to traffic congestion and this leads to poor service and long delays. In a straight contest with the motor car for urban road space (in the absence of special bus lanes), the bus can never win. By the end of the 1960s public transport in Britain was in retreat: demand for transport services from the large municipal undertakings was falling by 2.5 per cent a year, while in the big urban centres it was twice this rate.[51]

Table 7

Millions of Passengers Using Public Transport in Three Cities

	1910	*1930*	*1970*	*1980*
London	2350	4050	3100	2100
Paris	1160	1930	2000	2400
New York	1800	3100	2000	2000

Source: Tom Rallis, *City Transport in Developed and Developing Countries* (Basingstoke, 1988), p. 30.

In London between 1951 and 1967 the number of bus patrons fell by no less than 50 per cent, with the majority of the deserting passengers switching to the Tube.[52] With falling passenger numbers came falling revenue and London Transport's bus services fell into a vicious circle of under financing and poor service. The assumption that the bus system was self-financing and that a public subsidy was not needed took no account of the congestion on London's roads. When costs rose, London Transport was expected to cover them with increased revenue from higher fares; but raising fares was self-defeating. One 12 per cent fare increase in the 1950s resulted in an immediate loss of 60 per cent of bus passengers. Although most of them eventually returned, there was a permanent loss of 16 per cent, which was enough to wipe out any revenue gains from the fare increases. Sadly, this pattern was to be repeated several times in the next twenty-five years.[53]

The introduction since the 1980s of dedicated bus lanes in many cities, and the use of more economical minibuses seating no more than thirty people, has had some effect in improving the efficiency and lowering the running costs of urban bus services, but generally the decline of bus transport in cities has continued. Above all the *image* of the bus has suffered badly since the middle of the twentieth century. As the slowest form of motorised transport, and the mode with the shortest average distance, it is seen as the transport option of those who cannot afford to travel by car. Inevitably there is a strong preponderance amongst bus passengers of the young, the elderly, the poor and women.

Because buses are slow, their rivals in urban transport have tended to be not so much other motor vehicles as cyclists and pedestrians. The bicycle became an important part of British urban transport in the Edwardian period, although they had been around in some shape or form since the early nineteenth century when they were known as velocipedes or, appropriately, 'bone shakers'. The breakthrough in the adoption of bicycles as a regular mode of transport came in the late 1880s with the appearance of rubber tyres on the rear wheel-driven 'Safety' bicycle, the ladies' version of which launched a craze for cycling amongst women. Up until the Second World War the bicycle was a highly popular means of transport in Britain, not only with workers, who used them to get to their places of employment in towns and cities, but also with middle-class riders and Youth Hostel Association members. Bicycle use fell into decline, like urban public transport, in the 1960s. Cycle trips in London, for example, fell from 3,760,000 in 1952 to 610,000 in 1968.[54] With the phenomenal rise in the use of the motor car, the cyclists' needs, and cycling as a means of urban transport, was ignored. Cycling on roads now wholly given over to motor vehicles was a discouraging pursuit. Few of Britain's municipal authorities developed any kind of plan for bicycle users; their chief preoccupation being to *remove* cyclists from the path of motor traffic. Where once workers would cycle to work and children to school, the car prevailed and, as more and more cars struggled for space on the roads, so it became increasingly dangerous to ride a bicycle on them. Even the planning of new towns, such as Milton Keynes, neglected to provide for cyclists; it seems that planners in the 1960s simply assumed that everyone would and should drive a car.[55]

Fortunately for the British cyclist, the doctrine of giving priority to the car began to be challenged in the 1970s. Renewed recognition of the importance of the bicycle to urban transport was signalled by the 1977 Transport White Paper, which created a programme in which the Department of Transport shared the costs of experimental cycle schemes with local authorities. Cambridge, Nottingham and York are notable examples of urban authorities which have made use of the scheme to introduce pro-cycling transport policies and develop cycle path networks.[56]

If urban transport in the twentieth century has been a battle between competing modes, then there is little doubt as to the victor. From being an amusement for the Edwardian aristocracy, the motor car has become, in less than a century, one of the dominating features of modern life. With very few exceptions, cities throughout the world are held in its grip. In Britain the congestion that motor traffic causes acts like a kind of creeping paralysis on the mobility of city dwellers. From being welcomed as the answer to transport needs, and a clean and hygienic alternative to horse-drawn vehicles, cars have become the central problem facing urban transport planners.

In fact, urban opposition to the car developed early. In 1914 the Glasgow Corporation 'responded to growing concerns about the rising toll of fatalities and injuries occurring at tram stops'. Apparently passengers alighting from trams, which were of course positioned in the middle of road, were being knocked down by passing cars. A by-law had to be introduced to compel motor vehicles to stop if a tram in front of them was letting off passengers. By the end of the First World War urban hostility to the car was widespread, probably because cars were still a rarity in Britain and were closely identified with a monied elite whose lifestyle was in stark contrast to that of the typical tram or omnibus passenger. In Manchester there were repeated calls for speed limits on motorists as well as the implementation of Glasgow's tram stop law, the latter being bitterly contested by motoring interests in the city.[57]

It was in the 1960s that mass car ownership took off in Britain and it was also in the 1960s that British cities first became seriously congested with private motor vehicle traffic. Of course cities have always been congested with traffic, basically because people living in them tend to want to go to the same places at the same times. There is no doubt, however, that the motor vehicle, and the car in particular, caused a previously unknown degree of congestion. And it is an irony that traffic on many London streets at the end of the twentieth century moved no faster than the horse-drawn omnibuses of a hundred years before.

In response to urban congestion the government appointed a study group headed by the planner Colin Buchanan, who had already written an influential book on the environmental impact of the car. In his book, which was published in 1958, Buchanan wrote, with considerable foresight, 'it is not just the easing of traffic jams that is needed, but the recreation of centres for civilised life. There can be no compromise with the upstart motor vehicle that is pulling the whole fabric of cities about our ears'.[58] Buchanan was describing a problem which was to get much worse, but it is important to remember that his solution did not involve placing limits on the use of cars in cities or the encouragement of greater use of public transport. On the contrary, in the report *Traffic in Towns* (1963), which was based on an investigation of conditions in a number of British towns and cities, including Norwich, Leeds and London, he accepted the notion that traffic and towns were inseparable; the challenge was to build correctly-planned roads – and enough of them – to make it possible for people and cars to live together harmoniously.[59] In the years that followed the publication of *Traffic in Towns* (the Buchanan Report), this doctrine remained remarkably influential; indeed it is hardly an exaggeration to describe it as a road builders' mandate. In the meantime car ownership had a negative effect on public transport use, particularly of buses, as Table 8 shows for the morning rush hour in London between the 1952 and 1970.

Table 8

Passenger Journeys into Central London in the Morning Rush Hour, 1952–1970 (Thousands of Passenger Journeys).

	Public Transport			Private Transport	
	Rail		Bus	Car	Motor-Cycle
	BR	Tube			
1952	382	453	286	45	24
1955	400	472	270	60	24
1960	453	506	216	89	33
1965	456	543	180	117	22
1970	458	504	152	124	11

Source: D. L. Munby, *Inland Transport Statistics, Great Britain, 1900–1970*, i, *Railways, Public Road Passenger Transport, London's Transport* (Oxford, 1978), p. 542.

The 1968 the Labour government's Transport Act sought to bring some balance into urban transport policy, in that it recognised that subsidies to public transport could be justified on the grounds of 'social need' and it created Passenger Transport Executives in many of Britain's major cities. This gave some impetus to public transport development, but the growth in car ownership and use in cities hardly faltered until the oil crisis of the early 1970s brought the first general awareness of the motor car's inefficient use of fossil fuels and its detrimental impact on the environment. Already the streets of Britain's cities were lined with parked cars. The parking meter, which had been introduced in 1958, was followed by a programme of off-street car park construction, initially on bomb sites, later in multi-storey or underground structures. By the end of the 1970s, however, this trend had been halted and the ensuing shortage of parking space became part of a deliberate ploy to discourage car use in the inner city.[60]

From the mid 1970s attempts to build major new roads in London – the Buchananite solution – failed in the face of environmentalist opposition and 'nimby' (not-in-my-backyard) sentiment. Motorway building in London, where congestion was worst, became a political football kicked between Conservative (for) and Labour (against) councils. After Labour took over the Greater London Council (GLC) in 1973, most major new road projects were shelved and the GLC contented itself with building the outer orbital motorway, now known as the M25. Instead of new roads, London got new controls and traffic-calming measures like 'speed bumps' in residential streets where motorists sought to escape from the congested main roads. The downward spiral of public transport use nevertheless continued and by 1980 passenger journeys by public transport in London were lower than at any time since 1912. London buses, clogged in a state of almost permanent traffic congestion, now travelled on average at a slower pace than they had in the 1920s.

It is perhaps appropriate that this chapter should close where it began: with the 'walking city'. As motor traffic, and in particular bus transport, has slowed down to a walking pace in the choking congestion of Britain's cities, it is worth reconsidering the pedestrian transport mode that was universally accepted in the early nineteenth century. Walking has always been an important element in the transport 'mix' because many journeys by public transport begin or end with a walking stretch. What happened in the late twentieth century is that Britons' addiction to the motor car made them less inclined to walk short distances. According to the British Medical Association, in the years between 1975 and 1994 for instance, the number of miles walked declined on average by 17 per cent.[61] The single most obvious way of encouraging walking as an alternative short distance transport mode is to improve walking conditions in inner cities and to pedestrianise streets. Here Britain's record has been very poor compared with its European neighbours, where pedestrian precincts are common in city centres. The explanation for this is puzzling, but seems to be connected with resistance from retailers, who fear a fall in sales if they are isolated from car traffic.[62] In the final analysis, any improvement in walking conditions in British cities may depend on changes in the British attitude to the city itself. Unlike some of their continental neighbours, Britons have never felt genuinely at home in the urban environment. With industrialisation the British city became squalid and dangerous, and by the end of the nineteenth century a strong anti-urban sentiment had filtered down through British society, which remains to this day. Instead of creating cities in which it might be a pleasure to stroll, those who could fled the city for the new suburbs. The irony is that the twentieth-century suburbanisation of the British people, which followed the nineteenth-century process of urbanisation, and which was made possible by public transport in the form of trams and buses and the London Tube, can now only be sustained by the private car ownership which makes it possible for suburban families and commuters to 'get into town'.

8

Nationalisation

The idea that the nation's railways should be publicly owned is a long-established one. In his Railways Act of 1844 William Gladstone had made provision for the possible ownership by the state in 1865. In the latter year William Galt, in his book *Railway Reform*,[1] compared, unfavourably, the wastefulness of railway promotion and operation in Britain with the benefits of the planned state-owned system of the Netherlands. But its publication at that date was inopportune when ever-wider sections of the population were experiencing the advantages of railway communication. It was not until the closing years of the nineteenth century that the amalgamation of the railway companies into powerful regional monopolies aroused public concern and renewed demands for nationalisation. In 1893 James Hole's book, *National Railways: An Argument for State Purchase*,[2] stimulated discussion and was an influence persuading the Amalgamated Society of Railway Servants at its AGM in 1894 to pass a resolution in favour of the industry's nationalisation. When the Railway Nationalisation League was established in 1895 it recruited members of the general public to endorse this view.

The return of the Liberal Party to power in the general election of 1905–6, under the leadership of Sir Henry Campbell-Bannerman, spurred on by a group of thirty Labour MPs, produced a spate of private (Labour) member's Bills for the nationalisation of railways. Clement Davies, a senior Liberal revealed to the House of Commons on 16 December 1946 that Lloyd George had told him 'on many occasions' that, when he moved from the Board of Trade to the Exchequer in 1908, he had left behind him 'a complete Bill for the nation-alisation of the railways', and that there were in his documents with the Bill, letters from every one, he supposed, of the 113 managers of those companies, saying that it was the only thing to do. Nothing happened about that.[3]

In 1900 the Labour Representation Committee – the forerunner of the Labour Party – included in its general election manifesto the demand for 'Nationalisation of the Land and Railways'. In subsequent general elections transport was not always mentioned; but in the 1924 general election it was spelt out in some detail. The manifesto then included the promise of

A systematic reorganisation, in the national interest and on fair terms to all concerned, of the whole system of transport, including the more rapid development of an entirely unified railway and canal system in National Ownership and under exclusively public control, with greater use of electric power and in more intimate connection not only with the ports, but also with the increasing road motor services.

In *Let Us Face the Future*, Labour's general election manifesto in 1945, the party claimed that 'there were basic industries ripe and over-ripe for public ownership' and that these included 'the fuel and power industries' and 'inland transport' (among others).[4]

By the end of the Second World War there was widespread support for radical reform of transport policy in Britain. One reason for this was the 'apparent success of unified operation, through the Railway Executive Committee during the war'. Thus although the number of freight wagons in use fell by 8 per cent between 1938 and 1946, freight traffic rose by 27 per cent, and although passenger coaches in use fell by 12 per cent in the same period the number of passenger miles travelled rose by 10 per cent.[5]

The successful example of the reorganisation of London transport under the London Passenger Transport Act of 1933, which merged five railways, fourteen municipal tramways and sixty-one bus undertakings, and, through the issuance of London Transport stock of 113,000,000 pounds, made possible the extension of the Tube and bus network, was often cited as an example of what could be achieved by consolidation under public ownership.

Leaders of British industry were considering how well-equipped British firms would be to meet foreign competition under circumstances of peace, since transport costs were a significant part of the total cost of production. Table 3 shows that the British record in the electrification of rail tracks – a vital improvement for increasing speed and reliability in the movement of goods – was behind that of some of her industrial rivals.[6] (No resources were available for the development of the electrification programme in wartime Britain.)

It was also believed that a unified railway system would command more resources to back modernisation and investment. Some of the big four railways, notably the LNER, found it impossible both to pay acceptable dividends on their ordinary shares and keep up to date with improved signalling, track and passenger information systems. It was pointed out that two large but declining industries, coal and railways, employing some 1,750,000 personnel, 'needed a rescue act'.[7] It is significant that the Conservative Party's Industrial Charter in 1947 accepted the need to nationalise railways, coal and the Bank of England.[8]

There was even some support for nationalised transport in Churchill's coalition government in 1940. Sir John Reith, who was appointed Minister of Transport on May 14 that year, directed Alfred Robinson, Deputy Secretary in his department, to prepare a comprehensive plan for a National Transport Corporation and asked Dr Coates of the ICI to work with him. Meanwhile Reith wrote a cabinet paper which closely followed Sir Eric Geddes's 1919 plan for a comprehensive Ministry of Ways and Communications. But when Reith's paper was discussed in Cabinet on 3 September it was vigorously opposed by Lord Beaverbrook and on 3 October Reith was removed from office, to be succeeded by Lord Leathers, who soon shelved both his predecessor's cabinet paper and the Coates-Robinson report which had been presented on 17 October.[9]

Both the annual congresses of the TUC and the annual conferences of the Labour Party supported policies of railway nationalisation and the coordination of railway and road transport, but there were divisions of opinion on the role of labour in the proposed new public organisations.[10]

In the late 1920s and the early 1930s there were new arguments advanced for nationalisation in that 'the central objectives were to improve the efficiency of the railways and the co-ordination of transport as a whole, and additionally to contribute to the planning of the economy'. There was an underlining assumption that 'the professional skills and commitment of managers could be abstracted from their current context and applied to the disinterested service of the nation'.[11]

The most influential man on the railways from the late 1920s onwards was Herbert Morrison, MP for Hackney South from 1923, Minister for Transport from 1929–31, and successively Home Secretary and Minister of Supply in the Coalition government in the Second World War. He had played a large part in framing the London Passenger Transport Act of 1933 and favoured the public corporation type of organisation as exemplified in the Central Electricity Generating Board (1926) and the BBC, established in the same year. The governing body for a nationalised British transport should be a small group of, say six or seven, men chosen by the Minister of Transport solely on grounds of their suitability for the job. Representation of sectional interests, such as that of the trade unions,. should not have the right of appointment or election to the governing body.

When the annual congress of the TUC debated Morrison's proposals in 1932, John Cliff of the TGWU complained that they presumed 'the continuing commodity status of labour' and that that was their fundamental defect. The board, or corporation, would be 'a kind of benevolent sort of thing that would give to labour an opportunity to learn more about the job'. His comment on that was 'Good heavens, we can teach them more about the job than they ever knew'. The TUC's general council accepted Morrison's plan, however, and rejected Cliff's arguments. Undoubtedly political considerations influenced their decision and Morrison's attitude.

At the time the Socialist League, which included such influential figures as Richard Crosland, Sir Stafford Cripps and Professor Harold Laski, were campaigning for workers' representation on the board, and Morrison, who had no particular liking for academics regarded them as a divisive element in the party. The victory of the TUC general council and Morrison in 1932 and the publication of Morrison's statement *Britain's Transport at Britain's Service* in 1932 and his more substantial *Socialisation and Transport* in 1933, and the reappearance of these plans in the two TUC's booklets, the 'pink paper' *Post-War Reconstruction* 12 and the 'white paper' *The Public Organisation of Transport* in 1945, greatly influenced the structure of the British Transport Commission when it started work under the Transport Act of 1947. The large majority of the 800,000 employees of the Commission did not feel that things had changed much since the days of the private companies. They felt no affinity to the six members of the commission who were regarded as being out of touch with those who actually ran the railways.

With the help of Sir Cyril Hurcomb, the Director General (later Permanent Secretary) of the Ministry of War/Ministry of Transport, Alfred Barnes, the minister, drew up plans for a Transport Bill, the second reading of which was presented to the House of Commons on 16 December 1946. The structure of the new organisation was as follows:

British Transport Commission

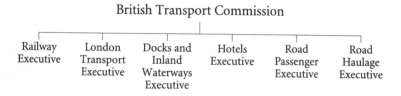

| Railway Executive | London Transport Executive | Docks and Inland Waterways Executive | Hotels Executive | Road Passenger Executive | Road Haulage Executive |

The six members of the commission were appointed by the minister. Their chairman was sixty-five-year old Sir Cyril Hurcomb, who had many years of experience in the ministry. The five other members of the Commission were Sir William Wood, who was president of the executive of the LMS, the largest of the 'big four' railways of the inter-war years, Lord Ashfield, Chairman of the LPTB; Lord Rusholme (formerly Robert Palmer) of the Co-operative Union, and John Benstead, the General Secretary of the NUR, who joined the commission despite the union's opposition to such a move.

When it came to the appointment of members of the six executives Alfred Barnes insisted – despite the opposition of his colleagues and the civil servants to the proposal – on making all the appointments himself.13 The minister made this decision after being influenced by the trade unions who thought that if the commission made the appointments those selected would be technocrats rather than those who had experience of the railway industry. But A. J. Pearson, the Chief Officer (Administration) at the Railway Executive wrote subsequently that in discussions in Parliament before the Act was passed it was agreed that 'in practice' the Railway Executive would largely be autonomous, certainly that they would have 'a great deal of freedom' from the commission.[14]

The Labour Party's manifesto for the general election of 1945 included the 'Coordination of transport services, by rail, road, air and canal'. It was clearly the purpose of the British Transport Commission to organise the executives under its jurisdiction. The fact that the executives tended to regard the commission as a meddling rather than a helpful adviser meant that the objective of transport coordination was more difficult to achieve. Yet coordination was vital to the survival of public transport if the challenge of the private motor car was successfully to be met.

In the second reading debate on the Transport Bill on 16 December it is remarkable that the Conservative leaders on the front bench did not challenge the idea of public ownership of the railways. Instead they mocked Alfred Barnes for slavishly following the TUC's post-war reconstruction booklets – he was no great orator though a reliable organiser. Major Sir David Maxwell Fyfe said, 'the Right Honourable Gentleman has got his Bill, practically idea for idea – I will not say word for word, out of the TUC document number two'.

Basil Nield led the attack in the Commons on the Bill's provisions for a financial settlement with the private railway companies' shareholders. There were, in fact, several days of hard bargaining between the minister and the railway companies in November 1946 on the terms of compensation given to shareholders in return for £907,800,000 government stock carrying a guaranteed interest of 2.5 per cent or £22,700,000. By the time of the transfer date, 1 January 1948, stock market prices had risen and the railway shareholders were allowed 3 per cent. This increased the Transport Commission's interest burden to £27,200,000 annually and Alfred Barnes was ironically chided by Opposition leaders for, in this one case, following the promptings of the free market rather than those of the TUC's booklet. These happenings did not deter Nield from drawing the Commons' attention to 'the tragic lot of the railway stockholders' ... who would be 'grievously harmed'.[15] C. R. Mitchison from the Labour benches experienced some difficulty in accepting Nield's case. He found it 'a very remarkable form of tragedy that railway stockholders were receiving the full market value of their shares'. He pointed out that in 1938 the GWR paid 0.5 per cent on its ordinary stock and the other three main line companies paid no dividend at all on their marginal stocks.[16]

When the debate in the Commons continued on the following day Hugh Dalton, the Chancellor of the Exchequer, likened the financial settlement to the employer offering his employees a barrel of beer:

> They drank it and he asked them how they liked it. They replied 'Well governor, it was just right.' He asked them 'What do you mean, just right?' They said 'Well, if it had been a lot better you would not have given it to us, and if it had been a bit worse we could not have drunk it'. That briefly is the philosophy of the Stock Exchange.[17]

The settlement was 'about right' solely in relation to political and administrative expediency. It was undoubtedly generous in relation to the future earning power, unless restraints were imposed on road transport. Furthermore, as Dalton said, 'What the railway companies had to offer was a pretty poor bag of physical assets'. Parliamentary exchanges aside, the financial settlement did have serious consequences for the British Transport Commission which was saddled with a burden of debt which added to its difficulty in meeting the Transport Act's requirement that its finances should break even 'taking one year with another'.

The single most important factor influencing the financial viability of the British Transport Commission was the growth of both passenger and freight road motor transport.[18] When the BTC began operations on 1 January 1948 there were 3,700,000 million motor vehicles of all kinds (private cars, buses, coaches and goods vehicles) on Britain's roads. By the time that the Conservative government abolished the railway executive in 1953 there were 5,300,000, and by the time the BTC was abolished under Harold Macmillan's government in 1962 there were 10,800,000. The number of motor vehicles in use was growing at the rate of 7 per cent compound in the early 1950s but at 8 per cent compound in the second half of that decade. The result of this momentous change in the predominant mode of transport was that, whereas until 1953 the 74,800 million passenger miles travelled by train or other public sector vehicles outnumbered the 42,100 million travelled by private car, in 1958 more (72,900,000 million) went by car than by rail and other forms of public transport. Furthermore, as motor vehicle manufacture became more sophisticated, people undertook longer journeys by car, and motor vans and lorries became more powerful, heavier and travelled longer distances. These were the circumstances causing the Railway Executive to cease covering its working costs by 1954 and the BTC to plunge into ever-increasing debt. No organisational changes such as the Railway Modernisation Plan in 1955 or the Beeching Plan of 1963 proved able to arrest the railways' decline.

Influencing this change of mode of passenger travel and of freight movement was the fact that the motorist, once he had paid his car licence, driving licence and petrol, was free to travel anywhere on the road, whereas the railway was obliged to pay rent for land use and rates (or council taxes). Robert Adley, Conservative MP for Christchurch during the lifetime of the BTC, resented the fact that motor coaches brought thousands of people each year to his Dorset constituency without having to pay for parking on the road, whereas visitors who came by train paid a fare which included an element of payment for station rates.

One area of policy unfortunately adversely affected by Alfred Barnes's insisting on the appointment of the members of the Railway Executive as well as the BTC, concerned locomotive building plans. In April 1948 Sir Cyril (later Lord) Hurcomb, BTC chairman, requested Sir Eustace Missenden, chairman of the RE, to appoint a committee to examine the relative advantages of diesel and electric locomotives, with a request for an urgent reply. Missenden, who lacked a good working relationship with Hurcomb, delayed the appointment of the committee for eight months and presented the committee's report over two years later. In the meantime the Railway Executive ordered a large run of steam locomotives on a standard pattern, on the grounds that the steam locomotives could be produced with the minimum of delay whereas 'a certain amount of fact finding was necessary for alternative forms of traction'. The delay caused by this dispute held back the modernisation of passenger and freight services.[19]

The Conservative Party's main transport policy expressed in the general election campaign of October 1951 was 'to reorganise rail and road services into regional groups', but its members were far more concerned to ensure that private road hauliers were 'given the chance to return to business' and that lorries should 'no longer be crippled by the twenty-five mile limit of their operations'.[20] The Transport Act of 1953 gave effect to these objectives. The Railway Executive was abolished. The BTC was required within twelve months of the passing of the Act, or such longer time as the minister might direct, 'to submit a scheme for the re-organisation of British railways'. The BTC's own plans suggested to the minister, A. Lennox-Boyd, from 7 May 1952 were subsequently published by him as a White Paper *Railways Reorganisation Scheme* in July 1954.

British Transport Commission

Six Area Railways Boards	London Transport Executive	British Road Services	Road Passenger Services	British Transport Docks	British Transport Waterways	British Transport Hotels	Other Classes and Catering

The Railway Executive went out of business in 1954 but its achievements in the very short space of time since 1948 should not be forgotten. The historian of British Railways considers that it succeeded in making a unified approach to railway working an established fact.[21] Michael Bonavia, who was a member of the BTC's headquarters staff and a witness of the very independent-minded approach of the Railway Executive, nevertheless gives it credit for establishing a 'sustained high level of traffic', with ton-miles of freight carried rising from 21,700 million in 1948 to 22,900 million in 1953, mainly due to an extended average length of haul, while passenger miles travelled by rail rose from 20,200 million in 1948 to 21,300 million in 1953.[22] Marshall Aid from the USA was suddenly stopped in September 1945. The Railway Executive, along with other organisations, had to 'make do' with essential components made in Britain; a new standardised passenger carriage, though unimaginatively designed, was put into service. There was a huge backlog both on maintenance and new investment. In the view of A. J. Pearson, who worked for the Railway Executive, the disadvantage of the abolition of the Executive was that the railways ceased to be managed by trained railway-men. In higher railway management, people were brought in who had no knowledge of the railways.[23]

Although in the early 1950s the economy was booming, both the Railway Executive and the BTC continued to make losses. Early in 1954 the government asked the BTC to draft a plan to make the industry financially more viable. The government appointed a planning committee mainly of head-quarters officers, with their assistant staff, to 'submit proposals for the modernisation and re-equipment of the railways, on the assumption that the plan would be capable of being launched within five and completed within fifteen years'.[24] The plan had four main heads: the improving of the track and signalling; the replacement of steam by diesel or electric traction; the modernisation of rolling stock and stations; and a radical remodelling of freight services. It was estimated initially that it would cost £1240 million; but because of inflation in the economy and the commission's underestimate it was raised to £1600 million in 1957. Under the (Railway Finances) Act of 1957, the government agreed to meet the financial deficits and declared that the plan was 'courageous and imaginative'. The cabinet agreed to this deficit financing as a better alternative to a continuing confrontation with the railway trade unions over their current wage claims.[25]

One third of the expenditure under the plan was spent on electrification and dieselisation. The general managers of the six regions' Railway Boards established under the Transport Act of 1953 favoured the electrification of both the main lines from London to the north: from King's Cross via Newcastle to Edinburgh, and from Euston via Birmingham to Glasgow. Only the east coast line was electrified in the years of the plan. Diesel power was used to good effect to speed up services elsewhere but these locomotives did not have as good a record on punctuality as did the electrified east coast line or the commuter trains into London and Manchester.

By 1958 it was obvious that the optimistic forecast of the BTC that the plan would serve to transform its finances and bring prosperity to the railways had not been fulfilled. Criticism of its conception and working were greatly increased. Matthew Stevenson told the Select Committee on Nationalised Industries in 1960: 'The plan was merely a hotch potch of things the commission was saying it was desirable to achieve by 1970'. BTC's record of investment during the years of the plan bore favourable comparison with the period from 1948–54. In constant 1948 prices the annual average investment of £37,700,000 in 1948–53 rose to £71,100,000 in 1954–62. Most of this new investment was spent on new rolling stock – larger wagons and more comfortable and smoother-riding passenger vehicles. An industrial recession in 1957 also did not help the financial position of the railways.

These improvements were in vain in face of the abolition of petrol rationing in 1950 and the threefold increase in the number of private cars on British roads between 1950 and 1962; at the same time as the number of road goods vehicles rose by 70 per cent, an increase in the latter case which disguises the fact that in 1962 the average capacity of goods vehicles rose far more rapidly than the increase in vehicle numbers.

To discover why the implementation of the modernisation plan had not eased the situation of the Railway Executive's finances, representatives of the Ministry of Transport and Civil Aviation agreed in 1958 the terms of reference of a reappraisal of the 1955 plan to be carried out by the BTC. In its report, published in 1959, it emphasised that the main objective for the next five years to 1964 would not differ greatly from those of 1955 but there would be changes in 'emphasis, priorities and timing'.[26] The report noted that between 1954 and 1958 the route miles of rail track was reduced by 300 to a total of 8850 miles still in service, but predicted that between 1958 and 1963 the reduction in route mileage was 'likely to exceed greatly the closures of the earlier years'. Foreshadowing Dr Richard Beeching's arguments four years later, the BTC claimed that, 'the construction of the railway system as a part of modernisation is far from being a negative process, because it aims at the revival of British railways as a whole'.[27]

It was a case of removing the dead wood to improve the life of the tree. The 'vigorous pursuit' of economy was to include the closure for freight traffic of many wayside stations and private sidings where they dealt with only small quantities of merchandise. Domestic coal traffic would be concentrated in 'a small number of destination stations'. Looking at broader issues for the future, the commission noted

> what the various transport services ... will be expected to plan ... On the one hand the services are asked to compete, and they must be asked accordingly, both by government and by general and business public, to act like a normal commercial undertaking and to base their decisions on business considerations, as regards both passenger and freight services and charges. On the other hand the Commission's services are often expected to be guided primarily by the public interest. Many of these services represent facilities which are essential to the life of a modern society ... *These two approaches, the commercial and the often unprofitable public service, frequently conflict, and though the economic benefits to the community are often substantial, they are not reflected in the revenue account of the Commission.*[28] (italics added)

The commission pointed out a major dilemma of transport policy but did not attempt to resolve it. Not until Barbara Castle's Transport Act of 1968 was a contribution made to its solution through Section 39, with its 'grants for unremunerative passenger services'. Later in the same year (1959), as the Reassessment Committee presented its report, the government set up a Select Committee on Nationalised Industries whose function was to find out 'on behalf of the House [of Commons] how the nationalised industries [had] been carrying out the activities required of them by statute, and then to make such comments as [seemed] appropriate'.[29] The Committee managed to squeeze in twenty-eight meetings, questioning dozens of witnesses in the six months allowed to it before reporting.

In contrast with the approach of the Ministry of Transport under Ernest Marples, the members of the select committee wanted to stress their view that they looked on all their activities as part of one general service. The Report's appendix 6 re-emphasised the view that 'neither the railways, nor the other forms of transport for which they are responsible can be treated in isolation. They are all inter-related and the Commission co-ordinates'.

Some subtle changes in terminology under the Conservative government were noted. Under the Labour government's Transport Act of 1947 the members of BTC were required to provide 'adequate railway services'. In the Conservative's Transport Act of 1953 the word 'adequate' was dropped and the words 'the railways could provide such services as they considered expedient' were substituted. In their general conclusions the members of the Committee stated that they had considered whether the losses on the railways arose mainly from the fact that 'they were competing against other, more modern, forms of transport'. They rejected this argument. On the evidence they had received they were convinced that a large-scale British railway system can be profitable. The number of improvements in hand, and the number of points at which further improvements can be made, lend force to this. The scientific and technical advances in other fields have not in recent years borne full fruit on the railways.[30]

The assumptions behind this optimistic outlook were that the economy would continue to expand and that there would be a continuing benevolent view of the future of the railways from Whitehall. Neither assumption could, in fact, be taken for granted.

Symptomatic of the growing predominance of the 'commercial' rather than the 'service' outlook in railway management was the gradual disappearance of the passenger porter. In 1958 the Central Transport Consultative Committee (the passengers' watchdog) discovered that the general manager of one of the railway regions had issued a press announcement that it was 'no part of the porter's duties to carry passengers hand luggage', that porters did so 'as an act of grace, and that by doing so they became agents of the passengers, so that the management was not liable for loss or damage to luggage'. The chairman of the consultative committee found this statement 'so much at variance with established understanding that he took it up with the commission forthwith, and found that the officer was under a misapprehension in both fact and law'. The consultative committee, however, found that inserted into the contract, which the passenger makes with the commission each time he or she purchases a ticket, was the assumption that a relationship of principal and agent existed between the passenger and a porter who carries his/her bag. But there came the subtle change. The contract ended at 'the termination of the journey' and that the journey did not terminate, as hitherto supposed, when the passenger left the terminal station, but at the moment when the bag was deposited on the platform beside the train in which it had been conveyed.[31] The consultative committee had no power to alter the regulations of the railway regional boards so that, before long, porters were declared redundant. Management in time could provide trolleys on main line arrival platforms but passengers might have to walk yards with their luggage to collect them. In vain the consultative committee observed, 'if the BTC wish to attract passenger traffic they should encourage porters to be as helpful as possible to passengers'.[32] Passengers increasingly found journeying by motor vehicle more attractive.

When General Sir Brian Robertson retired as BTC chairman after eight years in office, Ernest Marples, the Conservative Minister of Transport, appointed Dr Richard Beeching of ICI to succeed him. There had been intense bargaining. Marples promised Beeching his old salary of £24,000 a year (compared with Robertson's £10,000) in return for Beeching's agreement to serve for five years from 31 May 1961 and the ICI's consent to his

secondment for that term. The exceptional salary was given on the understanding that the new chairman was to introduce drastic reforms, including
very substantial reductions in the commission's manpower. When Beeching
left the post, after only four years, in 1965, his successor Sir Stanley Raymond
was paid a salary of only £12,500, the same as that of Lord Robens at
the National Coal Board but little more than half of what Beeching had
received.[33]

Less than six months after Beeching's appointment, Marples introduced
the second reading of the Transport Bill on 21 November 1961. He was no
great authority on his subject and read the whole of his speech introducing
the Bill – a departure from precedent. The principal changes it made
included the abolition of the BTC and the reallocation of its responsibilities
to four newly created boards: the British Railways Board; the London
Transport Board; the British Transport Docks Board; and the British Waterways Board. Each board was to have it own separate accounts and these
were to be managed so as to break even 'taking one year with another'.
The chairman of each board was to be appointed by the minister. In his
speech Marples argued that it was necessary to wind up the commission,
since the task of running all these activities at present was 'too big a job
for any single authority'. The BTC was 'overloaded with work'. Reorganisation, financial reconstruction and 'a different climate of operation' were
urgently needed. To this end each main field of the commission's activity
was to be placed under a separate authority and each such authority was
to have clearly defined responsibilities. The whole organisation was to have
greatly increased commercial freedom. Whilst welcoming the Bill's provisions for a reduction of the capital charges of the railways, G. R. Strauss
for the Opposition deplored its main purpose which was 'to destroy the
spirit and machinery of co-ordinated public transport' and to ordain that
'the individual transport elements should operate on their own as separate
competitive commercial concerns, without any unifying influence'. The
Labour Party considered this exceedingly damaging to the transport industry. Philip Noel-Baker who represented Derby South, still then an important
railway town, forecast that with continuing prosperity there would be a
massive increase in motorised transport and that 'the multiplication of
private cars could defeat the very purpose for which people want
them'.[34] Both Strauss and Noel-Baker pointed out that the overloading of
work at the BTC was the result of the Conservative's Transport Act of
1953, which had abolished the Railway Executive and transferred its work
to the BTC.

The Beeching Report, *The Reshaping of British Railways*, published in
March 1963, was a continuation of a slimming down process which had

begun with the Modernisation Plan of 1955, the Reappraisal in 1959 and the government's White Paper on *The Financial and Economic Obligations of the Nation*, published in 1961. For example the Reappraisal promised a reduction of 10 per cent, or 1800 route miles, in the rail network, and in 1960 the BTC, under pressure from government circles, produced a four-year modernisation programme which included lists of separate lines for closure. Beeching speeded up these proposals, pressed hard for more exact accounting and was ruthless in applying the remedies that these surveys indicated as necessary. He made a particularly searching enquiry into railway network and station utilisation. In freight, only the carriage of coal and parcels, and in passenger services only fast and semi-fast trains produced a surplus. Half the rail network produced only 3 per cent of the freight revenue. An appendix to the report listed 266 passenger services to be withdrawn and 2363 stations to be closed to passenger traffic. The existing railway network of 16,000 miles was to be reduced by about half to 8500 miles. Beeching's view was that after these unprofitable parts of the system were eliminated there would be a prospect of balancing the books, provided improvements such as liner trains, streamlining of stations and further electrification of signalling were put into operation. But the calculations of operational and capital maintenance savings were more accurate than the over-optimistic estimates of the extra revenue which would arise from the modernisation process.

Critics had stressed that the Reshaping Plan of 1963 consisted largely of cuts. To counter these objections, and also because it was in Beeching's programme for the future, he asked one of his senior assistants, James Ness, to prepare a more positive publication *The Development of the Major Trunk Routes*, which, after some delay, was published in 1965. By concentrating on 3,000 miles of the network, completely modernising their operation, the system could be made to yield a surplus. It was later pointed out that Ness had left out any consideration of feeder and commuter lines, which would add to the total of route miles it would be necessary to retain. There was growing doubt, however, whether the elusive 'profitable rail network' could ever be attained and Richard Marsh, chairman of the Railways Board from 1971 to 1976, told the Conservative Minister of Transport John Peyton, in a confidential memorandum in 1972 that he had found it 'impossible to find any network size which was viable'.[35] The reason why Beeching did not find a sustainable future either for the railways or for a balanced transport policy for Britain was that he analysed the railway system in isolation from what was happening in other forms of transport.

Under the leadership of Harold Wilson the Labour Party was returned to power in the general election of 15 October 1965 with an overall majority of only four MPs over the Conservative and Liberal Parties. In its election manifesto, *The New Britain*, it promised

> a national plan for transport covering the national networks of road, rail and canal communication, properly co-ordinated with air, coastal shipping and port services ... While these are being prepared, major rail closures will be halted.

Wilson's first choice for Minister of Transport was Thomas Fraser, an affable Scottish miner with little experience of government. The Premier asked him to devise a plan with Beeching and others covering all forms of transport; but, while this was being devised, he continued the Beeching policy of rail closures. This provoked a cabinet revolt which led to Fraser's resignation, the succession of Barbara Castle and Beeching's decision to leave his job as chairman of the British Railways Board as from 1 June 1965.

Barbara Castle worked with energy and enthusiasm, producing five White Papers on different aspects of transport policy before she introduced the second reading of her enormous Transport Bill to the Commons on 20 December 1967. In its final form the Transport Act (Elizabeth II 1968, ch. 73), with its ten parts and eighteen Schedules, ran to 2377 pages. The first part of the Act introduced a National Freight Corporation whose function it would be to coordinate the movement of goods by sea, road or rail, so that each form of transport was doing the task it was best suited to do – heavy, long-distance freight by sea or rail taken from the railhead or port to its final destination by road. The Act wrote off £760 million of the BRB's debts which had been suspended under the Transport Act of 1962 and £557 million of the railway's original capital debt. A reform which had been hinted at earlier in the Reassessment Plan of 1959, the singling out of socially necessary passenger services which did not cover their operating costs and – after careful costing to avoid sponging – sustaining them by Treasury grants for periods of three years, was arranged under section 39. A National Bus Company was to be formed to take over the bus and vehicle manufacturing interests hitherto under the control (rarely exerted because of inadequate funds and staffing) of the Transport Holding Company of 1962. A Scottish Transport Company was to assess these functions north of the Tweed. Provision of bus services outside London was to be the responsibility of local Passenger Transport Authorities which were to be helped by subsidies for the purchase of new vehicles and for maintenance of services in remote country areas.

Barbara Castle was less successful in controlling the growth of road freight transport in increasingly heavier vehicles. The weight limits of the vehicles had been raised from twenty-four tons to thirty-two tons by the previous Conservative administration. The original plan was to place an additional tax on vehicles of over three tons unladen weight to contribute to road upkeep in view of the damage they did. But this part of the Bill was dropped in favour of variations in the licensing fees for road freight vehicles. The lighter vehicles under 1.15 tons unladen weight were exempted from carrier licensing altogether. Even so the British Road Federation, the main road lobby, launched a ferocious campaign against the Bill. Whole page adverts were placed in the national press. Peter Walker, the Conservative Party's front bench spokesman on Transport, paid £10,000 out of his own pocket to set up a research group to provide arguments against the Bill.[36] Before the Bill became law it had attracted some 2500 amendments, more than two and a half times the number of amendments Barnes's Transport Act of 1947 had attracted and the committee considering the Bill met for a record 45 sittings.[37] Despite these obstacles, the Bill became law in 1968. The railways got their subsidies and the quantity licensing clauses emerged virtually unscathed. However, the quality licensing clauses were never enforced because of the opposition of Frank Cousins and the Transport and General Workers' Union. Barbara Castle acidly remarked 'Frank Cousins's socialism stops dead at the door of a lorry'.[38] Cousins's opposition effectively sabotaged Labour's plan for a coordinated transport system.

The failure of the 1968 Transport Act to arrest the decline of public transport by bus, taxi and railway, and the inexorable rise of the private motor car in passenger transport are illustrated in Table 9:

Table 9

Passenger Transport by Mode, 1979–1999
Billion Passenger Kilometres / Per Cent

Date	Buses and Coaches		Motor Cars and Taxis		Motor Cycles		Pedal Cycles		All Road		Rail		Air		Total
		%		%		%		%		%		%		%	
1980	45	9	395	80	8	2	5	1	453	92	35	7	3	1	460
1985	42	8	440	82	8	2	6	1	496	93	36	7	4	1	493
1990	46	7	588	85	6	1	5	1	645	94	39	6	5	1	689
1995	44	6	596	86	4	1	4	1	648	94	36	5	6	1	690
1997	43	6	619	86	4	1	4	1	670	93	41	6	7	1	717
1998	43	6	616	86	4	1	4	1	667	93	42	6	7	1	716

Source: Department of Transport, *Transport Statistics Great Britain* (1979 and 1999), table 1.1.

The decline in bus and coaches passenger kilometres was steeper in the south east of England than in the north east and Merseyside, where private car ownership was less pronounced than in the more prosperous south east.

Table 10

Goods Vehicles over 3.5 Tonnes Licensed at End of Year

Year	Rigid Vehicles	Articulated Vehicles	All Vehicles
1985	342,000	90,000	432,000
1990	353,000	106,000	460,000
1995	311,000	107,000	418,000
1998	308,000	111,000	419,000

Source: Department of Transport, *Transport Statistics Great Britain* (1999), table 3.7, p. 79.

It is notable that the number of rigid-axled vehicles declined (Table 10), though the tonne kilometres of goods carried increased. The reason for this was that goods movement shifted from two-axled to three-axled vehicles, often of thirty-eight tonnes. In 1992 there were 132,200 two-axled to 75,600 three-axled vehicles. By 1998 the number of two-axled vehicles had declined to 98,100 while the three-axled vehicles – the heaviest – rose to 131,800.[39] The environmental consequence of this change will be discussed in the next chapter.

After Barbara Castle was appointed Minister of Transport on 23 December 1965 it did not take her long to discover that the assets of the Waterways Board were in a run-down condition. The old principal standbys, coal and steel, were in decline. In their place liquid bulk and dry bulk cargoes, which accounted for more than three-quarters by weight of the cargoes carried. were to be found in the Kent and Thames areas. With the aid of her staff in the Department of Transport, she drafted a White Paper, *British Water-ways: Recreation and Amenity*, which was issued in 1967. It embodied her plans, idealistically motivated, for a revival of the canals as recreational centres.

In her speech introducing the second reading of the Transport Bill to the Commons on 20 December 1967 she said she was offering

new hope for those who love and use our canals, whether for cruising, angling or just walking on the towpath, or who want to see stretches of canal in some of our unlovely built up areas, developed as centres of beauty and fun.[40]

Part VII of the Transport Act (Elizabeth II, ch. 73, 25 October 1968) divided the waterways into two categories: commercial waterways and cruising waterways.[41] An Inland Waterway Advisory Council was to be created to advise the minister where there was a case for new canals to be dug or for services on some old ones discontinued. Canal links with railway stations or terminals were to be encouraged. Barbara Castle mentioned that under Clause 4 of the Act power was to be given to the Waterways Board to manufacture power boats, boat houses and 'any other objects which it considered could be advantageously done'. Peter Walker, for the Opposition, while approving the development of cruising waterways, raised a strong objection to Clause 45 which he claimed (rhetorically) provided the government with 'the possibility of the largest extension of nationalisation in British History'.[42]

Taking advantage of the cheaper licenses for the hire of pleasure craft, made possible by an increase in grants-in-aid from £1850 in 1970 to £5,300,000 in 1974, revenue from pleasure craft licences rose from £170,300 in 1970 to £368,400 in 1974. The revenues from the 'commercial' canals rose rather more modestly in the same period from £1,521,100 to £1,714,100.[43]

9

Technology and Transport

The rise of technology and the growth in the breadth and complexity of scientific knowledge is one of the critical factors in modern history. The relationship between technology and economic growth is well documented, as is the role of technology in industrialisation.[1] Transport has often been at the heart of this relationship, starting with the steam engine and its role in the creation of the railways at the beginning of the nineteenth century. Since then a number of technologies have appeared which have been crucial to the development of transport in Britain, and throughout the world.[2] This chapter looks at these inventions and innovations. The idea of technology is broadly defined here but it encompasses a range of developments emanating from and associated with four methods of locomotion or propulsion: steam engines, electric traction motors, internal combustion engines and jet engines. The chapter is loosely informed by the link between technology and social change, and by the degree to which technology is socially determined or 'constructed'.[3] It is also concerned to engage the discussion on transport technology's impact on the natural environment, an issue which became increasingly politicised in the last quarter of the twentieth century as 'green' activists sought to oppose the continued use of polluting technologies.

Locomotion and propulsion means the various ways of pushing or pulling transport vehicles along. As we have seen, at the beginning of the nineteenth century, locomotion depended on the human body and the ubiquitous horse (and it is remarkable for how long the locomotive strength of succeeding technologies has been measured in units of 'horse power'). The first successor to the horse was the steam engine.

The steam engine was the key technology in the creation of the railways and the power that drove the Industrial Revolution. It was also of great importance to shipping; indeed, as a source of propulsion, the steam engine's maritime use in wooden-hulled coasters and short sea craft predates its use on the railways by at least a decade. In Britain its long use on the railways is eloquent testimony to its efficiency and durability as a locomotive technology, as much as to its capacity for continual refinement.

The first functional steam engine, a stationary one for pumping water out of Cornish tin mines, was designed and built in 1712 by Thomas Newcomen.

In 1769 James Watt improved the Newcomen engine fundamentally with the addition of the separate steam condenser, but it was not until 1801 that the son of one of Watt's engineers, Richard Trevithick, made a steam engine with locomotive power; in this case a steam-driven carriage.[4] Finally, in 1813, the man generally credited with being the 'Father of the Railways', George Stephenson, put a steam locomotive to work hauling coal at the Killingworth colliery near Newcastle-upon-Tyne. He and his son Robert Stephenson improved the Trevithick design by coupling the wheels with connecting rods and putting the cylinders on the side of the boiler. It was the Stephensons' locomotive *Rocket* which won the contest to power the Manchester & Liverpool Railway at the Rainhill contest in 1829 and launched an epoch of steam engine development on the railways which would last for more than a century.[5] A symbolic climax to this development was reached in 1934 when Sir Nigel Gresley's Pacific Class *Flying Scotsman* reached 100 miles per hour on a stretch of railway track south of Grantham.[6]

The other successful application of the steam engine to transport was in shipping. Here the steam engine was coupled to paddle wheels and increasingly from the 1840s to screw propellers. It was innovations in marine engine technology that led to the raising of the steam engine's low thermal efficiency. In the 1850s John Elder's work on compound expansion, followed in the 1870s by triple and quadruple expansion, went a long way towards releasing a greater amount of the energy stored in coal – the steam engine's primary fuel source. Then, in the last two decades of the nineteenth century, the distinguished engineer Sir Charles Parsons adapted steam to a new method of propulsive power which overtook the reciprocating engine in marine use: the steam turbine. Instead of using steam pressure to drive a piston, Parsons used a jet of steam to turn a wheel directly by acting upon blades set densely around the circumference of a turbine. In this respect he was one of the forefathers of what became, fifty years later, the jet engine. Parsons began building static turbines for electricity generation in the 1880s. In the 1890s he turned his attention to ship propulsion and in 1897 his revolutionary craft *Turbinia* demonstrated the high speeds possible with turbine propulsion to an astonished crowd of naval notables at the Spithead Naval Review. In the Edwardian years the steam turbine was rapidly adopted in the merchant marine. Cunard began fitting their ocean liners with turbines from 1905. They made an even faster conquest in coastal and estuarial shipping, the first turbine-driven passenger vessel being the *King Edward* which was introduced into service on the River Clyde in 1901.[7]

Steam was also applied to other vehicles used for transport in Britain, but with far less success. On the roads cars were initially and experimentally powered by steam engines; indeed it was unclear at the beginning whether 'horseless carriages' should be powered by petrol engines, electric motors or steam engines. Steam power survived well beyond the First World War in heavy vehicles such as lorries and traction engines, although the difficulty of stoking the boiler while driving was only one of several problems faced by steam road vehicles. Steam traction engines enjoyed a long life and were still being used in the 1950s for heavy towing and lifting work, and as a stalwart power source for farmers, driving threshing machines and all manner of other agricultural equipment.[8]

After the steam engine the next major innovation in locomotion and propulsion came in the last quarter of the nineteenth century and stemmed directly from the harnessing of electricity. The main technological input for the development of electric traction came not from Britain but from Germany and the United States, although Faraday had shown the basic principle of generating electricity by rotating a coil in a magnetic field as early as 1831. Now the devices which flowed from Faraday's discovery – dynamos, alternators and others – were used in electric motors to convert electrical energy back into mechanical and propulsive power.[9] The German inventor Werner von Siemens, who was already producing dynamos in the 1870s,[10] was anxious to develop an electrically-driven street car and in 1879 his firm, Siemens & Halske, demonstrated the first electric-powered train in Berlin. The problem for Siemens was the rudimentary 'third rail' supply system he used; many German municipalities would not allow a live rail tram service on public safety grounds. The solution to this problem – an overhead power source – became a practical option when the American Frank Sprague perfected the spring-loaded pole collector in the 1880s, thus making urban tram systems efficient and generally acceptable. It was Sprague's achievement to solve not only the problem of how to feed electric current to tramcars moving along a city street, but also how to mount the electric traction motors on the cars' axles. These were mounted 'wheelbarrow fashion', partly on the tram's axles and partly suspended by springs from the tramcar frame. Meanwhile Siemens pressed ahead with its own design for overhead current collection. This was the spring-loaded bow collector, a forerunner of the modern pantograph, whose use on tram cars spread rapidly through Europe in the 1890s.[11]

As a means of locomotion, the vital characteristic of electric traction is that it gathers its power from a remote source. Electric traction is flexible in that its 'fuel' can be generated in a number of ways, although this flexibility does not extend to its operation since it is tied to both track and overhead wire or 'third rail'. The maintenance and operating costs of electric locomotives and trams are lower than equivalent steam or diesel systems and this can be manifested in lower fares. Thus electrification in urban transport meant lower tram costs, and lower costs meant that workers who had previously walked to work now rode. Electric traction, more than any other means of locomotion, gave mobility to the urban working class, but beyond the tram network it also had an important effect on urban railways. Because these railways were largely underground in 'tube' tunnels or 'cut-and-cover' trenches, they needed a propulsive system that did not pollute. When the Metropolitan Railway began operations in London in the 1860s, its steam locomotives quickly blackened the tunnels it passed through, and disposing of smoke and steam remained a major problem for the next forty years until electric traction was introduced in 1905. Electric traction and underground transport was therefore an ideal union of technologies; indeed it is impossible to imagine the London Tube network, or any other rapid transport system, without it. It should be remembered, however, that this marriage of technologies required stimulus from abroad. The London Underground was promoted after 1890 largely by American businessmen, notably C. T. Yerkes and Albert Stanley (Lord Ashfield), and their critical role in the electrification of the Underground should be seen against the fact that much of the equipment used on the new electric trains was manufactured by the British subsidiaries of American companies such as Westinghouse and Thomson-Houston, or imported directly from the United States.

Where electric traction was slower to establish itself was on Britain's mainline railway network. The electrification of British railways in the early twentieth century represented only a fraction of the national rail grid, the vast majority of which remained loyal to steam. It was also entirely concentrated at sections where there was competition from tramway systems, that is in urban and suburban areas. The Lancashire & Yorkshire Railway, for example, electrified part of its system around Liverpool in 1904 to stem the loss of passengers to local tramways, and the London, Brighton & South Coast Railway did the same in south London in 1909. The main technical system adopted by these main line companies was the 'third rail' positive conductor, although the London, Brighton & South Coast Railway initially used a 6600 volt ac overhead feed (this was converted to the familiar 750 volt dc third rail arrangement by the Southern Railway in 1926).[12] On London Underground trains, where the voltage was 600 to 650 volts dc, a fourth rail was added, so that the positive conductor rail lay outside the running rails and an insulated negative rail ran down the centre to collect the return current. This was to avoid the hazard of current escaping from the running rails into the surrounding tunnel structure and causing electrolytic corrosion. The first electrified line, the Metropolitan District (the District Line), set the standard for all future London underground railways with its 630 volt four-rail system, the earlier tubes also being converted to this standard.[13]

Apart from the Southern Railway's low voltage 'third rail' dc programme between the wars, which was only suitable for comparatively slow suburban trains, it was to be another half century before Britain's main line railways addressed themselves to the challenge of electrification. When they did it was to be part of the British Railways (BR) Modernisation Plan. This called for the rapid phasing out of steam locomotion and a shift to the high voltage (25,000 volt) overhead ac system already proving its worth on the French railways. Apart from cost savings on maintenance, high voltage electrification promised speed. Electric locomotives had always had the potential for high speeds and high speed trains were not new in the Britain of the 1960s when the Japanese first drew attention to their potential with the *Shinkansen* 'Bullet Train'. As we have seen, Gresley's A4 Pacific steam trains were built for speeds of up to 100 miles per hour, and in 1938 the *Mallard* had set the world speed record for steam traction at 126 mph. But Gresley's trains were an isolated innovation in an otherwise conventional and ageing railway system.[14] Their main technical significance lay in their streamlining, a vital part of which was the 'wedge-shaped' front-end which has remained the aerodynamic standard for high-speed trains ever since.

The prime obstacle to electrification in the BR Modernisation Plan was the very high capital cost involved. To electrify the British rail network with an overhead high voltage system required a massive investment which, in the event, made the programme a target for an unsympathetic Treasury and a hostile Transport Minister (Ernest Marples). Full electrification was therefore abandoned in 1959 and diesel locomotives were chosen to replace steam; the only electrification of BR's network at this time took place on the West Coast line, where a service from London to Manchester opened in 1966 with trains reaching speeds of around 100 mph.

This was the situation when engineers at BR's Advanced Projects Group in Derby proposed a new high-speed train whose performance would represent a quantum leap forward in British rail technology. This Advanced Passenger Train (APT) would use radical new technology, some of it pioneered in the aerospace industry, to create a train capable of speeds up 155 mph. The essential thing about the APT, unlike the Japanese *Shinkansen* or the highly successful French *Train à Grande Vitesse* (TGV), was that it was to run on conventional track; there simply wasn't the money to construct new track for modern high-speed running.[15] This meant that the APT had to be a 'tilt-train' with the capacity to go round curves at high speed without coming off the rails.[16] Work on the APT began in 1967. The first prototypes used gas turbines, but this technology was swapped at an early stage for electric traction. In 1975 a test model reached 150 mph on an experimental run between Swindon and Reading, but by this stage the APT was beset with problems. The computer-controlled tilting mechanism jammed, the advanced hydrokinetic brakes overheated, the articulated bogies gave a poor ride, and the positioning of the pantographs on the train's tilting roof presented serious difficulties. In late 1981 an APT passenger service was started from London to Glasgow, but it was abandoned within a week after a succession of breakdowns. By the end of 1982 BR had admitted that the APT was an operational failure.

In retrospect, the APT was an attempt to use high technology to modernise Britain's railways on the cheap. Its aim was to allow Britain to catch up with the French and other European nations experimenting with high speed trains, without the necessity of investing in elaborate new infrastructrure, especially track. From the beginning to the end of the project in 1982, the APT cost less than £50,000,000; yet over the same period expenditure on new motorways and other trunk roads in Britain totalled £5,300,000,000, while the Concorde supersonic transport project cost £2,000,000,000 from 1962 to 1976. As a further yardstick of comparison, a single line of the French TGV – from Paris to Lyon – cost about £1,000,000,000.[17] This idea that revolutionary (and untried) technology, and what was still widely perceived to be 'the genius of British scientists', could save money and allow Britain to leapfrog its competitors at low cost, was not confined to rail transport. In aerospace it was a widely-held creed and the Comet jet airliner of 1952 is a clear example of how Britain used a technological lead on a narrow front, in this case jet engines, to attempt to get ahead of the United States, its chief rival in aircraft manufacturing. The Comet project ended in a disastrous series of crashes which claimed many lives.[18] Fortunately there were no passenger fatalities involved in the APT's frequent break-downs, but the principle involved – that the APT was simply too advanced, and depended on the solution of too many technological problems on the frontiers of scientific knowledge – appears to be as valid as for the Comet.[19] There is some irony in the fact – and this seems to be an inherent feature of the application of technology to transport, indeed of the commercial application of technology in general – that the French, by settling for a simpler and less advanced technology with the TGV, had far fewer problems in its development, and got themselves a train which was substantially faster than the APT.[20]

One high technology transport project where Britain had no need to fear French competition was the Channel Tunnel. Since the eighteenth century, there have been numerous attempts to build a tunnel under the twenty-two miles of sea separating Britain from the European mainland, but until the end of the twentieth century they all failed.[21] A tunnel connecting south-eastern England to France required a collective psychological step for which the British needed two centuries to prepare: physical union with Europe and the loss of their island status.[22] The Channel Tunnel also had to wait for a viable electric transport system and in this respect it is reminiscent of the important relationship between electric traction and the construction of the London Underground tunnels a century before. Serious planning for the Channel Tunnel began in the 1950s, based on twin rail tunnels for car shuttles, a very similar concept to what was finally achieved in the 1990s. In fact many of the technical features of the tunnel were of considerable vintage. As early as the 1860s, when the London, Chatham & Dover and the South Eastern Railways reached the Channel coast, a pair of rail tunnels had been proposed, each containing a single track, with linking cross tunnels; ingeniously, the design would have drawn ventilation from the piston-like action of the trains in the tunnels 'pushing air in front and drawing fresh air from behind'.[23] After a number of engineering studies, a seven metre twin rail tunnel with a service gallery emerged in 1959 as the most viable proposal.[24] The project remained stalled until a new Channel Tunnel Planning Committee was set up as part of the Labour government's 1968 Transport Act. The government of the Conservative Prime Minister Edward Heath, a committed 'European', gave the Tunnel new impetus after 1970, but the enterprise was abandoned again, for various political and economic reasons, after Labour was returned to government in 1974. Finally, in 1986 a new agreement was signed by Britain and France and the Channel Tunnel Group proceeded with the boring of twin 7.6 metre rail tunnels with a third service tunnel of 4.8 metre running between them and connected by cross passages (for emergency evacuation) at 300 metre intervals. With the aid of modern computer-guided boring machines, progress through the soft chalk beneath the Channel sea bed was comparatively easy and the three tunnels were completed in 1991. The tunnel, which opened in 1994, offers two services: the car and lorry-carrying Shuttle and the high-speed Eurostar trains, physically connecting London with Paris and Brussels and, for the first time in its history, the British railway network with that of the Continent. By 2000 the Tunnel could be judged a success, at least in terms of passenger convenience: many businessmen and other Londoners found the Eurostar's city centre to city centre service faster than flying. The train, with electric traction, had become 'quicker' than the plane.[25]

It is four nineteenth-century Germans who deserve the credit for the invention of both the petroleum-driven engine and the motor car: Nicholas Otto, Gottlieb Daimler, Wilhelm Maybach and Karl Benz. The French also played an important role in pioneering the motor car in the years before the First World War; indeed progress in the motor industry in France was more rapid than in Germany.[26] The United States came somewhat later to automobile production, but when Henry Ford built the first low-priced car – the Model T – in 1910, and launched its mass-production, the Americans joined and very quickly dominated the world in car production and use.[27] By contrast the British contribution to the early development of the internal combustion engine and the motor car was more modest. Although the skills and ingenuity of early pioneers like Frederick Lanchester and Sir Henry Royce deserve a mention, the British were slower in establishing car manufacturing capability before the 1920s.[28] Like the steam engine, the internal combustion engine has proved capable of over a century's development and refinement – and, unlike the steam engine, the process is still continuing. Through improvements and innovations to its cooling, ignition and fuel supply, through rearrangements of the cylinders, through better transmission of power to the wheels, and through the use of lightweight alloys and plastics, the power, dependability and fuel economy of the internal combustion engine has been steadily increased.

The overwhelming triumph of the motor car and lorry as a means of transport is not so much a function of its speed as of its unique flexibility; 'what the motor vehicle has done essentially is to allow the exercise of far greater individual freedom in transport. The organised travel of the train and the tram-car has given way to the private and highly flexible car and lorry.'[29] From a technological point of view, the internal combustion engine has been supremely adaptable. The motor car has replaced the horse and carriage for shorter passenger journeys, and the railway carriage for longer; the bus has supplanted the tram and trolley; and the diesel lorry has made enormous inroads into the freight transport market of the railway wagon and canal barge.

The diesel engine's rate of adoption was slower than that of the petrol engine, although, after the eponymous Rudolf Diesel took out a patent in England in 1892, its use spread steadily to heavy transport vehicles, both on road and rail.[30] Apart from its use in lorries and coastal ships, the diesel engine's greatest application in British transport history has been in railway locomotives, where it exhibits a far higher thermal efficiency than steam engines. In Britain most diesel locomotives have been of the diesel-electric type, where the diesel engine drives a generator which provides current to electric traction motors, a system which was developed extensively in the USA in the 1930s. The diesel age on Britain's railways began in the 1950s when the high cost of electrification led BR to choose diesels in its sudden rush to replace steam.[31] The most powerful were the 3300 horse power English Electric Deltics, which used twin two-stroke diesel engines each driving a generator and associated traction motors. The Deltics spearheaded a modernisation programme which raised passenger train speeds substantially on BR's

East Coast line from 1962.[32] BR continued a major programme of diesel locomotive acquisition, bringing 1378 diesel locomotives into service between 1963 and 1973 as against a mere 181 electric ones.[33] In the 1970s, as the problems with the electric APT became intractable, BR's engineers swiftly developed an alternative diesel-electric high-speed train (HST) – the Inter-City 125. With two diesel power cars at each end of a fixed formation train this entered commercial service on the East Coast line in 1976. The HST was slower than the APT, although it did benefit from the research done on the APT in the design of its bogie and suspension systems. In its first year of service on the London to Leeds route, the HST showed an impressive 13 per cent increase in passenger numbers.[34] The age of the diesel on Britain's mainline railways was, however, comparatively short-lived. In the 1980s BR was able to advance the electrification programme which had been so abruptly abandoned in the 1950s and begin the process of catching up with the national railway systems of other European countries where electrification was more widespread. The 25,000 volt overhead system was gradually installed on the East Coast line and BR's Class 89 electric trains were introduced. The Class 89 was no faster than the diesel-electric HSTs, but in the 1980s greater speed was no longer the major criterion; electric locomotion would now provide significant savings on the maintenance and fuel costs which had always been high with diesel operation.

The only transport mode where the reciprocating combustion engine has suffered an actual retreat in the twentieth century is in air transport. The Wright brothers' first flight in December 1903 was powered by a twelve horse power petrol engine driving two propellers through bicycle chains.[35] For the next forty years all aircraft were powered by petrol-driven internal combustion engines (the Germans experimented briefly with diesel aero-engines in the 1930s), driving one or more propellers. Two main lines of development were followed: liquid-cooled engines with the cylinders 'in-line' and air-cooled radial engines where the cylinders were placed in a ring around the propeller. In the United States, two firms, Wright Aeronautical and Pratt & Whitney, concentrated on air-cooled radial engines and by the end of the 1930s they were producing sophisticated supercharged engines for commercial air transport.[36] In Britain, two main firms, Rolls Royce and Bristol, manufactured liquid-cooled and radial engines respectively. The former company produced the famous Merlin engine which powered many of Britain's warplanes during the Second World War and one or two airliners after it.[37] The internal combustion engine, however, with its reciprocating action, was an inefficient way to propel an aircraft through the air. The aero-engine designer Sir Stanley Hooker once remarked that 'the four-stroke piston engine had one stroke for producing power and three for wearing the engine out'.[38] Engines like the Rolls Royce Merlin represented the ultimate stage of their development and it was clear to a number of scientists and technologists that, if aircraft were to fly comfortably over 500 miles per hour, a radical new technology would be needed.

Of the four propulsive systems looked at here, the jet engine is the one that most clearly has its origins in the military. It is, as one of the leading researchers in the field has pointed out, 'a striking example of the commercialisation of military technology'.[39] Indeed civil aircraft technology, to a greater extent than with the other transport modes treated in this book, received its theoretical and practical stimulus from its evolution in the armed forces, although it must be noted that the Royal Navy did play an important role in the progress of British maritime engineering and communications, and the development of the steam turbine, before the First World War.[40]

The creation of a functional jet engine was the work of the Englishman Frank Whittle, a serving Royal Air Force officer, and the German physicist Hans von Ohain. They worked entirely independently from one another but at the same time and in the shadow of war. Ohain built and ran the first engine with the help of the Heinkel company in 1935 and flew the first jet plane in 1939. Whittle's first engine, the W1, powered a jet aircraft in 1941 and by the end of the Second World War both Britain and Germany had operational jet fighters: the Gloster Meteor with Rolls Royce Derwent engines, and the Messerschmitt Me. 262 with Junkers Jumo 004 engines – the latter using the more advanced and complex axial-flow compressors that were to form the basis of post-war jet engine development.[41] The Americans were behind the British and Germans but caught up rapidly after they secured a Whittle engine in 1941, and both General Electric and Pratt & Whitney were able to copy it. In the ten years after 1945 both British and American firms built jet engines, at first for military aircraft and then increasingly with commercial aviation in mind. The American Pratt & Whitney J.57 and the Rolls Royce Avon engines, for example, were equally at home in bombers (Boeing B.52/ Vickers Valiant) as they were in airliners (Boeing 707/ de Havilland Comet 4).

The jet engine was revolutionary in the context of aircraft propulsion, although it built upon a tradition of research in gas and steam turbines stretching back to Sir Charles Parsons.[42] It also benefited from the work that had been carried out by engine manufacturers on superchargers.[43] Jet engines work by sucking in air, compressing and heating it, igniting it by introducing a suitable fuel, usually paraffin, and finally expressing the burnt gas in the form of a jet out of the tailpipe at the rear. Apart from its ability to propel aircraft at far greater speeds than are possible with reciprocating engines, its main advantage lies in the fact that it is an altogether simpler concept than a piston engine; it suffers from less wear, it needs less maintenance and it has proved to be more economical in use. Because commercial jets operate at a much higher altitude than piston-engined aircraft, they are also able to fly 'above the weather' and save their passengers a great deal of discomfort from bumpy rides. All in all, the union of the aircraft and the jet engine is a technological marriage made in heaven, or at least in the upper atmosphere.

Of course it is the jet engine's speed which transformed commercial aviation. A glance at the performance of three generations of de Havilland commercial aircraft shows the dramatic increase in speed that jet engines brought about in the 1960s (Table 11):

Table 11

Fifty Years of de Havilland Aircraft

Year	Aircraft	Engines	Cruising Speed	Typical Number of Passengers	Time from London to Paris
1919	DH.4	1 x RR Eagle	100 mph	2	140 mins
1939	DH.91 Albatross	4 x DH Gypsy 12	200 mph	22	80 mins
1969	DH.121 Trident 2	3 x RR Spey jets	520 mph	110	50 mins

Note: The Trident was begun by a consortium led by de Havilland in the late 1950s. The company subsequently became part of the Hawker Siddeley Group.

Source: C. Martin Sharp, *DH: A History of de Havilland* (Shrewsbury, 1982), pp. 400–11.

The technical development of gas turbines and jet engines moved steadily in the years between 1950 and 1970 from 'straight' jets to quieter, more fuel-efficient engines that would appeal to airline executives as well as air force generals. For a brief interregnum in the 1950s its was thought that the turbo-prop engine – in which a gas turbine was coupled to a propeller – would best serve the needs of transport aircraft, particularly over shorter distances. Britain distinguished itself by producing the most successful turbo-prop – the Rolls Royce Dart – which gave good service, notably in the conventionally-designed short to medium-haul Vickers-Armstrong Viscount aircraft, the only British airliner to enjoy significant export earnings.[44] The turbo-prop brought some of the benefits of turbine power – reduced maintenance costs thanks to longer periods between overhauls, higher cruising altitude and less vibration – but because of the continued use of a propeller there was a limit to the cruising speed that could be attained.

The jet's real commercial triumph, the innovation that turned it from being a military engine with commercial possibilities into the power behind the enormous expansion of the airline and international tourist industries, was the by-pass engine.[45] The by-pass engine – what became known in practice as the turbofan – added additional thrust to the jet, lowered fuel consumption and, what was possibly of greater importance to the airlines, was substantially quieter than the deafening 'straight' jets. The first by-pass jet engine was the Rolls Royce Conway, which had a low 'by-pass ratio' of about 5 per cent. It entered service in commercial airliners like the Boeing 707 and the Vickers-Armstrong VC–10 from 1960 onwards. Thereafter the American engine manufacturers Pratt & Whitney (P&W) and General Electric (GE), and then Rolls Royce (RR), went much further and increased the by-pass ratio from 5 per cent to over 50 per cent, using huge front fans on the new generation of civil engines which included the P&W JT9D, the GE CF6 and the RR RB211; as with the Whittle engine in the 1940s and the Comet jet airliner in the 1950s, the Americans copied the idea of the by-pass engine in the 1960s and greatly improved upon it.[46]

There was an economic and social dimension to the direction in which the jet engine evolved. The by-pass engine can be seen as the key artefact in the transformation of the airline business from a travel opportunity for the adventurous elite into a transport industry for the masses. The international tourist industry, which took off in Britain in the late 1960s, and was centred around package tours and independent charter airlines, was possible because by-pass jet engines offered cheap and economical air transport. The direction in which air travel was headed, however, was not clear to everyone in the aerospace industry, at least not in Britain. The Bristol-Siddeley Olympus engine – a powerful 'straight' jet, designed in the 1950s for the Avro Vulcan V-bomber with military-style afterburner – was now installed in an aircraft that was a veritable symbol of elitist travel: the supersonic Concorde airliner. While the by-pass engine heralded air transport's coming-of-age as a transport mode, the Anglo-French Concorde seemed to revive the old notion that the rich should be able to travel faster than the poor. The Concorde, for which design work began in 1962, had engines which not only used a great deal of fuel – the Concorde requires more than three times the amount of fuel per passenger as a Boeing 747 'jumbo jet' – but were also appallingly noisy.[47] In operation with British Airways and Air France, the Concorde's Olympus engines were such an environmental hazard that they nearly destroyed the airlines' chances of operating commercially when the Americans initially refused to allow the plane to land in New York. The Concorde project was a fundamental misreading of the commercial air transport market in the 1960s. With jet engines, the speed of airliners had more or less reached their economic limit (about 575 mph) and the future belonged now to *bigger* not faster aircraft. Air travel would develop along a path quite different from the one that Concorde's supporters expected: towards leisure travel and the mass market. As the *Economist* sagely concluded, 'while Concorde sped off on a flight path to nowhere, the true advance in air travel has turned out to come from refinements of large jets, which have grown steadily cheaper and more reliable'.[48]

The Concorde drew attention to an aspect of modern technology which has become of increasing concern to the citizens of industrialised countries, including Britain, since the 1970s, and that is its impact on the natural environment. This 'green' concern has been particularly acute where technologies rely on the consumption of non-renewable energy resources like fossil fuels which produce atmospheric pollution when they are burnt. Heading the list of villains in the green critique of modern transport is the internal combustion engine and the vehicles that are built around it: the motor car, the lorry and the bus, and to a lesser extent the diesel locomotive. But jet aircraft are also part of the problem of environmental degradation because of the special damage that emissions from jet engines can do in the upper atmosphere to the ozone layer and the noise nuisance they cause to people who live around airports.[49] This is not to say that the other locomotion and propulsion systems considered above are environmentally clean. In its day the steam engine, whether stationary or in a locomotive, was the source of clouds of smoke and coal dust which blackened the surface of every building in Britain and clogged the respiratory systems of its inhabitants. Nor has the electric traction motor been entirely blameless. The difference in the latter case is that electricity can be generated in a variety of ways, some of which, like hydro-electric or even atomic power, have a low propensity to pollute on a daily basis. The Swiss, for example, who had electrified their entire rail network by 1950, clearly benefited from the abundance of hydro-electric power in building what is now a commendably 'green' transport system.

Without question, the most environmentally damaging transport system, at least in the second half of the twentieth century, has been the internal combustion engine. Attempts to improve the car's performance and reduce its environmental impact have centred on improving the engine's efficiency and cleansing its exhaust emissions. So-called 'lean burn' engines promise to reduce the fuel consumption of both cars and lorries and the amount of hydrocarbons, carbon monoxide and nitrous oxides which they eject into the air. Engines constructed of ceramics and polymers have the potential to be more efficient converters of stored energy into forward motion. Alternative fuels such as methanol, liquid hydrogen and liquefied petroleum gas are being tested and can be expected to become increasingly competitive with ordinary petrol and diesel fuel, as soon as some critical technical issues are resolved.[50] Other approaches to making engines more fuel-efficient include the integrated flywheel, which when mounted on buses, for example, can release energy from braking action for subsequent acceleration. It is doubtful, however, that there will be any major new technological break-throughs in vehicle propulsion in the foreseeable future and improvements to the internal combustion engine are more likely to be of an incremental nature. Much has been made of the potential of electric cars, and cars powered by electricity have been around as long as those powered by petrol engines; but the critical weakness of the electric car – the short-lived nature of the power stored in the large and awkward batteries it must carry – does not show signs of any solution in the near future.

The most significant technological breakthroughs in transport in the last quarter of the twentieth century came not in propulsion but in navigation, guidance and control systems, brought about by the headlong introduction of computers. The application of computers to almost every facet of transport activity represents a change comparable with the arrival of the telegraph in the nineteenth century. Computers revolutionised reservation and ticketing systems in the airline industry, and somewhat later, on the railways. Yield-maximising computer programmes are now an indispensable part of the marketing effort in these transport modes. Computers control the positioning of rolling stock in railway companies, and computers linked to navigation satellites help lorry drivers plot their course. The most dramatic changes are promised by the computer's application in cars, where diagnostic aids and 'drive-by-wire' systems borrowed from aerospace technology practically take over the driving of motor cars from human beings. Real breakthroughs have been made in computer-controlled guidance and regulation of travel by motor car. Electronic control and navigation systems, linked to central computers, can make road traffic flow more easily. Combined with radar, computers with access to information on traffic conditions and under-road guidance systems, can organise 'tight convoys' of cars, or lorries, which can be 'driven', a metre apart, at a steady seventy miles per hour.

These new computer-dependent solutions to road traffic congestion as-sume a willingness on the part of the individual driver to adopt, or return to, a collectivist philosophy of travel and transport. A car in a computer-controlled 'tight convoy' will no longer be an individual vehicle with the flexibility and freedom of movement promised by early twentieth-century propaganda for the motor car – 'the open road beckons' – but rather an element within a moving group similar to the carriages that make up a railway train. It is clear that an essential factor in the application of the computer to the problems of road traffic congestion and environmental pollution is the willingness of human actors to accept the solutions they offer. The technology for road pricing is a obvious example. Tolling sensors mounted on roadside masts can engage electronic meters fitted in vehicles which use tolled roads and a central computer can charge the car owner at monthly intervals according to how long, and at what time of the day, he or she used the tolled road.[51] The technology exists, but the social and political will to use it may lag behind. So-called 'cordon systems' can use traffic lights programmed by a central computer to shut off, in tourniquet fashion, the road traffic flowing into a major urban area until congestion in the inner city is relieved. But drivers cannot be forced to leave their cars and make use of 'Park and Ride' bus facilities. Where traffic lights stay red for twenty minutes or more, this can simply lead to long queues of very angry motorists. The city of Nottingham tried such a 'collar' scheme in the early 1970s, giving priority to bus access into the city centre, but it failed; inexplicably, drivers chose to remain in their paralysed cars rather than park them at the 'collar' and ride into town on free buses.[52]

By way of conclusion, it is worth considering the contemporary value of the oldest means of locomotion and propulsion known to man. The human body is a marvellous piece of transport technology and, despite all the achievements of science discussed in this chapter, walking has never been totally superseded. In some ways it is the best method of travel and in certain parts of the world it remains more or less the only one. However, although walking is both healthy and efficient, in Britain it declined in popularity as a transport mode for most of the twentieth century, particularly in the last quarter, as Table 12 demonstrates. The human body is even more efficient when combined with one of the simplest artefacts of transport technology – the bicycle. Indeed on a bicycle a man or woman is a more effective converter of energy into forward motion than any other form of locomotive power. Moreover he or she is using a transport mode which is non-polluting and entirely in sympathy with the natural environment.

Table 12

Average Distance Travelled in Britain by Walking, Cycling and Private Car, 1975–96 (Miles Per Person Per Year)

	1975–76	1985–86	1989–91	1994–96
Walking	255	244	237	200
Bicycle	51	44	41	38
Car (as driver)	1849	2271	2891	3141

Source: Transport Statistics Report, *National Travel Survey*, 1994/96 (London, 1997), p. 6.

The earliest bicycles were produced in Britain in the 1860s, so as a manufacturing industry bicycles are the oldest locomotive system except steam.[53] Within fifty years Britain had become a nation of cyclists and cycling was firmly established as a mass transport mode along with the railways. In 1931 there were only one million private cars on British roads, but an estimated ten million cyclists.[54] The quarter-inch scale Ordnance Survey maps of Britain in the 1930s were aimed as much at cyclists as motorists, and their covers were typically decorated with a stylised couple, resting with their bicycles under a tree at the top of a hill. In the next fifty years, however, cycling lost popularity as a transport mode. As car ownership grew, and the needs of cyclists and walkers were ignored by road designers and transport policy-makers, cycling over short urban distances became increasingly dangerous.[55] The resurrection of cycling in Britain since the 1970s coincided with the metamorphosis of the humble bicycle into a new piece of sports equipment in the form of the mountain bike. And bicycles are not the only locomotive technology to have re-emerged as a sporting pastime. Steam engines have passionate bands of followers, whether they are railway locomotives or traction engines, and veteran motor cars evoke the same kind of nostalgic reaction. What was once the indispensable part of a transport system has over the course of two centuries become an attraction for hobbyists, what was once the best way to get to work is now a source of family entertainment.

10

Air Transport

It has been said that Michael Curtiz's famous 1942 film *Casablanca* was a sign of recognition, by Hollywood at least, that the age of the train – and of farewells in steamy railway stations – was giving way to the age of the aeroplane. The film ends, of course, with the image of Humphrey Bogart watching Ingrid Bergman's plane (a Lockheed Electra) disappearing into the clouds.[1] In the United States domestic air transport was already well established by 1942, and the so-called 'big four' trunk carriers (American Airlines, Eastern, TWA and United) had carved out impressive transcontinental routes, as well as a wide network of lines connecting America's major cities.[2] In Britain, however, the story was very different. The great distances which ensured that air transport would be a success in North America were completely lacking in Britain. Up until the 1950s the railways still held sway and only a tiny number of passengers – government officials and a few businessmen – travelled by air. Indeed even in the 1990s the proportion of total passenger travel within the British Isles undertaken by air was still under 1 per cent.[3]

When we talk about passenger air transport *within* Britain, therefore, we are talking about a minority transport option. Air transport is the fastest and most costly of transport modes, but it is also – like shipping, but unlike rail or road transport – an inherently *long-distance* mode. Indeed the economics of air transport are such that it only becomes really profitable over long distances. British airlines have always made more money flying passengers from London to New York than from London to Manchester. Because, traditionally, regulations have made it difficult for an airline to change either the capacity it offers or the price it charges, it has been of paramount importance that its operating costs are held down. Yet these costs, which weigh heaviest at take-off and landing, are more easily spread the longer the aircraft remains in the air, in other words the longer the route being flown. For this reason, short-haul operations, which means all British domestic air services, have always been costly to operate and difficult to make profitable, although the recent (and one might say overdue) appearance of really efficient short-haul aircraft has alleviated this problem to some degree.[4]

Commercial air transport in Britain began in 1919. This was sixteen years after the American Wright brothers had carried out the world's first powered flight in 1903 and ten years after the Frenchman Louis Bleriot had flown across the English Channel from Calais to Dover in 1909. Even before the First World War a number of aircraft enterprises were being set up in Britain by aviators and engineers, including Claude Graham-White at Hendon, whose French Farman biplane duelled unsuccessfully with another Farman in 1910 for a £10,000 prize for the first flight from London to Manchester.[5] Other firms which began building aircraft in Britain before the war were Handley-Page, Blackburn, Sopwith and A. V. Roe. The war itself, besides producing the first generation of competent pilots in Britain, advanced aeronautical science considerably, so that manufacturers were capable of converting their production from military to civilian needs. It must be remembered, however, that the very idea of transport aircraft was novel in 1919; aircraft were closely associated with the recent war and few people saw in them the potential to be anything other than a new and sophisticated weapon. That commercial airlines got off the ground at all in Europe is largely thanks to the enthusiasm and advocacy of pioneers like George Holt Thomas. In August 1919 Holt Thomas, who had already set up the Aircraft Manufacturing Company with Geoffrey de Havilland, launched Aircraft Transport & Travel (AT&T) with the first regular international passenger air service between London and Paris. London to Paris was an obvious route to begin with because it was the right distance for the aircraft of the time with their highly limited range, had good traffic potential between the two European capitals, and involved a sea crossing – a critical advantage which air travel has always enjoyed over surface transport. AT&T was soon followed on the Paris route by Handley Page Transport, set up by the aircraft manufacturer, and in February 1920, by a third airline established by the shipowners Instone. British civil aviation began therefore with international operations and open competition, but the latter did not last long. Although in the summer months traffic looked promising, it was far too thin for the market to support so many British firms, not to mention the subsidised French carriers which had also entered the field. Operating with the most rudimentary and uneconomic aircraft – often converted bombers – the airlines' costs were so high that they did not have even a theoretical possibility of breaking even. Beginning with AT&T, they folded one after the other, until for a while in 1921 there was not a single commercial airline left in the country.[6]

In this way the first characteristic of air transport became painfully apparent to government and public alike: it could not survive without wide-ranging support from the state. The British government had hoped that British airlines would be able to fly by themselves, but this was not going to be possible for many years to come. Instead the immediate and humiliating prospect presented itself that cross-channel air services would now become entirely dependent on foreigners (the Dutch carrier KLM was also flying into London). This was a state of affairs which the government decided it could not allow. A subsidy scheme for the London-Paris route was quickly drawn up and British companies were guaranteed a 10 per cent profit on gross receipts from March 1921; then, from April 1922, a more complicated scheme was introduced which benefited three companies on the London-Paris route and one on London-Brussels. Neither arrangement worked and traffic did not increase appreciably, so from October 1922 competition between the four British airlines was abandoned and they were given separate routes. Instead of subsidy per income they now received subsidy according to the number of flights, with a minimum number necessary to receive the funding. There was now some increase in the share of traffic on British aircraft, but little improvement in the airlines' financial situation. In January 1923 a further committee under the chairmanship of Sir Herbert Hambling began considering the whole future of Britain's international air transport effort and concluded that competition between airlines would never be effective until demand had increased very substantially. It recommended that the policy of subsidising competing companies be stopped altogether and a single monopoly with a 'privileged position as regards subsidies' be created instead.[7] The government accepted this and in April 1924 the four airlines which were still operational were merged to form Imperial Airways.[8]

This is not the place to consider the history of the privately-owned, state-subsidised Imperial Airways, which was Britain's international 'flag-carrier' between 1924 and 1939.[9] Already in the 1920s it was clear to the authorities, not only in Britain but throughout Europe, that only international air services stood any chance of financial success, because of the need for aircraft to operate over distance. Moreover, Europe alone would also not provide the range necessary to make operations worthwhile for the British. In 1925 the chairman of Imperial Airways, Sir Eric Geddes, said at the first annual general meeting of the company:

> It is axiomatic in civil aviation that the greater the distance the greater is the advantage of flying that distance, and your company must stretch forth its services so as to reap that advantage over older and slower methods of transport. Confined to short routes such as London-Paris and London-Berlin, the progress of commercial aviation must be slow ... the very name of your company implies that we should not be justified in confining operations to short European routes (hear, hear).[10]

Both Imperial Airways' management and Sir Samuel Hoare, the Secretary of State for Air for much of the 1920s, decided that 'distance' meant 'empire' and that Britain's new airline should concentrate on developing mail and passenger services to the colonies in Africa, India and ultimately Australia. By 1928 the emphasis in British international air transport policy lay firmly with Imperial Airways' future operations in the Empire – to the detriment of its services to the European Continent.[11]

Internal air services in Britain during the 1920s developed very little. The high cost of operations and the unreliability of available aircraft made domestic air transport quite uncompetitive with surface transport systems, notably the railways, except where there was a major geographical obstacle involved, such as a river estuary or a stretch of sea. An experimental scheduled air service was opened between Manchester and Blackpool in 1919, and in 1923 a passenger service was inaugurated between London and Manchester by Daimler Hire Ltd, but it was not continued after the absorption of Daimler into Imperial Airways.[12] The only significant British destination which could be reached by air in the 1920s was Guernsey in the Channel Islands. British Marine Air Navigation operated a flying boat service there from Southampton and Imperial Airways continued weekly flights from 1924 until 1929.[13] The number of passengers carried on internal air services in the 1920s is hard to establish from official sources, but a more or less reliable annual figure can be reached by subtracting the number of passengers on services from Britain to the Continent from the total figures carried by British air transport. The results, which confirm the insignificance of domestic services in the 1920s, are presented in column 1 of Table 13.

Table 13

Air Passengers on British Aircraft in the 1920s

	Internal Passengers	Passengers between Britain and the European Continent	Total Passengers
1922	903	9490	10,393
1923	1394	11,947	15,552
1924	3365	10,456	13,601
1925	3126	10,602	11,193
1926	1325	15,450	16,775
1927	2341	16,533	18,874
1928	2849	24,810	27,659
1929	3130	26,182	29,312

Note: The figure for 1929 includes 1228 passengers on *Imperial Airways*' new London to Egypt service, so the internal passenger figure for that year was under 2000.

Source: Air Ministry, Directorate of Civil Aviation, *Annual Report on the Progress of Civil Aviation*, HMSO, 1927; Cmd 2844; 32, 34, (1928); 39–40, (1928); 39–40, (1929); 54–55.

In the 1930s the picture changed dramatically. Between 1932 and 1936, as the air transport industry became more confident and major breakthroughs in aircraft design and construction were made in the United States (and to a lesser extent in Europe), a rash of independent airlines appeared in Britain. Lacking the prestige factor that had made the government so concerned about international services in 1924, these small domestic carriers flew unsubsidised, in open competition with one another, free to decide their frequencies and fares. They were not profitable (see Table 14) and they were short-lived; 'flitting', in the words of one knowledgeable commentator, 'like brief shadows across the scene'.[14]

Table 14

British Civil Air Transport, Operating and Financial Results, 1919–38

	1919–24	1924–38	
		Imperial Airways	Domestic Airlines
Revenue Passengers	31,870	575,870	824,800
Capacity (Ton-Miles)	1,716,000	89,446,500	24,596,400
Load (Ton-Miles)	1,007,200	60,620,600	8,540,700
Load Factor (%)	58.6	67.7	34.7
Expenditure	£762,300	£15,427,700	£3,231,000
Revenue	£235,600	£9,659,100	£1,721,700
Deficit	£546,700	£5,768,600	£1,509,300

Source: Peter G. Masefield, 'Some Economic Factors in Air Transport Operation', *Journal of the Institute of Transport* (1951), p. 87.

But it was these new entrepreneurs, flying different routes from Cornwall to the north of Scotland, who laid out the foundations of the British internal air transport network.[15] (The range of these different routes is shown in Table 15). One of the first was Hillman Airways, founded by the bus entrepreneur Edward Hillman, which began a short air service between Romford and Clacton in 1932, and the following year started flying to Paris and Brussels in competition with Imperial Airways. In 1934 and 1935 Hillman opened air services from his Romford base to Liverpool, Hull, Glasgow and Belfast. Others joined Hillman from 1933 onwards, including other bus operators like George Nicholson of Northern and Scottish Airways. Scotland with its mountains, islands and circuitous surface communications seemed a highly promising field for air transport. In 1931 Edmund Fresson had flown across the Pentland Firth from northern Scotland to the Orkney Islands and recognised the potential of an air link across that turbulent stretch of water. In May 1933 his airline, Highland Airways, began a regular air service from

Inverness via Wick to Kirkwall in the Orkneys, cutting the nine hour trip by train and ferry to one and a half hours. Flying six-seat de Havilland DH.84 Dragon aircraft, Highland began carrying mail and passengers from mainland Scotland to many of the Scottish islands as well as operating a service from Inverness to Aberdeen, where it encountered competition from fellow air transport pioneer Eric Gandar Dower and his Aberdeen Airways. By 1935 Highland's lack of profits and access to capital for expansion had forced Fresson to consider surrendering his independence. In London Clive Pearson's United Airways had been formed with the backing of the Whitehall Securities group and was soon to merge with Hillman Airways and Spartan Air Lines to form British Airways Ltd. In May 1935 Highland was taken over by United, and later became a British Airways subsidiary, although it continued to operate under its own name until 1938.[16]

The most important entrant into domestic air transport in the 1930s was not an individual entrepreneur but the railways. In the early 1920s the railways had ignored air travel and its potential threat to their business, but gradually they changed their mind and in October 1928 the four mainline companies, LNER, LMS, Great Western and Southern, decided on joint action. Within nine months a Bill had passed through Parliament allowing the railways to operate air services, although they made no immediate attempt to use their new powers. Only with the appearance of independents after 1932 did the railways respond, first with a service for the Great Western between Cardiff, Torquay and Plymouth (a long and difficult rail journey), and then in March 1934 with the establishment of Railway Air Services (RAS) in conjunction with Imperial Airways. Backed by the resources of the railway companies, RAS established services on routes where the independent airlines were offering an alternative to existing rail connections. The service between London (Croydon Airport), Belfast and Glasgow, in LMS territory, seemed to have the greatest potential, but results for the summer of 1934 were disappointing and in the next four years RAS lost over £200,000. The railways carried these losses seemingly as part of a strategy to dominate domestic air transport in Britain and prevent outsiders from developing it to the detriment of the railways' main transport operations. RAS represents the first time an airline was owned and directed by a competing form of transport, and there is no doubt that it exhibited strong monopolistic tendencies.[17] Where they could not take over competing airlines, the railways applied pressure on the independents by banning railway-accredited travel agents from taking bookings from them; an extraordinary practice which persisted until the 1938 Air Navigation Act, by which point the railways had a financial stake in all but five of the sixteen companies operating air services within the UK.[18] On the other hand, it must be recognised that the RAS's aim of consolidation amongst the competing independents and its wish to see regulation of the domestic industry was logical in view of the weak and highly seasonal traffic demand that still characterised the market, and the experience gained with the international carriers in the early 1920s. This was certainly the view taken by the government-appointed Maybury Committee in 1937, which took evidence from the RAS and heard the railway's criticism of 'unrestricted competition' in domestic air transport.[19] The committee concluded that 'if air transport is to become fully self-supporting, it is a pre-requisite that cut-throat competition must be eliminated and that some measure of restriction must be applied to avoid indiscriminate multiplication of services'.[20]

Table 15

Main British Internal Scheduled Air Services, 1933–36

Airline	Year of Registration	Routes	Passengers		
			1933	1934	1936
Portsmouth-Southsea-Isle of Wight Aviation	1932	Portsmouth–Ryde Shoreham–Shanklin			
		Heston–Ryde–Shanklin	9640		
		Shoreham–Portsmouth –Ryde–Shanklin	34,900	28,690	
		Portsmouth– Bournemouth–Shanklin			
Hillman's Airways	1933	Romford–Paris			
		Romford–Clacton			
		Romford–Manston	n/a		
		Abridge–Paris	5300		
		Abridge–Liverpool– Isle of Man– Belfast–Glasgow	n/a		
Spartan Air Lines	1933	Heston–Isle of Wight	1459		
		Croydon–Ryde	6794		
Blackpool & West Coast Air Services	1933	Liverpool–Blackpool– Isle of Man	1863	5098	30,000
Jersey Airways	1933	Portsmouth–Jersey	n/a	30,061	
		Heston–Jersey			
		Southampton– Portsmouth–Jersey	19,867		
		Jersey–Paris		105	
Highland Airways	1933	Inverness–Wick– Kirkwall	1582	1971	6060

Airline	Year of Registration	Routes	Passengers		
			1933	1934	1936
Midland & Scottish Air Ferries	1933	Glasgow–Campbeltown			
		Campbeltown–Belfast	3658		
		Campbeltown–Islay			
		Romford–Birmingham–Liverpool–Renfrew	n/a		
Norman Edgar/Western Airways	1933	Bristol–Cardiff	1671	n/a	15,101
North Sea Aerial & General Transport	1933	Hull–Grimsby	1300		
Aberdeen Airways	1934	Aberdeen–Glasgow	n/a	2334	
Guernsey Airways	1934		1877		
Northern & Scottish Airways	1934	Renfrew–Kintyre–Islay	31	15,117	
Railway Air Services	1934	Plymouth–Haldon–Cardiff–Birmingham–Liverpool			
		Birmingham–Bristol–Southampton–Cowes			
		Croydon–Birmingham–Manchester–Belfast–Glasgow	2237	22,103	
		Manchester–Isle of Man–Belfast			
		Croydon–Liverpool–Belfast–Glasgow			
British Airways	1935	Various		19,642	
United Airways	1935	Heston–Blackpool–Isle of Man			

Note: British Airways, which took over Hillman, Spartan Air Lines and United Airways in 1935, operated both domestic and international (European) routes.

Source: Air Ministry, *Annual Report on the Progress of Civil Aviation, 1933* (1934); 13, *1934* (1935); 14, *1936* (1937); 86. There are no records of passenger numbers for a number of airlines.

Not surprisingly the railways' strategy drew hostile comment from aviation interests, who felt that they had only entered the field in order to strangle it. But the railways were instrumental in securing legislation arising from the Maybury investigation for licensing domestic air traffic. This resulted in the setting up of an independent Air Transport Licensing Authority in 1938.[21] With its power to issue licences to operators on approved routes, this body brought some measure of order to the domestic air network which had hitherto been inadequately supervised by the Air Ministry.

With the benefit of hindsight, it is possible to see two notable consequences of the brief appearance of independent domestic airlines in the 1930s. First, it prompted a defensive reaction from the railways, a response that was to have further echoes in wartime policy formulation for British civil aviation, towards which both the railways and Imperial's successor, the British Overseas Airways Corporation (BOAC), made substantial contributions.[22] British European Airways, created in 1946 to handle both European and domestic services, had a hostile attitude towards the British independent (non-scheduled) airlines which appeared from the late 1950s. This seems to have been inherited from its RAS legacy.[23] Secondly, it encouraged the British aircraft industry to produce short-haul airliners. There is a common view that British manufacturers in the inter-war years allowed the aircraft industry to fall seriously behind the United States and the leading European nations, notably Germany, in both output and technical quality.[24] Although this view is largely justified in the case of long-haul types, the British did develop considerable expertise in the building of short-haul aircraft and the new independents undoubtedly fostered the development of successful aircraft like the six-passenger DH84 Dragon. The models that the de Havilland company developed from it, such as the four-engined DH86 Express Air Liner and the DH89 Dragon Rapide, were the only British civil aircraft to be exported in significant numbers between the wars.[25] In the post-war years this British expertise in short-range aircraft, in contrast to the catalogue of commercial disasters with long-range aircraft (de Havilland Comet, Bristol Britannia and Vickers VC10), was carried forward with such notable types as the de Havilland Dove and Heron, the Vickers Viking and Viscount and the Avro 748.

With the outbreak of war in 1939 commercial flying in Britain became highly restricted. Civil aircraft could only take off and land at certain specified airports in the west of the country, while night flying and all activity by private flying clubs were forbidden. During the war the domestic services which had been established in the 1930s were run on the government's behalf by a group of companies controlled by the railways, known as the Associated Airways Joint Committee (AAJC).[26] After the war, with the passing of the 1946 Civil Aviation Act, the post-war Labour government added the nationalised British European Airways (BEA) to the state-owned BOAC, which had been formed in 1939 by the Conservative government.[27] For a few months the AAJC companies continued flying domestic services as agents for BEA, until it was ready to absorb them in January 1947.[28] There was some resentment on the part of the pre-war independents at being forced into a nationalised monopoly, and they gained some limited support beyond the realm of civil aviation from advocates of free enterprise, but, essentially, responsibility for Britain's internal air network now passed without much controversy into the hands of BEA. By combining continental European air services and British domestic operations in a single airline, Labour may be said to have missed the opportunity of establishing the latter as a controlled environment for competing independents (much as the Maybury Committee had envisaged in 1937), while letting BEA 'carry the flag' in Europe. This course might well have led to the creation of a private monopoly controlled by the railways along the lines of RAS (although the railways themselves were now in the process of being nationalised); what is certain, however, is that BEA's obligation to run a full schedule of domestic services, in addition to its European routes, saddled the airline with a financial burden for much of its life.[29]

The reason BEA made such bad losses on its domestic services was that they were very difficult to make money on; in fact, with the available short-range aircraft, they were inherently unprofitable. This point had been obscured during the 1930s by the energetic activity of the independents as start-up enterprises and the widespread assumption that eventual consolidation amongst the different companies would bring efficiency and profits. But thin traffic and the high costs of internal services – at many of the isolated destinations, staff waited around at a tiny airport for a single flight per day – coupled to the low fares which the airlines were permitted to charge, combined to make them intractable loss-makers. Passenger demand was weak because travellers still did not think in terms of flying. Their choice stemmed from impulse and tradition, and this meant going by a familiar surface transport system, usually the railways. Although the war had greatly increased the British people's consciousness of air power, it would be some time before they became accustomed to the idea of air travel for themselves, at least as a transport option within Britain. On the supply side, an additional factor which made internal services more costly to operate than international routes was the wide seasonal variation in demand; this meant, for example, that in the summer of 1960 three times the aircraft capacity had to be provided at the height of the summer season than in the winter months.[30]

Certainly, BEA was able to expand its passenger services rapidly in the 1950s and it was a self-supporting enterprise by 1955, in that it no longer required an annual Treasury grant to cover its operating deficit.[31] Yet this happy state of affairs was because it made decent profits on its international European network, where fares were maintained at a generously high level by the airline cartel IATA (International Air Traffic Association), and it was able to use the money to cross-subsidise its domestic routes. BEA had no statutory constraints on the level of its domestic fares and could have charged whatever it liked in theory, but in practice it accepted a situation in which it sought the government's approval for any fare change in Britain.[32] The result was that BEA never charged domestic passengers more than two thirds the rate per mile of the average international fare, so, whenever BEA's international revenue fell, for whatever reason, it was more difficult to cover the losses on domestic operations.[33] The *Economist* magazine, true to its free-market principles, disapproved of this and in 1963 inquired as to why the airline's fare rate was 8.25 pence per mile for a trip from London to Rome, but only 5 pence per mile for a flight anywhere in Britain. 'Is there any valid reason', it asked, 'why the man who flies to Glasgow should be subsidised by the man who flies to Rome?'[34]

The domestic air routes which BEA set about developing in the 1950s consisted of three types: trunk routes from London to major centres such as Glasgow, Manchester, Belfast and Edinburgh, as well as services from Glasgow to Belfast, Aberdeen and Inverness; holiday routes to the Channel Islands, the Scilly Islands and the Isle of Man; and social services to the Highlands and Islands of Scotland. The Islands services, from their Renfrew (Glasgow) hub, radiated out to the Orkneys and the Shetlands, to Campbeltown (Kintyre), Islay, Tiree, Benbecula and Barra (at Barra, in the Outer Hebrides, there was no airstrip at all and the aircraft landed on the beach – tide allowing!). The aircraft used were initially pre-war DH89 Rapides, American Douglas DC3s (the wartime Dakotas which were now to be seen in large numbers around the world as the workhorse of new airlines), and even some German Junkers Ju-52 trimotors which Britain had acquired by way of reparations from the former enemy. In the 1950s and early 1960s these obsolescent types were replaced with modern British aircraft: the de Havilland Heron, the Vickers Viscount and the Handley Page Herald. The fourteen-seat Heron was particularly suited to BEA's 'outback' operations amongst the Scottish Islands and often served as a flying ambulance in the manner of Australian Flying Doctor.

While BEA's trunk and holiday routes had the potential to cover their costs and make profits, this could not be said about the social services. The Scottish network was, however, *politically* essential: alternative surface transport in that part of Britain was very poor and air services were considered vital in maintaining its isolated communities. The dilemma of how to finance such an uneconomic, yet socially vital, domestic air transport as the Highlands and Islands service was to persist for the next twenty years. Should it be covered by an open and direct subsidy, such as was the norm in the USA and many European countries, or should it be paid for by cross-subsidisation from profitable international operations? The government consistently took the latter view and treated BEA's obligation to fly services for the public good as beyond negotiation. BEA enjoyed monopoly profits on its high-revenue international routes and should bear the losses incurred on its uneconomic domestic ones through cross-subsidisation – taking, in the words of successive ministers, 'the rough with the smooth', as the railways had done for over a century.[35] Although several official committees of inquiry, including the magisterial Edwards Committee Report in 1969, rejected this view and supported the idea of an open subsidy for the Scottish services,[36] BEA itself behaved somewhat ambivalently, initially complaining about the lack of subsidy and then accepting its public service role in Scotland with the acquired stoicism of a nationalised industry.[37]

One area where BEA was unquestionably a pioneer in the 1950s was in the use of helicopters. Since air transport with fixed-wing aircraft over short stages showed only the smallest time saving over surface transport between city centres, helicopters seemed a potential alternative. BEA's chief executive, Peter Masefield, looked forward in 1951 to a time 'twenty years hence', when 'I hope that the journey time from the centre of London to the centre of Paris may be reduced from 3.5 hours to not much more than 1.5 hours – by helicopter'.[38] BEA had already established a Helicopter Experimental Unit in 1947 to build up operational experience and the following year began helicopter mail services in East Anglia, using American Sikorsky S-51s.[39] In 1950 the airline operated the world's first regular scheduled passenger helicopter service between Liverpool and Cardiff, also using the S-51s.[40] This was discontinued the following year, although a new service between London and Birmingham was run briefly in 1952. The Sikorskys, which seated only three passengers, did not meet operational costs. BEA obviously needed something bigger to make helicopter services into a commercial proposition. In the summer of 1955 helicopters ferried passengers from Heathrow airport to BEA's London terminal at Waterloo; this time bigger (five-passenger) Sikorsky S–55s were used, but it was still impossible to operate them economically and the experiment was ended in 1956.[41] The major obstacle to profitable passenger helicopter operations, which BEA and other interested short-haul airlines (like the Belgian flag-carrier SABENA) were unable to foresee in the 1950s, was the difficulty in reducing passenger-mile costs – something which fixed wing aircraft did much more effectively as their capacity grew. A further factor was the extraordinary growth of private car ownership – a big rival on the short-haul intercity routes that were envisaged for the helicopter. Although BEA had on order a large (thirty-five passenger) British helicopter, the Fairey Rotodyne, the airline was losing interest in passenger helicopters by the end of the 1950s and sought to break its commitment to the project.[42] By 1963 all Britain's commercial helicopter projects were dead and the main British manufacturer, Westland, had virtually given up building civil types. BEA's only helicopter service now remained on the sea route from Land's End to the Scilly Isles, using American

Boeing Vertol machines, and this service needed a government subsidy.[43] For major civil transport work, helicopters turned out to be too costly, too noisy and too unreliable. Outside military operations, which is their main role today, they remain most useful in emergency situations such as medical evacuations and helping the victims of natural and man-made disasters.

In 1960, with the passage of the Civil Aviation (Licensing) Act by the Conservative government, a new British licensing authority – the Air Transport Licensing Board (ATLB) – was created and it became possible for the first time since 1947 for independent airlines to operate competitive scheduled services on BEA's domestic routes. Two airlines took up the challenge: British Eagle and after 1965, British United Airways (BUA). In addition, this partial liberalisation of air transport called forth a number of new independents contesting international routes and the fast-growing inclusive tour market in Britain, chief amongst which were Caledonian and Britannia Airways (See Table 16). For the monopolist BEA the competition was thoroughly unwelcome, as it threatened its revenue base on what were already unprofitable domestic routes. Its response varied between attempts to block the granting of operating licences to the independents by the ATLB, using its much larger resources and aircraft fleet to smother the competition's services with its own – 'sandwiching' as it is known in industry jargon – and taking a stake in independents with 'services complementary to those of BEA'.[44] BEA had already acquired a 33 per cent interest in the Welsh airline Cambrian Airways in 1958. Cambrian flew the pre-war route from its Cardiff hub to Bristol and Southampton, and in 1964 it took over BEA's Isle of Man services, demonstrating in the process that a small independent could operate short-haul internal routes with substantially lower costs than BEA. In the 1960s BEA extended its joint venture programme to Jersey Airlines and in 1964 acquired a minority stake in BKS, an airline based in the north east of England at Newcastle-upon-Tyne. In 1967 BKS (which was shortly after renamed Northeast Airlines) and Cambrian became wholly owned subsidiaries of British Air Services, which was 70 per cent owned by BEA.

It was on BEA's three trunk routes – London-Glasgow, London-Edinburgh and London-Belfast – that domestic competition began in the 1960s. The Glasgow route had the highest passenger numbers, with Belfast and Edinburgh at about two thirds of the Glasgow level. In the ten years between 1958 and 1967, BEA's Glasgow traffic increased from 164,172 to 577,557, while the independents on the route (British Eagle and then BUA) rose from zero in 1962 to 103,576 in 1967; with that rate of growth and with far fewer frequencies than BEA, it is hardly surprising that the nationalised undertaking felt threatened.[45]

TRANSPORT IN BRITAIN

Table 16

Total British Airline Scheduled Passenger Numbers on International and
Domestic Routes, and Independent Inclusive Tours, 1958–67, in Thousands

	BOAC	BEA		Independent		
		International	Domestic	International	Domestic	Inclusive Tour
1958–59	470	1638	1191	471	299	180
1959–60	587	1864	1425	585	367	167
1960–61	785	2207	1784	774	545	199
1961–62	855	2282	2112	846	815	311
1962–63	896	2530	2385	1,082	930	387
1963–64	984	3021	2584	1,126	1241	526
1964–65	1167	3326	2793	1,158	1514	832
1965–66	1329	3819	3024	1,197	1711	1191
1966–67	1459	4260	3064	1,343	2144	2027
1967–68	1548	4267	3068	1,201	2179	2316

Source: British Air Transport in the Seventies (Edwards Report) (London, 1969), appendix 9, p. 296.

In November 1963 British Eagle had inaugurated services to Glasgow and Belfast using four-engined turbo-prop Bristol Britannias formerly operated by BEA's sister BOAC on long-haul routes. Having failed to stop British Eagle in the ATLB, BEA now declared 'total war' on the independent and resorted to 'sandwiching' its flights.[46] It seems that BEA was particularly aggrieved at the effect of competition on its aircraft procurement programme, and it should be remembered that it had been the chief sponsor of a number of important British airliners in the 1950s and early 1960s (including the Airspeed Ambassador, Vickers Viscount and Vanguard, and de Havilland/Hawker Siddeley Trident). For example, in response to the use of jet aircraft (BAC1–11s) by competitors on its domestic trunk routes, BEA had had to introduce its own jets (Tridents and Comet 4Bs), with a consequent rise in unit operating costs, before it wished to do so and before the turbo-prop Vanguards, which it had planned to use, were fully depreciated.[47]

Competition for BEA's trunk routes also came from surface transport in the 1960s. In 1966 British Railways (BR) opened its newly-electrified train service from London to Manchester and immediately made serious inroads into the revenue on what had always been BEA's weakest trunk route; according to the airline itself the 25 per cent reduction of air traffic on the route was mainly attributable to BR's electrified service.[48] On the other hand, BR also felt threatened by the state airline. BEA's objective had been to get its fares on the longer trunk routes down to 'within a few shillings of second-class rail fares', and in September 1961 it applied to the ATLB for a three guinea fare on winter night flights from London to Belfast, Glasgow and Edinburgh. The application was strongly opposed by the British Transport Commission. BR's chairman, Dr Richard Beeching, took a personal interest in the appeal against it in February 1962, although the flights had already gone ahead, with some success, in November.[49]

In 1974 BEA lost its separate identity in the merger with BOAC which created British Airways (BA). The new British flag-carrier had one of the largest route networks in the world, a big fleet of diverse aircraft and a vast labour force brought together by an amalgamation process which had guaranteed the staff of the two constituent airlines that there would be no redundancies.[50] The 1970s was a troubled period for the airline industry in which sharp rises in the price of fuel combined with slower rates of growth in passenger traffic. In the United States a long debate on the merits of airline regulation culminated in the 1978 Deregulation Act which opened the huge American domestic industry to more or less unfettered competition. In the 1980s the doctrine of deregulation crossed the Atlantic and began to influence the aviation policies of some European countries. In Britain, where the Conservative Party under Margaret Thatcher was in government throughout the decade, deregulation was blended in selective fashion with a programme of privatisation of state-owned industries, as a part of which BA itself was privatised at the beginning of 1987.[51]

Deregulation, or 'liberalisation', of the air transport market had various consequences for domestic air services in Britain. The most obvious was the appearance of serious new competitors to BA, such as British Midland Airways. The background to this development was the establishment, on the recommendation of the 1969 Edwards Report, of a new licensing authority to replace the ATLB, the Civil Aviation Authority (CAA). The CAA had a greater measure of independence from central government than its predecessors and was more inclined in its decisions on licensing to favour competition to the state-owned monopoly. BA, not surprisingly, was unhappy about this and had an often confrontational relationship with the CAA in the years to come. The second factor which began to change the character of British domestic air transport in the 1970s was Britain's entry into the European Economic Community. With greater orientation towards continental Europe, the rigid centralisation of domestic services on London, which had distinguished the BEA years, became more difficult to justify. People, particularly businessmen, wanted greater emphasis on services originating in the provinces and an increased number of direct flights to the Continent so that they could avoid having to travel through London.[52]

Britain's domestic internal network thus became more closely integrated with its European services (Table 17). In recognition of this, BA created a 'UK and Ireland Division' in 1978, which was to be responsible not only for operations within Britain and to the Irish Republic, but also for flights from Manchester, Glasgow and Birmingham to the Continent.

In the late 1970s BA benefited from the North Sea oil boom and new traffic growth to the 'oil capital' of Aberdeen. From this northern Scottish city, a new business was also developed by the BA subsidiary, British Airways Helicopters Ltd, flying workers to the oil rigs now dotting the North Sea. But the Scottish internal services remained loss-makers for BA and in 1979 several routes were closed. Two years later, with John King now chairman of BA, it was decided that the Scottish services would either have to cover their costs or be withdrawn. This meant massive staff cuts in the Scottish Highland Division, and a new 'lean' regime – in stark contrast to the public service image of BEA – in which co-pilots helped load and unload cargo and mail, and cabin crew doubled as check-in clerks. Remarkably, by 1983 the Highland Division was making a small profit.[53]

Table 17

British Airways International and Domestic Passenger Services

	International Services			Domestic Services		
	Passengers millions	Load Factor %	Revex £ millions	Passengers millions	Load Factor %	Revex £ millions
1972/73	6.29	51	16.04	3.28	62	−3.8
1973/74	6.55	54	19.18	2.19	60	−0.6
1975/76	9.34	55	6.6	4.41	57	−1.7
1976/77	9.99	58	90.4	4.51	56	0.4
1978/79	11.37	62	75.3	4.39	54	0.9
1979/80	12.53	65	31.2	4.78	58	−8.6
1980/81	12.03	61	−86.6	3.88	54	−22.2
1981/82	11.55	63	10.7	3.67	55	−9.8

Note: In 1972–74 the figures are for BEA's accounts only. Revex = operating revenue less expenditure. In 1982 three profit-accounting divisions were created at BA and the European and domestic scheduled services were no longer presented separately in the accounts (the other divisions were Intercontinental and British Airtours).

Source: British Airways, *Annual Report and Accounts*, 1972/73 to 1980–81.

The most significant innovation in internal air services at this time was BA's introduction of an inter-city Shuttle service – meaning a guaranteed seat on a flight with no advance booking – which was developed on the airline's trunk routes from London to Glasgow, Belfast, Edinburgh and Manchester between 1975 and 1979. Within three years of its launch the 'no frills' Shuttle had carried around five million passengers, undoubtedly attracting substantial additional traffic to the domestic air market – for example, there was an increase of 23 per cent on the London-Edinburgh route when the Shuttle was inaugurated there in 1976.[54]

The success of the Shuttle attracted competition from British Midland (BMA). This independent had already gained routes based on Liverpool from BA when, in 1982, it was granted a licence by the CAA to begin services in competition with BA on the London-Glasgow route, and from 1983 on London-Edinburgh routes as well. The BMA services, which, unlike BA's, were bookable and provided hot meals and bar on board, were a success and the newcomer had achieved a 29 per cent market share on the Glasgow route within the first year, although it must be noted that the market itself expanded by 10 per cent, which suggests that there was room for both airlines. Nonetheless, BA fought characteristically hard to stop BMA, challenging in the courts the CAA's decision to give it a licence for a third route to Belfast in 1983.[55] BA lost the case and the CAA recommended further competition for the flag-carrier, as well as a reallocation of its routes, in a report published in 1984.[56] BA's commercial response was to announce its own Super Shuttle in 1983, with the same 'frills' as the BMA service, to Glasgow, Belfast, Edinburgh and Manchester. The Super Shuttle recorded an average growth rate on the Manchester, Glasgow and Edinburgh routes of 25 per cent 'thanks to a general upturn in demand and a range of low fares which attracted passengers away from rail and road'.[57] The rapid growth in traffic on both BA's Shuttle and the BMA services is testimony to the effect of deregulation on prices, for both airlines were free to set their own domestic fares in the 1980s. Between 1982 and 1987 there was a significant degree of liberalisation and fares no longer needed prior government approval, merely having to be filed with the CAA. For the first time, inter-city air transport in Britain became genuinely competitive with the road and rail options. For BA, in preparation for its privatisation, it was an opportunity to focus with greater emphasis on its profitable Shuttle services on the trunk routes; many of its less rewarding domestic destinations – inherited from the 'public service' days of BEA – it had hived off to franchisees or partner airlines like Brymon, Loganair, Maersk and Manx Air. In the financial year 1985–86 BA carried five million domestic passengers, nearly half of them on its four Super Shuttle trunk routes between Heathrow Airport and Glasgow, Edinburgh, Belfast and Manchester. In thirty years these routes had grown six times in capacity – what a thirty-seat BEA Douglas DC3 had handled in 1955 now required a 180-seat Boeing 757. In

1989 Super Shuttle was 'relaunched' in a twin format designed to appeal both to businessmen, who appreciated the last-minute check-in, 'turn-up, take-off' approach (Super Shuttle Executive), and to the leisure traveller, who could book in advance (Super Shuttle Saver).[58]

By the beginning of the 1990s domestic air transport in Britain had evolved into something quite different from what it had been fifty years earlier. Three key developments seem to have guided it towards maturity. First, Britain's entrance into the EEC, and more importantly, the tremendous growth in air tourism from the 1960s onwards, familiarised the average Briton with foreign travel and the airline business. The vast majority of commercial flights originating in Britain remained, as they had always been, international services. The difference was that now people used domestic services like the Shuttle to begin their journeys; the airlines used the domestic networks as feeders for their international routes. BA's management of its internal services as an integral part of its European operations in the 1990s was a recognition of this reality and British routes and revenue were no longer distinguished from European routes and revenue in its annual accounts.[59] With the appearance and rapid growth in Britain of a new generation of very low fare, 'no frills' carriers like EasyJet and Ryanair in the second half of the 1990s, this feeder principle became a central part of airline marketing strategy.[60] Moreover, the development of direct air links to Europe from British provincial centres like Manchester, Glasgow and Birmingham (the latter the object of a major investment by BA in 1991) signified that domestic services were no longer just about flying within Britain, but also about decentralising away from London. This has been an important change and one where the air transport mode appears to have advanced beyond the more (perhaps necessarily) rigid approach of the national railway system. The second development in the half century of air transport since the end of the Second World War, and one of the main reasons why British domestic routes finally became profitable in the 1980s, was the appearance of much more economical short-haul aircraft. Many of the aircraft used in the 1950s and 1960s by BEA were not designed for optimum performance on British domestic routes. The DC3, and the Viscount, Vanguard and Trident, all 'retired' onto domestic routes as if they were in some way quiet pastures for old workhorses, were not conceived for the short-haul domestic role. Even an aircraft like the BAC1–11–500 twinjet, which seated around a hundred passengers and was introduced by BEA in 1968, was not as efficient as aircraft which entered service two decades later. The 1–11 had a take-off speed of about 180 mph and a fuel consumption of 3085 litres per hour. By contrast the British Aerospace BAe ATP, which has twin turboprop engines, seats sixty-four passengers and was introduced

16   Traffic congestion on Ludgate Hill, London, 1900.

17 Horse buses in Tottenham Court Road, London.

18 A tram and hansom cabs crossing Westminster Bridge.

19   The Prince of Wales in a car, 1900. Cars were originally the preserve of a monied elite.

20   A Baby Car, 1923. By the 1920s car ownership had begun to move down the social scale.

21 Inappropriate transport: a heavy lorry in the narrow streets of a village. (*Peter Lyth*)

22 Prince Charles opening the first section of the Jubilee Line to Charing Cross, 1979. (*London Transport Museum*)

23 Buses at Ryde Esplanade, Isle of Wight. (*Philip Bagwell*)

24 Croydon Tramway, 2000. (*London Transport Museum*)

25 A BEA Viscount landing on the island of Islay, Scotland. (*British Airways*)

26 A BEA helicopter lands at Battersea Heliport, London. (*British Airways*)

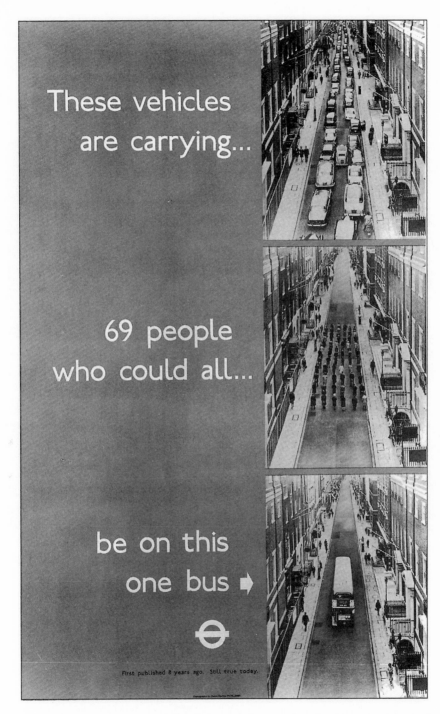

27 Congestion as seen by London Transport in 1965. (*London Transport Museum*)

28   Traffic congestion in London, 1965. (*London Transport Museum*)

in 1989, has a lower take-off speed of about 130 mph and fuel consumption of only 763 litres per hour.[61]

The third development influencing British domestic air transport has been the profound changes which have taken place in the rival surface modes of road and rail transport. When air travel within Britain began in the 1930s there were few cars and no motorways; instead the railways were the predominant and natural means of travel across the country. It was indeed, as we have seen, the railways which felt threatened by the first domestic airlines and sought to buy them up or put them out of business, a ridiculous notion in the changed circumstances of the 1990s. In the sixty years in between the railways have clearly lost their position of pre-eminence, although their decline has been relative rather than absolute, while road transport has grown into the all-pervasive means of travel for the average Briton. Where once the domestic airline faced competition from British railways, its rival is now the motorway, except where there is some extreme natural obstacle to surface transport. The best way to the Orkney Isles from the north of Scotland in the year 2000 is by air, just as it was when Edmund Fresson started Highland Airways in 1933. However, in an age of increasing traffic congestion on the roads, the railways may yet prove the more potent rival for air transport's passengers, particularly as domestic airlines concentrate increasingly on inter-city services. The experience of the French since the 1980s, with their TGV trains, suggests that high-speed rail is a serious competitor to domestic air services, primarily because it carries its passengers from city centre to city centre instead of depositing them in a crowded airport in the suburbs. Railways in Britain were regarded for most of the twentieth century as a downmarket, public service industry, far removed from air travel, which has continued to enjoy an association in the public mind with path-breaking new technology. But this attitude may change if high-speed rail inter-city links are opened; in the meantime it is worth noting that many inter-city air routes, such as BA's Super Shuttle, have hourly departures throughout the day in the manner of a train service.

11

Privatisation

The Conservative General Election manifesto of 11 April 1979 contained a foreword by Margaret Thatcher, who had been elected as party leader four years earlier.[1] It read:

> For me the heart of politics is not political theory, it is people and how they want to live their lives. No one who has lived in this country during the past five years can fail to be aware of how the balance of our society has been increasingly tilted in favour of the state at the expense of individual freedom. This election may be the last chance we have to reverse that process and to restore the balance of power in favour of the people. It is therefore the most crucial election since the war. Together with the threat to freedom there has been a feeling of helplessness, that we are a once great nation that has somehow fallen behind and that it is too late now to turn things round. I don't accept that. We not only can but we must.

In many ways the new leader of the Conservative Party was right in considering the 1979 general election 'the most crucial election since the war', but not for the reasons she gave. The manifesto marked a decisive break with the consensus between the main parties over the previous thirty years that the achievement of an efficient transport system could not be left to the vagaries of the free market but required substantial government regulation and control. One of her predecessors in the office of Prime Minister, the Conservative Harold Macmillan, who held that office from 1959–64, had advocated in his trail-blazing book, *The Middle Way*, the formation of a public trust for the supervision of the railway system.[2] He professed a love for the railways (though railwaymen's representatives were unsure of this when he interviewed them on 22 April 1958 and told them they must increase their productivity before receiving a wage increase).[3] In his party's general election manifesto of October 1959, however, the railways were promised three thousand new diesel locomotives and electric traction was to be increased by 60 per cent.[4] These promises reflected the Premier's view that the railways should be modernised.

By contrast Margaret Thatcher disliked the railways and all other forms of public transport. Following the Conservative Party's general election victory of 3 May 1979, with an overall majority of thirty-seven seats in the

Commons, the new government was not slow in implementing its promise to curtail the influence of the state. On 12 June 1979 the Chancellor of the Exchequer, Sir Geoffrey Howe, in his budget speech, announced a reduction in the Public Sector Borrowing Requirement (the payment limit imposed by the Treasury on loans for support of industry) of one billion pounds: from £9,250,000,000 in 1978–79 to £8,250,000,000 in 1979–80. He assured his backbenchers that 'savings are also being made in transport'.[5]

Consistent with this policy of reducing Treasury outgoings on the railways, the Public Service Obligation Grant (the grant for the social railway which had been introduced in Barbara Castle's Transport Act of 1968) was reduced as shown in Figure 1.

Figure 1

Passenger Grant from Central Government (PSO)
£m at 1988/89 Prices

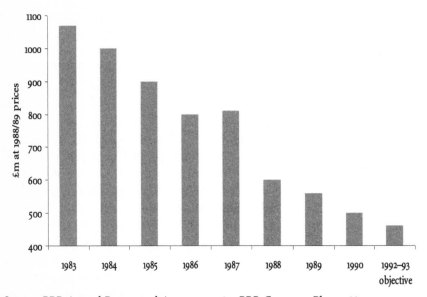

Sources: BRB Annual Report and Accounts, 1983; *BRB Corporate Plan*, 1988.

The government also imposed a limit on the amount of money the British Railways Board might borrow from sources outside the industry. This was known as the External Financing Limit (EFL) and it was reduced from £1000 million in 1983 to under £400 million in 1988–89 (both at 1988–89 prices).

Another way of viewing the generosity or meanness of government grants to railways is to compare what the British government allocated with the railway grant allocations in other European countries. This is shown on Figure 2:

Figure 2

Government Subsidies in £s per Train Kilometre, 1986

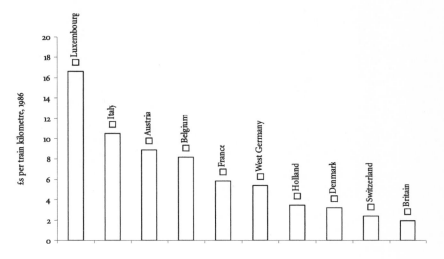

Sources: BRB, Annual Report and Accounts, 1986; *Observer*, 2 July 1989

One result of British Railways having had lower levels of subsidy than did the railways of her European neighbours in the 1980s was that standard passenger rail fares were, and still are, higher than theirs. Figure 3 shows the situation in 1992 when subsidies were higher in the UK than they were in the 1980s because of investment in connection with the future Channel Tunnel.[6]

The attack on the publicly owned parts of the road transport industry came principally via two measures: deregulation and privatisation. Deregulation is the removal of government controls over the behaviour of firms in the industry. Privatisation is the sale of government-owned assets in a company, either through the sale of some or all of its shares or through the sale of specific assets.[7]

The first target of the Thatcher government in the campaign to reduce the power of the state in transport was the bus industry. Within thirteen months of the Conservatives' general election victory the government's Transport Act had entered the statute book. It came into operation on 30 June 1980. It was an attempt to apply the principles of the free market to

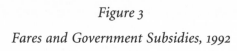

Figure 3

Fares and Government Subsidies, 1992

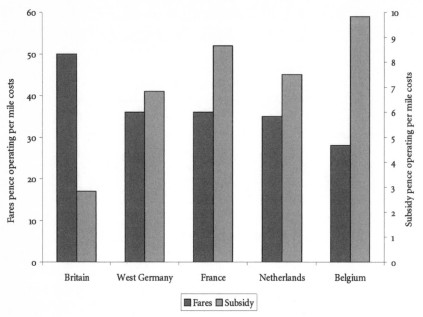

Source: *Financing Public Transport: How Does Britain Compare?* (1992).

road passenger and freight services. Part one of the Act removed all restrictions, except those concerning safety, on express bus and coach services covering over thirty miles between stops. All restrictions were also removed on excursions and tours by coaches. Part two provided for the privatisation of the National Freight Corporation. In a press release, issued on 1 July 1980, Norman Fowler, the Minister of Transport, claimed that he would reshape the system in ways specifically designed to benefit the travelling public.

To what extent were these expectations fulfilled? Under the new competitive system, long-distance coach and bus passengers benefited from lower fares and increased frequencies of services. Contrary to government hopes, the large publicly-owned National Bus Company and the Scottish Bus Group captured the lion's share of the expanding express and long-distance market. Between 1980 and 1983 the NBC's passenger carryings on express routes rose by 50 per cent and express mileage covered increased by 35 per cent. At the same time the private sector's share of passenger journeys on express routes declined from 40 per cent in 1981 to 28 per cent in 1982.[8]

It must be emphasised that the government's claim was that the Act would result in new operators coming forward, especially in the rural areas. Inevitably, however, the expansion of the express and long-distance services was at the expense of the local bus services. On 4 December 1984 Rupert Brook, chief executive of the NBC, told the Commons' Transport Committee how the introduction of a more 'market-oriented' economy influenced the company's decisions: 'When competition emerged, we as commercial people, applied our resources to where they were most productive – on motorways. We did therefore withdraw several cross-country services.'[9]

The effect of the 1980 Act was to reduce substantially the amount of cross-subsidisation by the large bus companies of their rural services. The NBC's route mileage fell by 8 per cent in the year 1981 through the withdrawal of a considerable number of its country services. The Bus and Coach Council, which represented the large majority of the operators, explained clearly why the Transport Act had led to a decline, rather than an increase, in rural bus services.

The hopes of the legislature have not been realised because the market has invariably not justified the commercial investment.[10] One of the government's objectives for the 1980 Transport Act was to reduce the influence of the NBC and the Scottish Bus Group (SBG) through competition with private operators. This plan completely misfired. A new tactic was therefore adopted in David Howell's Transport Act of 1982. The NBC's profitable subsidiaries, National Express and National Holidays, were privatised. A further Act was passed in 1983, paving the way for privately operated bus services within the Passenger Transport Authority areas. The Passenger Transport Executive was given powers to invite tenders from private operators to run local bus services.

Despite the fact that for five years the government had been busy sweeping aside regulations for the control of road passenger services, and a large measure of competition had been introduced, the number of passenger journeys by bus and coach fell from 6204 million in 1980 to 5686 million in 1984.[11] These facts did not deter Nicholas Ridley from asserting, in his second reading speech on a new Transport Bill on 12 February 1985, that 'One of the principal causes of decline was the system of regulations and near monopoly. The Bill is about competition. Competition is the key to increased patronage'.[12] When John Prescott, Labour's front bench spokesman on Transport, pointed out in a further Commons debate on 25 April 1984 that, since the Tories came to power in 1979, something like a thousand million passengers had been driven off the buses,[13] Ridley was unperturbed. In a couple of sentences, remarkable for their naivety, he replied:

The number of rail passengers is down by 5 per cent and bus passengers by 17 per cent, but the Labour Party must realise that transport is for the benefit of the traveller, not the operator. If travellers prefer to go by car and can afford to do so, that is a sign of progress.

He therefore proceeded with his Bill, which became law as the Transport Act of 1985. Gwyneth Dunwoody MP, noted that the government had deliberately not delayed the introduction of the Bill by a few weeks until the Transport Committee had reported on the 'Buses' White Paper. She declared that

> The government feel that they need not indulge in consultation to discover what is really important for the public. They do not believe in constructing legislation based on research and investigative work done by those with knowledge of the bus industry. For this government it is sufficient to move fast towards certain shibboleths that are important to the Secretary of State.[14]

Research into the working of bus deregulation was carried out in experimental areas in Strathclyde and in Hereford. In the Strathclyde area it was found that, after bus deregulation, the total level of service provided increased, although this was not reflected in an increase in patronage. Competition between bus operators meant that some areas received considerable increases in services but that poorly-used services were discontinued. In Hereford a questionnaire revealed that the numbers of the public questioned were about equally divided between those who thought that after deregulation services were better and those who thought that they had deteriorated.[15]

From 26 October 1986, when the Transport Act 1985 came into operation, all road service licensing (apart from the roadworthiness of the vehicles) came into operation and local authorities were forbidden to subsidise any bus service without the consent of the Secretary of State for Transport. Within three years the NBC was to sell off its seventy remaining subsidiary organisations, which were mostly regional bus undertakings. Local authorities and Passenger Transport Authorities were given power to secure public transport services by subsidy agreements in cases where private contractors failed to come forward.

Was it the case, as Nicholas Ridley had asserted, that 'competition was the key to increased patronage'? By 26 October 1986 only two hundred new operators entered the bus business to challenge the approximately 1500 already established before deregulation. According to the Department of Transport own statistics, the number of passenger journeys made per year in local buses and coaches continued to decline – from 5684 million in 1984 to 5340 million in 1987–88.[16] It was not a spectacular decline but then Fowler, Howell and Ridley had each in turn proclaimed that their market economy approach would reverse the downward trend in bus and coach usage.

Far from it being the case that the spate of Thatcher government legislation on the buses would increase competition and increase patronage, as Nicholas Ridley had assured the Commons, the consequence of the passing of those Acts was that a few giant companies, including Stagecoach, Badgerline, Go Ahead and Arriva, came to dominate the industry. There was a stampede to the stock market. The bus war that took place in the town of Darlington was subject to investigation by the Monopoly and Mergers Commission in 1994. Busways, a subsidiary of Stagecoach, wished to acquire the ninety-year-old, municipally-owned Darlington Transport Company (DTC). When the terms for a purchase could not be agreed, Busways ran free buses for five weeks over the routes covered by the Darlington company, its buses running just a few minutes ahead of the local company's vehicles. After five weeks the DTC was put on the market by the Darlington borough council with the loss of fifty jobs out of its 170, the balance of 120 being taken over by Busways. Running the free services for five weeks cost the private firm £100,000, but as Nick Wallis, the chairman of Darlington Council's transport committee, declared, 'that's a lot cheaper than having to buy DTC'.

What happened in Darlington was an extreme example of the consequences of a market-oriented economy; but it was by no means untypical of the forces or work. The changes in Britain after 1985 worsened the hours and earnings of bus workers. According to *New Earnings Survey*, in 1986 average gross weekly earnings for all types of bus and coach drivers were 7 per cent above average male manual earnings; in 1994 they had fallen to 14 per cent below. Actual working hours, apart from contractually negotiated ones, had fallen by shortening meal breaks and employing men and women at basic rates, instead of overtime rates, for overtime working. The morale of the bus industry workforce was adversely affected. The large bus companies which dominated the industry in the later 1980s and 1990s were frequently preoccupied with purely commercial objectives, with the result that many uneconomic country routes were less well served or not served at all. Where they could afford to buy a motor car, more and more people living in the countryside did so. Fifty-six billion passenger kilometres were travelled by bus or coach in Britain in 1979. This represented 12 per cent of all journeys made when 365 million journeys or 77 per cent of journeys were made by cars, vans or trains. By contrast in 1997 44 billion passenger miles were travelled by bus or coach, or 6 per cent, while 390 billion passenger miles, or 86 per cent of journeys, were travelled by cars, vans and taxis.

In the summer of 1989 the refusal of British Rail to offer railway workers a rise of more than 7 per cent, when the basic wage of those in the 'railman' grade was no more than £96.80 a week, led to a series of six one-day strikes. Members of British Rail were working an *average* of eleven hours a week overtime to achieve earnings barely sufficient to pay for basic items of household expenditure. In case the 8.8 per cent rise agreed following the conclusion of the strike should seem overgenerous, it is worth emphasising that the *new* basic pay of those in the railman grade of £105.31 was still well below the £144.00 minimum laid down by the low pay unit or the British government's £128.83 Income Support Earnings Equivalent.

The consequence of the British Rail Board being under increasing pressure to make financial savings was a deterioration in the service to passengers at the same time as fares were increased above the level of the rise of the retail price index. The Annual Report of the Central Transport Consultative Committee for 1988–89 noted that, in the provincial sector, there had been 'the largest cutback in the number of passenger vehicles' with 'overcrowding the inevitable result'. Over the country as a whole it found that the complaints of overcrowding had increased by 24 per cent in one year. It warned that planned reduction in rolling stock had 'already gone too far and should be put into reverse'. The fact that British Rail staff were leaving for better-paid employment elsewhere was having a damaging effect on the reliability of services. The report noted that an acute shortage of train crews in the London area had forced BR to introduce a substantial number of planned cancellations, including some peak trains. In the provincial sector there was 'de-staffing of a high proportion of stations, with many more being staffed for limited periods only'.[17]

The impact of soaring rail charges, growing overcrowding, increasing passenger train cancellations and deterioration in punctuality induced more passengers, whenever it was within their means, to buy a car, new or second-hand, and travel by road, incidentally increasing the pollution and congestion on the nation's highways.

On 28 November 1990 Margaret Thatcher, having lost the confidence of the Conservative Parliamentary Party, was obliged to resign as Prime Minister, to be succeeded by John Major. One of the reasons for her dismissal from office was her high-handedness with her colleagues, but there was also her failure to secure a clear lead on transport policy. It is true that both Margaret Thatcher and John Major were agreed on the objective of privatising British Rail, but they took ten years to settle how it might be done. In 1982 a small committee of Conservative MPs explored different methods of transferring the ownership of railways to the private sector. Chris Ridley, as Secretary of State for Transport in 1985, favoured the 'Big Bang' policy of selling off British Rail as a unit. This had the backing of the Prime Minister and the chairman of British Rail, the first Sir Bob Reid (who supported the policy only as a political tactic, to keep British Rail as a unit). In view of British Rail's losses, however, and the huge sums which would be involved in carrying through the project, it was realised that any flotation would be a flop.

A second option, favoured by John Major and the Downing Street research team, was to revert to the 'big four' main line railways which functioned between 1923 and 1939. Nostalgia and visions of a Golden Era of rail operation lay behind this unrealistic proposal – the four main line companies made meagre or nil profits in the inter-war period.

The third option, the brainchild of a right-wing think-tank, the Adam Smith Institute, and the Department of Trade and Industry, was the one that prevailed: splitting British Rail into two parts, a track authority and an operational authority; complying, it was thought, with EC Directive 91/440 – though this directive was primarily concerned that the split would simplify accounting procedures. There would be an outright sale of British Rail's freight business and the leasing of trains to private operator franchises to run passenger services.

After considerable delays – it was suspected because of the difficulty of reaching agreement in the Cabinet – the White Paper, *New Opportunities for the Railways*, came out on 14 July 1992. There was to be no major stock market flotation. Instead there was to be a piecemeal and gradual transfer of British Rail's assets to the private sector, the one exception being the freight and parcels business which was to be sold off soon after the legislation planned for 1992–93. British Rail was to be split into two parts. Railtrack would own and manage the infrastructure, including the tracks, stations and signalling. There would be a Franchising Authority which would contract with railway operators (franchisees) to run the trains, Railtrack's revenue would be gained from the railway operating franchisees, who would pay access charge for a (negotiable) number of years for the use of the track. There was a great deal left over for subsequent 'arrangement' between the parties.

Interdepartmental disagreements over the best method to choose to expose the railways to more competition delayed the publication of the White Paper, promised for the end of 1991, beyond the date of the general election.[18] In its leading article on the White Paper, the *Financial Times* gave its opinion that 'without further changes in transport policy the White Paper is unlikely to improve rail services greatly and could even accelerate their decline'.[19]

A most notable omission from the White Paper was any reference to a comprehensive transport policy. The Institution of Civil Engineers expressed its concern, in its memorandum to the Commons' Transport Committee on 11 November 1992, at the absence of any policy in the White Paper for coordinating the different means of transport:

> The key requirement is to coordinate transport provision through strategic planning to maximise the use of different modes. This would require the creation of a national coordinating group reporting directly to the Transport Secretary.[20]

The House of Commons all-party Transport Committee heard various key persons' views on the subject of railway privatisation after the appearance of the White Paper, but before the Bill was published and the Commons at the Second Reading debated it. Major General Lennox Napier, the Chairman of the Central Transport Consultative Committee (after privatisation renamed the Central Rail Users Consultative Committee), was heard on 11 November 1992. He said:

> We are thoroughly clear that we would wish to keep the track and infrastructure in public ownership ... if anybody disintegrates the network advantages, the network effect, privatisation will not work, nor will it work unless there is a high level of sustained investment.[21]

The White Paper had suggested that one justifiable economy which might be adopted by the Railway Operating Companies would be to make use of 'a healthy second hand market'. The Consultative Committee scorned this proposal.

> This downgrading of equipment is precisely what has happened since bus deregulation; fleet ages have increased enormously, because there is no central body which can order vehicles in sufficient quantity to enable economies of scale to reduce unit prices.[22]

The proposal to allow operating companies 'open access' to all lines was dismissed equally derisively:

> Open access will increase the commercial risks of all train operations perceived by private sector franchisees because it will make assessment of market share and operating revenues more uncertain.[23]

It is significant that, less than a month later, as a result of this warning and the hesitations of potential franchisees of operating companies, John MacGregor, the Secretary of State for Transport, announced the abandonment of the plan for open access. It is also significant that commercial, rather than safety, reasons prompted his withdrawal on this important point.[24]

In its Second Report, completed in February 1993, the Transport Committee noted that 'the government's proposals [had] undergone a process of evolution since the basic principles were first enunciated in the White

Paper'. It found that in one sense such developments were welcome, since they showed that the government did not have 'a closed mind' as to the final character of the proposals. On the other hand, the committee's task had been made more difficult because of the 'constantly shifting nature of the target.'[25] When the committee heard witnesses, and the individuals giving evidence were being asked questions, Peter Luff MP drew attention to the fact that there was a strong feeling in the country that franchisees should be allowed to control the infrastructure as well as the operation of trains. When he asked Robert Horton, chairman-designate of Railtrack, what he thought of the proposal, Horton replied 'We are at the behest of our shareholders and if our shareholder decides that he wants to change his mind and do it differently, one would make it work'.[26] This answer, given by the man who would have charge of the whole of the railway infrastructure if the Bill under discussion became law, is indicative of the fact that the claims of shareholders would be given priority over what needed to be done to secure a reliable and efficient transport system.

In the last weeks of the parliamentary session of 1992–93 there was a storm of opposition to the Railways Bill which transcended party lines and the opposite sides of industry. Four former Secretaries of State for Transport, John Peyton, Richard Marsh, Nicholas Ridley and Barbara Castle, and three former chairmen of British Rail, Richard Marsh, Peter Parker and Bob Reid, were all on record in opposition to the proposals. Nicholas Ridley, who was Margaret Thatcher's Secretary of State for Transport from October 1983 to May 1986, wrote an article in The Times in December 1992, headed 'Simply No Way to Run a Railway', arguing that the separation of Railtrack from the franchise operators was 'a recipe for confusion'. The former Secretaries of State (now Lords) Peyton and Marsh, led the opposition to the Bill when it came to the Lords being ably backed by Baroness (formerly Barbara) Castle. According to Robert Adley, the new Conservative MPs elected in the General Election of April 1992 had expressed their enthusiasm for the Bill. He declared, with some derision, 'They probably want to privatise everything.'[27]

Although the Conservative Party was elected with a clear majority of twenty-one seats over all other parties on 9 April 1992, and John Major enjoyed a rating of over 50 per cent support in Gallup poll findings at the time of the election, it dropped like a stone to only 23.3 per cent in November 1992 and to a mere 18.4 per cent in June 1993 when the Transport Bill still had not completed its progress through Parliament.[28] To add to the party's woes they sustained dramatic by-election defeats. At Christchurch on 29 July, the Liberal Democrat vote rose to 65.1 per cent compared with their general election tally of 37.2 per cent, and at Staffordshire South East, the

Labour candidate's vote in the by-election rose to 60.1 per cent from a general election figure of 32.2 per cent. From May 1993 to May 1997 the Conservatives sustained ten by-election defeats. Urgent action had to be taken to persuade their traditional supporters to return to the party. Revenue from the sale of companies under the provision of the Railways Act 1993 was needed to finance (what was assumed to be vote-winning) tax reductions. By the mid 1990s 'revenue from sales had become an integral part of the budgets arithmetic'.[29]

In view of the Major government's intentions it was unfortunate for the cabinet and the party that the proposal for railway privatisation was unpopular. A Gallup survey conducted on behalf of the *Daily Telegraph* found that 71 per cent of rail users were against the government's plans. Only 18 per cent of those questioned were in favour of privatisation. When passengers were asked for their preference between privatisation and more investment in British Rail, 84 per cent opted for the greater volume of investment and only 9 per cent favoured privatisation.[30]

John MacGregor, the Secretary of State for Transport, introduced the Second Reading debate on the Railways Bill on 2 February 1993. The arguments he used to justify the major changes in the ownership and organisation of British railways were summarised in the second paragraph of his speech:

> We begin with a railway regime not fundamentally changed since nationalisation in 1948. It is not in the interests of customers – or of management and staff – to persist with that regime. As an organisation BR combines the classic shortcomings of the traditional nationalised industry. It is an entrenched monopoly. That means too little responsiveness to customers needs, whether passenger or freight; no real competition, and too little diversity and innovation. Inevitably also it has the culture of a nationalised industry; a heavily bureaucratic structure; an insufficiently sharp awareness on the part of employees that their success depends on satisfying the customer indeed of attracting more customers; and an instinctive tendency to ask for more taxpayers' subsidy.

He claimed that, in order to get more freight back on the rails, breaking British Rail's monopoly was 'crucial'. He defended the clauses which provided the separation of the ownership of the track, signalling and stations as necessary on grounds of producing more competition. The White Paper had proposed that Railtrack should be owned by BR. He surprised some of his hearers when he said:

> We have now decided that BR ownership of Railtrack is now no longer necessary or desirable ... Railtrack will be a truly independent commercially driven body, a government owned body separated from BR in April 1994.

Separate, privately owned companies would run the freight services.[31]

In the debate which followed MacGregor's speech there was opposition to the proposed Bill from members of all three of the main political parties. Robert Adley, the Conservative MP for Christchurch and Chairman of the Commons' Transport Committee, declared that 'the hostility of the government under Lady Thatcher to anything in the public sector formed the background to the Bill'. The latest figures, on a dollar per head basis, showed that in support of their railways (West) Germany spent $24, France $37 and Italy $50, compared with Britain's $7, yet 'there was no mention of any investment regime in the Bill'.[32] Keith Hill, Labour MP for Streatham and a member of the Transport Committee, supported Robert Adley. 'There [was] an immediate crisis in under-investment in the railway industry', he said.[33] David Howell, the Conservative MP for Guildford, spoke for the 'stockbroker belt' commuters, expressing concern at the possible threats to safety of railway operation through the fragmentation of passenger services. John Prescott, the Labour front bench spokesman on transport, both in the Commons and in the press, cited the Health and Safety Executive's warnings on dangers to safety of operations under the very fragmented system of passengers services which were being proposed. Despite these expressions of concern, party loyalty prevailed. The second reading of the Bill was carried by 307 votes to 292. The doubters fought hard to secure concessions during the committee stage of the Bill. No less than thirty-five sessions were needed to deal with the 250 proposed amendments tabled. At this stage it became clear that Railtrack was to be a privately owned, not government owned, organisation.

The concessions granted by MacGregor included giving the Franchising Director powers to control fares to ensure that any rises were reasonable; the requirement that the department should publish an investment plan in its annual report; and that concessionary railcards should be available for the young, the elderly and the disabled. On one important issue, however, he refused to give way to the Opposition and his own backbench rebels. Under Clause 22 'neither BR nor any of its subsidiary organisations [was] to be allowed to bid for any of the operating franchises'. No doubt Mac-Gregor had in mind recent happenings in Sweden. SJ, the national railway, separated the infrastructure into an independent company, Banverket, to comply with EU requirements; but the government had allowed SJ to bid for operating franchises and it had won over 95 per cent of them in terms of mileage covered.

It was on this question that the Lords crossed swords with the government when the Bill came before the Upper House on 5 July 1993. All the former Secretaries of State for Transport were decisive in their opposition to the plan to exclude British Rail from any part in running the new railway.

Lord Peyton moved an amendment to Clause 22: 'nothing in subsection (1) above shall prevent the British Railways Board ... or (b) a wholly owned subsidiary of the Board, from being a franchisee'. [34] He said: 'the amendment would let British Rail in. In effect it would be a step back from the clear intention of the Bill to kill off British Rail and bury the corpse at an early date.' This amendment was opposed by the Earl of Caithness, who put the government's case for the Bill and declared that he favoured management buy-outs. He said he was firmly against British Rail being allowed to bid as it would 'undermine private sector interest due to the implicit government guarantee that it would have. Many in the private sector would probably think they were wasting their money in even preparing a bid against British Rail'.[35] Baroness Castle declared it was a total tyranny to brand British Rail as a failure: 'The noble Lord does not wish it to be allowed to prove whether it can compete.' Certainly he had not convinced the majority of their Lordships, who voted 150 to 112 in favour of Lord Peyton's amendment.

During the summer recess there was widespread talk in the Commons and in the papers that John Major was on the point of abandoning the Bill. The *Financial Times* 8 July headline read: 'Defeat in Lords Threatens Sell-Off of British Rail'. But Patrick Brown, Permanent Secretary at the Department of Transport, was a determined man. He urged John Major and John MacGregor to stand firm. In addition, although a number of Conservative rebel MPs had pressed MacGregor to accept the Lords amendment, they were without the influential leadership of Robert Adley, who had died of a heart attack at the age of fifty-eight on 13 April. As the obituary in the *Financial Times* observed, his death left 'the unease among Tory backbenchers without a clear focus or spokesman'.[36]

The Commons did not consider the Lords amendment until the evening of 2 November. MacGregor had earlier promised the Lords that he would need to amend the Peyton amendment to improve its wording. It later transpired that he had changed it to deny the right of BR to bid for franchises except in cases where there was no other bidder. The Lords considered the Commons treatment of Lord Peyton's amendments on the evening of 3 November in the knowledge that every page of the 243 page Bill had to be agreed by the following morning. Nevertheless, Lord Marsh's proposal that the peers should stand their ground was approved by 170 to 160 votes. Only after the Commons declined an opportunity to make a compromise did the Lords surrender to the Commons decisions (on the grounds that they must defer to the decision of the elected House) at 11.30 p.m. on Wednesday 3 November (the day before the end of the session) and the Bill received the Queen's signature on 5 November 1993. The Act came into force on 1 April 1994.[37]

Privatising the British railway system cost the Exchequer and the British public a great deal of money. According to the all-party Public Accounts Committee, the initial stage – getting the Bill through Parliament – cost no less than £629 million.[38] John MacGregor, in his speech introducing the Railways Bill, claimed that one of the reasons for privatisation was that the publicly-owned industry had an instinctive tendency to ask for more tax-payers' subsidy. In fact, following the Bill's enactment, the PSO (the subsidy given to support the socially necessary railway) was increased from £930 million in 1993–94 to £1740 million in 1994–95.[39] Robert Horton, chairman of Railtrack, was in a strong bargaining position vis à vis John Major, the Prime Minister. He knew that the government was anxious to complete the transition to a privately-owned railway system and gain part of the proceeds of the sale before the coming general election.

The first big transaction was the sale of Railtrack itself. In British Rail's *Annual Report and Accounts* for 1994, the gross value of 'Buildings and Infrastructure', including the stations, track, signalling and offices and land round all of these, was £6464 million as at 1 April 1994.[40] At the sale of these assets to the Railtrack consortium on 20 May they were published as being worth only £1900 million, an outrageously low figure, but one designed to attract investors to a very good bargain, promising a return of 15–20 per cent. The enormity of the downgrading of this essential public asset can be seen when it is realised that the Major government sold off the entire rail network of 16,656 miles of track, 2615 stations with adjacent land for less than the £2100 million needed for the projected cross rail link between Paddington and Liverpool Street in London.

According to the *Financial Times*, what cleared the way for the sale of Railtrack was the reduction of its inherited debt.[41] In negotiations with the Treasury, Horton at first argued for a reduction of £1600 million; the Treasury offered to wipe out £600 million and a final figure of £1000 million was agreed.

One area of great waste of publicly-owned resources which took place during the privatisation process was in the formation and sale of three rolling stock companies, known as ROSCOs, which had ownership of 11,258 vehicles (carriages and locomotives, but not Eurostar or freight wagons). British Rail, which had established the three companies in March 1994, sold them for a total of £745 million to the Secretary of State for Transport. The sale by British Rail of the three companies was completed with all possible speed as the government was aware that some of the twenty-five Train Operating Companies (TOCs) had not yet been launched and it wanted to persuade potential investors that there was big money to be gained in the privatisation process. The transactions which took place are summarised in Table 18.

Table 18

Privatisation of Rolling Stock Leasing Companies

Company	Price Paid to BR November 1993	Price Paid on Resale and Date	Profit fromResale	% Gains to ROSCOs
Porterbrook	£527m	£826m August 1996	£298m	56
Angel	£580m	£1.1 billion December 1997	£520m	58
Eversholt	£518m	£726.5m February 1997	£206.2m	40

Source: National Audit Office, *Privatisation of the Rolling Stock Leasing Companies*, 5 March 1998, p. 47, section 2.

It will be seen that the total profits from the resale made by the three management teams exceeded one billion pounds, a sum which could have made a substantial contribution to train operating safety apparatus installation.

Railtrack was floated on the stock market in May 1996. The company's prospectus emphasised its marketable assets in land. These were thousands of acres of unused land by former goods and marshalling yards and railway stations. In the House of Commons on 17 April 1996 David Chidgey cited one 'share shop' whose brochure stated: 'Railtrack is essentially a property company and the land that Railtrack will own could be regarded as one of the most valuable pieces of real estate in the United Kingdom'.[42] Railway land surplus to requirements had been sold by previous Secretaries of State for Transport; but in those cases the proceeds had gone to the Treasury. The proceeds of sales of land after April 1994 went to the privately-owned Railtrack's shareholders.

An important accompaniment to the privatisation process was a sharp decline in capital investment and in maintenance work in the industry. Figure 4 shows the extent of their decline.

In April 1994 when Railtrack took over responsibility for track, signalling and stations from British Rail, Robert Horton, its chairman, promised to make 'substantial cuts in maintenance and repair bills'. It is therefore not surprising that the Railway Industries Association reported that 'orders from Railtrack for signalling and track components had fallen steeply since Railtrack was formed ... purchases of rails, rail fastenings and switches had declined in the previous two years'.[43] Meanwhile the Institute of Railway Signal Engineers warned that 'the age and safety of electrical signalling introduced in the 1950s and 1960s was causing concern. Lack of finance would appear to have delayed both renewal and improvement to

Figure 4

UK Public Investment in Railways, 1991–1995

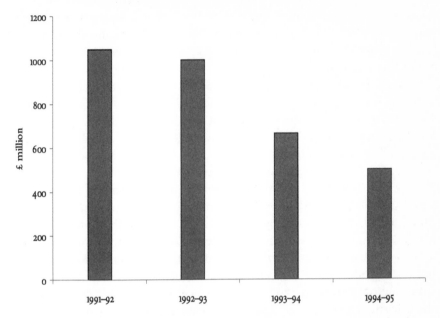

Source: Commons Hansard, 6th series, vol. 260, 17 May 1995, col 342 and vol. 261, 6 June 1995, cols 49–50. Written answers to questions by Michael Meacher, MP

these safety systems and the current indications are that this situation will worsen'.[44]

Railtrack's preoccupation was making better commercial returns from the largest railway stations by letting shop space. The launching of the company on the stock market in May 1996 was accompanied by the payment of huge bonuses to the directors and executives. Tom Winsor, who was appointed Rail Regulator in 1999, announced on 23 August 2000 that he had 'reviewed the whole bonus system, and you can be sure that from April 2001 these nonsenses are going to be swept away'.[45]

In 1999–2000 at least three organisations, the Health and Safety Executive, the Rail Passengers' Council and the Central Rail Users Consultative Committee, issued warnings about threats to the safety of passenger travel. Mr Coleman of the Health and Safety Executive said that the number of incidents of broken rails had risen from 654 in 1994–95 to 937 in 1998–99. The number of signals passed at danger (SPADs) rose from 583 in 1997–98 to 639 in 1998–99.[46]

The best-known example of a SPAD occurred on 5 October 1999 at

Ladbroke Grove in London, when thirty-one people were killed and about 400 injured, some horrifically so, from burns and other injuries. Two miles away at Paddington Station, Railtrack had spent many millions of pounds in modernising and beautifying the terminal. In Railtrack's Annual Report and Accounts for 1998–99, the chairman boasted: 'the results of the £1 billion station refurbishment are everywhere to be seen'. This report was published before the Ladbroke Grove disaster.

In both this accident and in one at Southall two years earlier, there had been a failure to install the Automatic Train Protection (ATP) system which would have prevented the collisions. It was a tragedy that these and other accidents spoiled the railway's record over the previous decade when deaths from collisions fell from 296 in 1988 to 126 in 1997–98 – a good performance for Britain compared with its European neighbours.[47]

How did passengers and traders react to the changes brought about by privatisation? Through the railway companies' own records, and through more extended media coverage as public discontent with the railway service increased, transport historians are better able to give an informed opinion on recent developments than was the case fifty years ago. Under the Transport Act of 1947, the Attlee government established the Central Transport Consultation Committee to voice the concerns and champion the cause of the railway passenger. The agitation by this organisation persuaded British Rail to publish the Passengers' Charter in March 1992, which recognised the passenger's right to claim compensation for delays and cancellations. Under the Railways Act of 1993 the CTCC was abolished and replaced by the Central Rail Users Consultative Committee (CRUCC) whose annual reports contained a fuller analysis of passengers' complaints and are one of the best indicators of the travelling public's reaction to the performance of the privatised railway.

On the positive side, passenger journeys by rail increased by 20 per cent in the years 1997–98 and 1998–99, the first two full years of privatisation.[48] There was also a slight improvement in the figures of traffic in freight from 101.7 million tons in 1998 to 102.1 million in 1999.[49] The dismal general picture, however, was that in the late 1990s only 6 per cent of passenger journeys were made by rail, while the volume of freight traffic carried by rail was a mere 5 per cent.[50]

The complaints from passengers reached their highest ever level in the year 1998–99 at 18,771, 27 per cent more than in the previous year, a fact that some critics have tried to explain away by pointing out that, in a booming economy, a record number of people were in work, more were enjoying holidays and there were more CRUCC offices to provide the public with information on how to make their complaints known.[51] The CRUCC's reply was that the number of claims for redress on particular instances of trains being late, shortcomings or mistakes in the provision of information and so on, were in line with the actual state of the railway. In the years 1998 and 1999 the aspects of the service which saw the biggest increase in complaints were on train reliability, suitability of service, train punctuality, overcrowding and travelling environment. These had been broadly the same as the CTCC had received over many years. It is clear that the greatly increased number of complaints since the Railways Act were to a large measure due to Railtrack's failure to maintain adequately the condition of the tracks and the signalling. These causes seriously affected train reliability and punctuality. The Railway Regulator, Tom Winsor, issued repeated warnings to Railtrack to improve its performance by target dates set. On 9 October 2000 Railtrack revealed that it had missed its performance improvement target for the second year running. Gerald Corbett, Railtrack's chief executive, also announced that because of heavy rainfall in April and May 2000, it might mean 'a larger leaf fall' which would affect train punctuality (shades of British Rail's 'leaves on the line' explanation in the 1960s). However, Derek Patch, director of the Arboricultural Advisory and Information Service, said, 'There is absolutely no evidence there will be an extra growth of leaf this year'. It looked possible that, because of its shortcomings in 1998 and 1999, Railtrack would be paying out £70 million in 2001 – the biggest fine in British corporate history.[52]

12

The Decline of Public Transport

Government policies on transport are influenced by a wide variety of factors. They may range from practical considerations, like budget restrictions, to overtly political objectives, such as providing a piece of transport infrastructure in a region where there is a forthcoming election. More usually they are focused on the economic and social benefits which are expected to flow from investment in transport. Not surprisingly they vary between countries according to geography, culture and political philosophy. At a more fundamental level transport policies are informed by the concept known to economists as 'externalities', which recognises the possibility that transport can benefit people and companies in ways that do not necessarily bring profit to transport providers. It may therefore be worthwhile for a government to run transport services, without prospect of profit, for the greater good of society.

Whether a government will accept this duty, we believe, is the defining attribute of transport policy. In Britain governments have customarily shown reluctance in this regard; while it is taken for granted that the state runs schools and hospitals without expectation of profit (it is assumed that the greater good of a healthy and educated population is worth having), when it comes to transport more commercial principles usually apply. To give a single example, the cuts in rail services to rural areas following the Beeching review of British Railways operations in the 1960s were justified on the grounds that they were unprofitable. What was not considered by Beeching or the British government was the wider costs of the cuts – their 'negative externalities'. These quickly became apparent as the people who lived in areas which were now deprived of rail links and who were forced to resort to cars and bus services to meet their transport needs, adding to road congestion – and the necessity for the government to increase its investment in new road construction – as well as to atmospheric pollution from exhaust fumes.

Britain's transport 'policy', and the dilemma it always seems to face in reconciling the cost of transport operation with the wider needs of the community, began in the nineteenth century. In the early part of the century, when roads and canals, and then railways, were the dominant transport mode, the prevailing attitude of the government can be truthfully described as *laissez-faire*. Having participated in the ordering of canal and railway construction, as it thought, through the parliamentary Private Bill process which launched any new enterprise, the government had no wish to encroach any further on the liberty of private capital. As the century progressed this attitude was attenuated and the government saw fit to increase its control of the private railway companies; but this, it should be stressed, was regulation, not *planning*. Its aim was to avoid the abuse of power by an oligopoly, to ensure competition, and to force the railways to accept certain social obligations, including providing cheap fares and special trains for workers. Its intervention was not designed to bring about the integrated or planned rail system which might have brought more lasting benefit to rail passengers or freight customers; and it did not encourage or even recognise the need for a balance between transport modes. This explains why it took little interest in the fate of the canal system at the end of the nineteenth century and did not make any attempt to protect canals from the monopoly power of the railways. The slow atrophy of British canals can be attributed directly to the lack of planning in government transport policy; no attempt was made to prioritise the assignment to them of the freight business for which they were best suited. Left to stand on their own, they withered away until today they serve little purpose other than as a recreation ground for tourists.

This lack of coherence in transport policy became more serious in the twentieth century when it was the railways' turn to become the victim of a new transport mode – the motor vehicle. It is hard to recall that a century ago the motor car was actually seen as a step towards greater cleanliness in city streets strewn with manure and urine from thousands of working horses. The new motor vehicles that first appeared in Edwardian England were wonderfully liberating, but it would be another half century before they were adopted by Britons as a genuine means of mass transport. In the meantime British public transport had its heyday.

The years between 1890 and 1940 saw the universal introduction of electric trams and motor omnibuses in British cities, and the completion of the London Underground railway network. The mainline railway companies, shrunk in number to four after 1923, offered a comprehensive passenger and goods service, although in the 1930s they were already feeling the heat of competition from road and even air transport, and asking the government for help in their 'Square Deal' campaign.

Above all, these years saw the consolidation of Britain's urban transport systems. The municipal ownership and administration of tram systems in cities like Glasgow showed what could be achieved with the right management and policies by transport providers in public ownership.[1] There was little policy guidance, however, from central government on urban transport and in particular on the control of privately owned bus companies which sprang up like mushrooms in the 1920s. Sir Henry May complained to a Royal Commission on Transport in 1928 that the competition between buses and trams was unnecessary and wasteful, and would drive the latter out of business.[2] The government's continued reluctance to engage in transport planning continued until Herbert Morrison, Labour Minister of Transport from 1929 to 1931, presented the case in his book, *Socialisation and Transport*, not only for public ownership of transport but for the planning of a national transport system. Transport, he said, 'must be brought together and its problems dealt with as a whole. That will enable us to destroy the biased railway mind and the biased road mind and substitute a big transport mind'.[3] A step in this direction was achieved in 1933 with the passage of the London Transport Passenger Act, which brought all of the capital's passenger transport modes, except mainline railways and taxis, under the administration of a public corporation. Unfortunately, the other regional transport boards which were proposed at the time, for Manchester, Merseyside, West Yorkshire and Tyneside, were not adopted and those conurbations had to wait until 1968 before they had a similar transport planning apparatus. London Transport was an undoubted success, not only because it proved the viability of a publicly-owned transport monopoly in the challenging environment of a major city, but because it vindicated *planning*. As one commentator noted, five years after the London Passenger Transport Board came into existence, it demonstrated the 'positive advantages in the planned provision of transport as against regulation by spasmodic and necessarily limited competition'.[4]

After the Second World War the new Labour government was able to bring large swathes of Britain's transport system into public ownership. In fact the nationalisation of transport undertakings in Britain had already begun with the creation of the publicly-owned British Overseas Airways Corporation (BOAC) by the Conservative government in 1939 – in Charles Mowat's telling phrase, a 'piece of Tory socialism'.[5] In 1945 transport stood at the head of Labour's nationalisation list and the railways, canals, road transport, coastal shipping and air transport all came under public ownership and control; but the vital question, more easily seen in retrospect, was how far would this initiate a new government planning regime. The answer is: not enough. There was certainly the hope of planning in the 1940s nationalisation programme amongst those members of the Labour government responsible for transport. The British Transport Commission (BTC) was established to introduce planning and create an integrated transport system out of the disparate and compartmentalised transport modes which Britain had had before the war. The progress with integrating transport services was, however, painfully slow and overshadowed by the generally dilapidated state of the infrastructure. The pressing need to rebuild the system, particularly the railways, took precedence over the more fundamental question of integration, and this was still the situation when the Conservatives were returned to government in 1952.

The Conservative governments of the 1950s heralded a boom in consumer spending and a partial retreat from nationalisation. In transport, although British Railways (BR) remained in public ownership, the attempt at planning represented by the BTC was abandoned in favour of competition between transport modes and between individual transport companies. With the passing of the 1953 Transport Act, the Conservatives crippled the BTC and began to dismantle the planning apparatus; there has been no serious attempt to restore it since. The 1953 legislation favoured cars and road haulage over the railways. Encouraging car ownership was now part of the political agenda of the Conservative government which famously proclaimed 'You've never had it so good!' Meanwhile road haulage was to replace the railways as the primary overland freight transport mode and by 1955 it had in fact replaced rail as the largest mover of cargo in Britain.[6]

In 1959 Britain built its first full-length motorway, the appropriately labelled M1, which linked England's first and second cities, London and Birmingham. This event probably deserves more attention in the chronology of twentieth-century British social history than it usually gets because it marks the beginning of the full motorisation of British society and the adoption of the car, forty years after the Americans, as the preferred mass-transport mode. From now on the railways would have to fight hard to maintain adequate levels of investment against an alliance of car manufacturers, lorry drivers' unions, motorway builders and unsympathetic members of the government and civil service – the road lobby. The long-overdue rail modernisation programme, which had already been put in hand, was now reversed; it was decided that the £1,200,000,000 earmarked for rail investment was not warranted and would not be continued. The consequence of this was that the investment which had already been made was utterly wasted: bridges were raised to cater for the overhead wires needed for electrification, but the wires were never installed. 'Track works, signalling and junction improvements were left half completed such that any operational advantages were minimal. It was the typical mess that stop-go policy produces.'[7] It was in fact a perfect example, all too familiar in the modern history of British transport, of what happens when planning is neglected or ignored and a dogmatic reliance on market forces is allowed to determine the course of transport policy.

Two men and two reports set the tone and agenda for Britain's motorisation in the 1960s: Professor Colin Buchanan, a highly influential thinker
on road planning, and Dr Richard Beeching, a former director of ICI and
chairman of the British Railways Board from 1963 to 1965. Beeching, in his
report, *The Reshaping of British Railways* (1963), brought a narrow, accountant's approach to the evaluation of Britain's national rail services. Like Sir
John King twenty years later, who was asked to prepare another nationalised
transport undertaking, British Airways, for privatisation, Beeching went
through BR's business 'weeding out' unprofitable lines.[8] The idea that rail
services, particularly in rural areas, might be retained for social reasons,
even if they were unprofitable, appears to have been ignored. The results
of Beeching's Report, when its recommendations were put into practice,
were close to catastrophic in the British countryside. Once BR had closed
a line, the replacement bus services were rarely satisfactory and a large
percentage of BR's former customers did not use them. The buses themselves
could then be withdrawn on the grounds that their passenger loads were
not high enough. The final result was that a rural area which had once had
a functioning rail link now had no public transport at all. Everyone had the
choice of buying a car, and joining the growing congestion on the roads,
or accepting a state of immobility almost equivalent to that of a century
and a half before.

The Beeching Report is significant in the analysis of British transport
policy, not only because of the wholesale cuts it precipitated in the rail
network but also because it signalled the end of any attempt to develop an
integrated transport system. By singling out the railways for treatment in
isolation from the rest of the national transport infrastructure, it represents
a clear break with planning for a balanced approach. Beeching's vision of a
much reduced role for rail in British transport was all the more persuasive
because it appeared at the same time as another report on British transport:
Colin Buchanan's *Traffic in Towns* (1963). Buchanan entered the debate on
the state of British roads at a time when road transport planning was in the
grip of the engineering community. Motor transport was in the ascendant
and the notion that car and lorry use might be controlled to reduce the
need for road space was heresy. The engineer's job was to provide sufficient
road space for the safe and expeditious movement of motor traffic; in
the words of one critical authority, 'all traffic demands should be met'.[9]
Buchanan accepted that people wanted to drive their cars and assumed that
unrestrained car growth was not only inevitable but also desirable. Like the
engineers, he saw the problem of traffic congestion, in towns as elsewhere,
as one of insufficient road space, but he went further by saying that road
space had to be carefully planned in urban areas; it was not just a question

of meeting demand with new roads wherever they were required, but rather there was a need to channel demand to minimise the negative impact of road traffic on the urban neighbourhood. The car had to be tamed, but not restricted in its access to towns and cities.[10] Buchanan was influential for the next twenty years in the planning of roads in towns; thanks to him the thinking in transport administration changed from coping with traffic to designing Britain's towns and cities with the car in mind. All kinds of ring and radial roads were devised to steer cars into and around cities, leaving – in theory at least – islands of calm residential areas in between. Buchanan recognised the need to preserve a certain quality of life for people who lived in towns and had to share their living space with cars and lorries. What he did not advocate however, or even consider, was that the freedom of mobility and access of those cars and lorries should in any way be restricted; in short, that the car should give way to people. The fact that Beeching's study of the railways and Buchanan's into road traffic in towns were conducted separately from one another, and the results of one were not considered by the other, is highly indicative of the isolated 'single-mode' approach to transport policy that became an orthodoxy in government and in Whitehall.

With the return of Labour to government after 1964 there was some hope that the integrative approach to transport might be revived. The 1968 Transport Act, drawn up by Transport Minister Barbara Castle, did not restore the BTC, but the minister did indicate that she wanted more planning in transport services and that different transport modes should not be allowed to go 'their own sweet way'.[11] The Act represented a shift in urban transport policy away from private transport towards more regulation, and the long-overdue Passenger Transport Authorities (PTA) were established in London, Liverpool, Manchester, Birmingham and Newcastle. In the 1970s the idea of the car's environmental cost was first recognised and the oil crisis of 1974 began to bring into question the high energy consumption of the motor vehicle and its efficiency as a mass transport mode. In the urban setting, the obsession with road construction, so typical of the 1960s, gave way to a greater emphasis on subsidised public transport and traffic management. It was a revision of Buchanan, but by no means an abandonment of the doctrine. Car owners would now pay more for parking in towns, but there was strong reluctance to actually preventing them driving into city centres or taxing them for road use. London Transport passed under the jurisdiction of the Greater London Council in 1969, although the amount of transport integration that occurred in the capital before the GLC was abolished in the 1980s left a lot to be desired; in particular surface rail travel into London remained separated from Underground operations. Although London was something of a pioneer in traffic limitation in the 1970s, and did not follow the United States and other European cities in building costly city motorways, it did not succeed in reversing the trend away from the use of public transport either. Unlike more enlightened European cities, there was no attempt to pedestrianise streets or make any significant provision for cyclists. In general, as London entered the 1980s, there was no plan and no initiative for transport.[12]

In 1979 the Conservative government of Margaret Thatcher came to power and hopes for a more integrated transport policy, in fact any transport policy at all, were crushed. The new government was unashamedly pro-car and had no interest in planning Britain's transport services or trying to create greater balance between what it saw as competing transport modes. Planning was not even given lip service. Instead the government championed the doctrine of free competition and the idea of privatising publicly-owned transport undertakings. Over the course of the next twenty years the scale of this disaster in national transport management – and in particular, the government's treatment of the railways – became clear.

Privatisation and deregulation began with the nation's bus services in 1980. In the 'free-for-all' amongst the bus operators that followed, the bus transport mode lost over a quarter of its market share and nearly all of these deserting passengers chose to switch to private cars. But the government waited another decade to tackle the railways. When eventually it did so, it was by a rushed and ill-conceived piece of legislation that was forced through Parliament in 1993. According to its supporters, privatisation would make competition possible, although exactly how rival private train operators would use the same track seems to have been understood by no one. In the nineteenth century the privately-owned rail companies had given up the idea as early as 1830 and had indulged in the expense of laying different tracks between the same places. This lesson from history seems to have been ignored by Britain's modern privatisers, who then compounded their difficulties by separating track ownership (Railtrack) from train operation. Despite the claims of the supporters, it is doubtful that this arrangement has the potential to yield any benefits; experience shows that what economies are available to railways come rather from the common management of track and train services. In fact, there are few efficiency gains to be had from rail privatisation that cannot be gained from more efficient management of rail in the public sector. Ironically the publicly-owned BR was quite efficient when judged by the amount of subsidy-per-kilometre it received. For example, in 1989 its trains travelled 49 per cent 'more kilometres per employee than the West European average, with only a sixth of the subsidy.'[13] It is too early to make a historical judgement on the privatisation of Britain's railways, but some critics did not wait. The *Economist*, a traditional champion of market forces, announced in 1999 that rail privatisation had 'proved a disastrous failure ... a catalogue of political cynicism, managerial incompetence and financial opportunism. It has cost taxpayers billions of pounds and brought rail travellers countless hours of delays.'[14] The crash of a passenger train in October 1999 on the approach to Paddington Station galvanised public opinion against privatisation and prompted the *Guardian* to castigate the new Labour government, perhaps a little unfairly since it had only been in government for two years, for its 'hand-wringing ineptitude'.[15]

One of the most serious effects of the return to *laissez-faire* conditions in transport in the 1980s was the impact on goods traffic. Because rail transport had been required to meet its commercial costs, including the upkeep of its infrastructure, and passenger and freight rates were raised continually under the Thatcher governments of the 1980s, it was cheaper to ship goods by road. As lorry weights rose steadily to forty tons by the early 1980s, they gained an increasing cost advantage over both rail and coastal shipping. Lorries received a hidden subsidy, in that the fuel and licence dues they paid did not come close to equalling the damage that these heavy vehicles did to the roads. By the late 1990s they accounted for over three quarters of freight transport in Britain, less than 10 per cent being carried by rail.

In the absence of an integrated transport policy, and in an atmosphere which favoured privatisation as the solution to industrial problems, the compartmentalisation of the transport industry was increased. When people or goods travel they generally make their journeys by a combination or road, rail, sea or air, but the companies which provided these services rarely operated more than one kind of transport mode and coordination was not encouraged by a government which had turned its back on planning. The administration of transport at government level was also divided between departments responsible for different modes, each with separate junior ministers and each treated in isolation, although not equally. In this structure road transport was favoured to an extraordinary degree over other transport modes, despite the growing evidence that the uncontrolled use of the private car and lorry threatened to paralyse the transport infrastructure. Under the Conservative administrations of the 1980s and early 1990s the government's approach to transport actually encouraged road vehicle use; the growth of suburbia, the neglect of the city centre, the proliferation of shopping malls in greenfield sites, and spiralling levels of road congestion followed naturally in its train. Between 1979 and 1989, for example, car traffic grew almost twice as fast in Britain as in the Federal Republic of Germany, and Britain had more car traffic, measured per unit of Gross National Product per capita, than every other European country except France.[16] In 1990 Britain (and the Benelux countries) had 1500 vehicles per kilometre of trunk road compared to 800 in Germany and just 780 in France.[17] The economic costs of road congestion, according to figures published by the Confederation of British Industry in a report of 1989, totalled fifteen billion pounds,[18] while its medical and social costs were laid bare in a report of the Royal Commission on Environmental Pollution in 1994, which unambiguously linked exhaust gases from cars and lorries – and the stress caused by driving them – with the increased incidence of heart and lung diseases.[19]

Britain's transport problems, some of which have been outlined here, have been developing in fits and starts over the last two hundred and fifty years. Because, as the nation enters the twenty-first century, those problems seem to be overwhelming, there is a tendency to see them as something of recent origin. They are not. They are long standing and fundamentally political in nature. For a long time, and not just during the last quarter of the twentieth century, British governments have been incapable or unwilling to arrive at coherent, long-term transport policies for the nation and then to stick to them, and they have been unable to resist cutting the funding for investment in transport, usually in the face of short-term budgetary pressures, on the occasions when policies have been agreed. The British, it seems, have always been suspicious of funding transport out of tax revenue and, in particular, providing subsidies for transport operations which have no prospects of profitable operation, but which nonetheless provide an overriding social or political benefit. The refusal of government to provide proper subsidies for socially indispensable air services to the Highlands and Islands of Scotland in the 1960s, like Beeching's refusal to consider the wider social costs of cutting rail services to isolated rural areas, reflects a basic philosophical predisposition in British government which it is beyond the scope of this book to analyse. A comparison with the transport policies pursued in other European countries, however, is salutary.

Perhaps because Britain is an island, its transport decision makers have rarely looked abroad for guidance on transport policies. Whatever the reason, the British reluctance to put money into public transport in general and into railways in particular stands in stark contrast to policy in continental Europe, where the railways are seen in the context of a broad range of social and economic benefits and invested in accordingly. Britain's rate of investment in railway infrastructure has been at, or close to, the bottom of the list of European nations. This is despite occasional high-tech prestige projects such as the Advanced Passenger Train (APT) in the 1970s and the Channel Tunnel a decade later. Both France and Germany have shown a solid political commitment to the development of their railway systems which is vital when large long-term investments, such as new track construction, are being made. Moreover, both governments see railway planning as part of an integrated transport system. Whereas the British government, after Beeching and up until privatisation, treated the railways as an industry that had to earn a commercial rate of return on its capital, France and Germany viewed their railways in terms of their benefits to the community at large, including reduced road congestion. New lines for high speed trains, for example, could not therefore be built by BR, because the servicing of the capital investment would have had to be included in the price of a railway ticket, making it higher and even less competitive with road transport. By contrast the French and the German railways secured appropriate loans from the government to carry out these major investments. Strong central government direction and dedication throughout the 1980s and 1990s ensured that the highly-praised French TGV high-speed train programme was carried through without any breaks in financing, while in the Netherlands a national plan for transport covering the next twenty years was agreed in 1990.[20] With the exception of the years of the Labour government and the BTC after the Second World War, such long-term dedication to a plan for transport has been almost completely lacking in Britain in the twentieth century.

13

Problems and Possibilities

'The aim of all good histories', observed the Earl of Clarendon, 'should be to teach the lessons of what has been fortunately or unhappily done.'[1] In answering the question 'What can history tell us about contemporary society?', the historian Eric Hobsbawm cites the old proverb 'the child who burns his fingers keeps away from the fire!'[2] We learn, or at least we should learn, from experience.

We believe that a study of British transport history over the last two and half centuries can teach us useful lessons on the direction of transport policy at the present time. As the last chapter aimed to show, that policy has been in disarray for the last thirty years. The reasons for this are partly of an economic and social nature, but they are also the result of political unwillingness on the part of successive governments, Labour as well as Conservative, to accept the need for a well-planned transport policy. Perhaps it is impossible to carry out systematic transport policies in a democracy like Britain, where long-term infrastructure investments tend to bring a political reward only after the initiating government has left office. We hope not. It is an unfortunate fact, however, that Britain invests about half as much in transport as other European countries such as France or Germany, resulting in what the *Economist* has called 'an overcrowded, underplanned and undermaintained transport system'.[3]

Britain has never had a properly integrated transport plan. The British Transport Commission did have integration as one of its objectives in the late 1940s, but this came to very little before the Conservative government stripped the commission of its powers in the early 1950s. This lack of the integrative element in transport planning has had serious consequences. Not only has it permitted a penny-pinching attitude towards transport investment to become entrenched in the Treasury and other decision-making centres in government, it has allowed transport to be treated as a collection of separate and independent modes. These modes are now severely out of balance and impact negatively upon each other in ways which could hardly have been predicted by even the most prescient of engineers and planners in the 1950s. One notable exception, however, was Professor Colin Buchanan who published a little book in 1972 in which he wrote the following:

One would expect to be able to look back over twenty-five years and see a steady implementation of plans for developing a national transport system closely integrated with the social and economic needs of the country and especially with the planning of urban areas which are the main generators of movement. But it has been a haphazard story in which for most of the period the railways stood right outside the planning system, and road development was bedevilled by the lack of common understanding between planners and engineers.[4]

Buchanan was himself a planner, so it is understandable that he saw the lack of integration in transport as a planning deficiency. Considering the problem a quarter of century after him, the authors of this book put the *consumer* of transport at the centre of the debate.

We began by addressing the meaning of travel. Why do people travel? Why do they need transport at all? We believe that when one considers the requirements of human mobility, rather than how to facilitate the movement of cars, buses, or trains, the *interdependence* of transport networks becomes clear. Providers of transport services must not lose sight of the consumer's needs and experience. They must remember why people travel: that they commute to work, or have to go shopping, or that their children need to get to school, or that they want to go on holiday. This should be the starting point for any analysis of transport problems, rather than the narrower, production-orientated question of how to get vehicles moving along a road or track. And because it starts from the perspective of the consumer, and his or her experience of travel, it is a multimodal approach, providing for the coordination of car with bus travel, of trains with bicycles, of planes with trains, and walking with everything.

What follows is a discussion of what we identify as the main problems with British transport today, and what we consider are the possibilities for the future.

There is more or less universal agreement today that, while it is undoubtedly the chief means of passenger transport, the motor car is also transport's biggest problem. The car is out of control and this is due to a failure of government policy. Of course road congestion is experienced all over the world and particularly in Europe, but in Britain it is especially bad and the British people are becoming increasingly aware of the fact. Britain has more vehicles per mile of trunk road than almost any other major European country. In urban centres, where the vast majority of the British people live, we are literally choking on the car.

Cars and lorries are appalling polluters. The list of complaints against them is a familiar litany, but it bears repeating. Their exhaust gases contaminate the air with hydrocarbons, carbon dioxide and nitrogen oxide (the latter from diesel-engined lorries and buses), particularly in cities where they are usually moving very slowly in heavy traffic. The rising incidence of respiratory diseases like asthma, especially amongst children, is now widely attributed to the noxious effect of cars and lorries. Diesel lorries, of which there are over 400,000 of the largest type in Britain, emit nearly 50 per cent of 'particulates', the main contributor to respiratory illnesses. Yet, in seeming disregard of this sombre statistic, the government raised the maximum permissible weight of these juggernauts in January 2001 from forty to forty-four tons.[5] Cars and lorries ruin the countryside, with their insatiable need for new roads, and the centre of old towns, with chronic vibration that damages the foundations of ancient buildings. They cause high levels of stress amongst drivers and anti-social behaviour in people who would otherwise be passive and well-adjusted citizens; the increasing occurrence of the phenomenon known as 'road rage' is evidence of the fundamental cost to society of car and lorry use. Cars are socially divisive in so far as non-car users are disadvantaged by car use and the congestion it causes. This means economic and social inequality for children, old people and women, as well as lower-income earners. Cars kill and injure people in accidents at a far higher average rate than any other transport mode, although the publicity given to spectacular crashes involving trains and planes can lead us to overlook this fact.[6] Lastly, and notwithstanding the attempts of manufacturers to make them more economical, cars are highly inefficient users of the most important non-renewable energy source on the planet – oil.[7] Their dependence on it leads to economic, political and even military crises when the oil producers' prices rise too high, or too fast, for the consumers of the industrialised world to bear. Moreover, as we enter the twenty-first century, 'green' issues can no longer be ignored in transport analysis. The Intergovernmental Panel on Climate Change found that average earth temperatures were rising faster in 2000 than in 1995 and concluded that 'the burning of fossil fuels and emissions of inanimate chemicals has contributed substantially to the observed warming [of the earth] over the last fifty years'.[8] In the light of the panel's and other research findings, Michael Meacher, the Environment Minister in the Labour government, noted in 2000 'that motor vehicles are world-wide the single fastest rising cause of CO_2 emissions and the main driver of climate change'.[9]

Yet, despite this register of complaints against them, we love our cars. They are flexible and, if we believe the television advertising that promotes them, they are even fun. In fact the advertising of cars has for a long time had more to do with power, youth, sex and personal attainment than with any useful system of transport. Cars seem to signify liberty and self-expression.

When Toad exclaimed the 'bliss' of motor cars and driving in *Wind in the Willows*, he meant the sense of power and freedom which cars give their owners, something which was probably true in the Edwardian England of the author Kenneth Grahame. Today they rarely give their owners any feeling other than frustration, but this does not seem to have dampened our passion for them. The British are buying more and more cars, and use them more than any of their European neighbours. Despite intolerable congestion on the roads in and around London and other urban areas, and heavier and heavier traffic on the nation's arterial motorways, we steadfastly refuse to leave our cars at home. We seem to be addicted to them. It is a paradox that as cars themselves, as artefacts, become seductively close to a state of technological perfection, they are increasingly unsatisfactory as a means of transport because their freedom of movement is restricted by self-imposed traffic congestion.

The second problem is the lamentable state of public transport in Britain, and the low regard in which it is held. This may have something to do with the individualisation of society in the second half of the twentieth century; public transport is, after all, a collective experience compared to car travel. It is more likely, however, to be the result of a decline in the standard of public transport itself.

The obvious example is the state of Britain's railways. British governments have repeatedly cut financial support for the railways (Fig. 1) and Conservative ones have been anxious to demonstrate that publicly-owned railways are not compatible with a car-owning democracy. In the years that followed the nationalisation of the railways, an influential 'road lobby' in the House of Commons was all too willing to blame it for the shortcomings of Britain's transport system. During the period when Ernest Marples (1959–64) and Nicholas Ridley (1983–86) had ministerial responsibility, the number of staff at the Ministry of Transport concerned with motor transport was disproportionately increased, so that the department's civil servants acquired a strong pro-car and pro-lorry disposition. Rather than following the example of continental Europe, where railways have been properly maintained, British governments adopted the inappropriate model of the United States which more or less abandoned passenger rail services in the 1950s. As car travel became established as the norm in the 1960s, the British ceased to take their railways seriously. Nationalisation became associated with the earlier failure of the railways and, sadly, British Rail was never able to shake off this stigma before it was privatised in the 1990s. Meanwhile public antipathy was compounded by a palpable anti-rail culture in government. Instead of being sustained as a public service, the railways were required to follow narrow commercial objectives and manage with a minimum of financial support from the state. The result now shows all too clearly in poor service and shabby equipment, as any traveller will know who has had the opportunity to compare Britain's railways with those of France or Germany. Worse still, British rail fares, measured on a per mile basis, are amongst the highest in Europe.

The final indignities to Britain's once-proud rail service have taken place since its privatisation in the 1990s. It now consists of a collection of individual private companies trying to please their shareholders, operating in a spurious railway transport 'market'. Those responsible for the privatisation clearly ignored the lesson from Britain's railways in the early nineteenth century: that separating train operations from track ownership and responsibility is doomed to failure. At the centre of the new constellation of British rail companies lies the track-owner, Railtrack plc. On its foundation in April 1994 Railtrack was given the vitally important task of maintaining and improving the track, signalling and stations of the British rail network. Yet it promptly announced that it would 'make substantial cuts in maintenance and repair bills', a feature of which would be a reduction in the rate of rail replacement from 2.5 per cent of the track per year, as was the practice with British Rail and most European rail systems, to a mere 1.5 per cent. The result was an inevitable increase in the number of broken rails. In addition, Railtrack put out to sub-contractors the work of track maintenance, with the result that the number of qualified trackmen fell from 31,000 in 1993, their last year of employment with BR, to just 15,000 in 1999.[10] The real cost of these 'cost savings' became clear in October 2000 with the train derailment at Hatfield, where four passengers lost their lives.

What can be done? We see a number of potentially fruitful avenues, but stress that nothing can be achieved without the political will and a leadership dedicated to carrying out a long-term policy.

The result of the Hatfield crash, and the far more serious disaster at Westbourne Grove on the approach to Paddington Station in 1999, was a total collapse of whatever confidence the British travelling public still retained in their railways. Railtrack has failed the nation and, we believe, it should be bought back for the good of the British people. The cost, on the company's present valuation, would be around five billion pounds, a sum which can be easily afforded by the Treasury. A public trust should be formed, to be financed by loans at fixed interest rates and placed under the democratic control of Parliament. There are plenty of successful examples of public trusts in Britain and abroad. For instance, the Port of London Authority, established by Act of Parliament in 1909 to replace the chaos in London dockland, is still functioning well. In France, the French railways

(SNCF) created a public trust, financed by loans, to build and manage the TGV line from Paris to Bordeaux.

Meanwhile the Railway Operating Companies (ROCs), with two exceptions, have been massively supported by Public Service Obligation grants from the Treasury. There was provision under the 1993 Railways Act for these grants to be gradually reduced in the closing years of the ROC's franchises, which were mostly of seven years duration. Where the companies have not been able to sustain these reductions, the Department of Transport and Environment has stepped in with ad hoc grants. This system has been compared to a bucket with holes in it; instead of this method we suggest the government buy shares in the companies to increase its control of how taxpayers' money is spent.

The restoration of Britain's railways should be coordinated with a comprehensive plan to bring the car under control. Motor vehicles no longer provide unlimited mobility, and already in some urban areas they do not even fulfil the basic requirements of a transport system. There needs to be a fundamental shift in the emphasis of the government's thinking on transport, away from individual car usage and towards collective public transport. Given, however, that in the foreseeable future car usage will remain the most important transport mode in Britain, whatever policy initiatives are taken, there should be a change in the focus of car control from ownership to *usage*. Hitherto, the fiscal burden on British motorists has been concentrated on fuel tax and the vehicle licence fee; both penalise ownership, but they are blunt instruments for controlling the use of cars. The licence fee bears little relationship to the amount of car travel undertaken and does not take any account of where journeys are made. A car owner in central London pays no more than one in the wilds of Northumberland. Similarly fuel tax is non-discriminatory and ignores the traffic congestion that motor vehicles create.

In future, taxation on motorists should concentrate on the actual use of cars on roads. This means the introduction of a variable form of road pricing by which the full cost of car use can be identified and made clear to the people who choose to use this form of transport. Road pricing is precise in its effect and also democratic because it is a tax on the congestion and delays a vehicle causes to other road users. Of course it is not new; the concept originates in the turnpikes which were common in Britain up until the early nineteenth century and the tolls which were levied on some of London's bridges until the 1870s. The difference lies in the greater sophistication of modern road pricing, which charges road users directly for the road space they occupy according to rates determined by the demand for that space at different times. Thus the rush-hour use of a busy London highway would cost more than driving on the same road at midnight. It brings demand for road space into balance with supply and as such is the economist's solution to congestion. Kenneth Button has put it in the characteristic terms of the transport economist:

> The congestion problem is ... essentially an economic one: motorists are not paying the full cost of their journeys and consequently urban road space is not being allocated optimally. Quite simply, the price of motoring in towns is below that required to equate the supply of road space with demand for its use – an excess demand has consequently developed. The logical economic solution in these circumstances is to raise the price of driving in towns until equilibrium flow is reached.[11]

For a long time the technical difficulties of tolling road users posed an obstacle to the introduction of systematic road pricing, but now electronic charging, using roadside or overhead radio signals and car-mounted sensors, has solved these problems. What remains is the political hurdle. British politicians are extraordinarily reluctant to alienate car owners. They fear that making voters pay for something that has always been free will result in disaster at the next election, although this has never been put to the test. This is not the place to discuss how best to introduce and 'sell' new policies to the electorate in a democracy, but it seems clear, intuitively at least, that the British motorist will be more willing to pay for using a road (and, incidentally, less aggrieved at paying a high rate of duty on petrol) if he or she knew for certain that the revenue from road tax would be invested in better public transport. Where road pricing has been introduced, for example in Singapore and some Norwegian cities, not only has road congestion been reduced but a valuable new source of revenue has become available for improving public transport.[12]

Road pricing will only achieve its full purpose if the revenue that it generates is dedicated to enhancing the extent and quality of public transport options for those people who choose to leave their cars at home. A long-term programme of public transport investment will be necessary and the travelling public must be convinced that this will be carried out. The authors of this book agree that public transport must be revived, if necessary, by drawing on the tradition of British public transport in the first half of the twentieth century when it was efficient and well-appreciated. The role of public transport is to provide a *service* for passengers. But the task of coaxing people back onto public transport will amount to more than providing a few extra buses; it will require a radical improvement in its status. Inner-city bus usage has been declining steadily and there is little hope that car drivers will relinquish their vehicles in any significant numbers if the only alternative is a bus ride. Notwithstanding the useful contribution made by dedicated bus lanes in urban areas, the fact is that buses are usually as stricken as any other motor vehicle by road congestion because bus lanes are not enforced.

Instead, the key to reversing the negative trend in public transport's usage, and to reburnishing its image, is to embrace what history has shown to be the paradigmatic public transport mode: vehicles moving on tracks. We believe that it is trains and trams, or light rail systems, which hold the key to public transport's revival in Britain in the twenty-first century. As the earlier chapters in this book have shown, these are nineteenth-century technologies, but ones with extraordinary longevity; nostalgia can be replaced with modernity if high-speed trains and light rail systems are allowed to solve the problems of intercity travel and urban transit. Railways provide a large transport capacity and therefore relieve congestion. They are also environmentally-friendly when powered by electricity from power stations, where the optimal use of energy and the most efficient control of pollution can be practised. Railway infrastructure uses far less space than roads: a double track of ten metres width can carry the same number of passengers as a British motorway 135 metres in width.[13] Meanwhile modern trams, and light rail systems, are adaptable to both suburban and inner city conditions and are attractive to urban travellers; they have the reassuring and predictable performance of the train combined with the accessibility of the omnibus.

These possibilities and projects for the future will amount to little more than empty rhetoric unless there is the *political* will behind their execution. One thing that becomes obvious from a view of transport over the last two and a half centuries is that transport only works when the government sets clear policy and then adheres to it. This has not happened during the last half century in Britain; there has been little leadership and, where there has been, it has been of too short a duration. Too often the politics of transport has degenerated into a clash of lobbies and interest groups, as if transport policy is no more than a market place of ideas and vital interests. The authors of this book make no apology for calling for clear leadership in transport matters – the British people are entitled to expect transport to receive as much attention from government as health care or education. There have been men and women who have played a distinct leadership role in transport over the course of the last century – Sir Eric Geddes, Herbert Morrison and Barbara Castle are names which come to mind. They have set agendas and fostered legislation, but in the end their policies have not survived. Too often transport has been treated as a poor relation which can safely be ignored by politicians and civil servants alike, particularly when it competes for government funds with other more glamorous and politically rewarding enterprises.

G. M. Trevelyan wrote that 'social history might be defined negatively as a history of a people with the politics left out'.[14] We believe that for too long now Britain has conducted transport policy 'with the politics left out'; it is time to bring transport into the centre of the public debate and to make it a political priority.

Notes

Notes to Introduction

1. Jack Simmons, *Transport* (London, 1962), p. 1.
2. Rick Szostak, *The Role of Transportation in the Industrial Revolution: A Comparison of England and France* (Montreal and Kingston, London, 1991), p. 11.
3. Simon Ville, 'Transport and the Industrial Revolution', *Journal of Transport History*, third series (September 1992), pp. 180–85.
4. James A. Dunn Jr, *Miles to Go: European and American Transportation Policies* (Cambridge, Massachusetts, 1981), p. 68.
5. Phyllis Deane, *The First Industrial Revolution* (Cambridge, 1969), pp. 69–70.
6. The much-publicised Heathrow Express merely takes passengers into the centre of London, a job which is already accomplished (admittedly more slowly) by the Piccadilly Line of the Underground; there is no provision for travellers who want to travel directly from Heathrow to destinations in the rest of Britain.

Notes to Chapter 1: Inland Navigation

1. While a packhorse on a bridlepath could carry around two and a half hundredweight, a horse on a towpath could haul as much as thirty tons in a river barge and even fifty tons on the deadwater of a canal. Philip S. Bagwell, *The Transport Revolution, 1770–1985* (London, 1974), p. 1.
2. W. T. Jackman, *The Development of Transportation in Modern England* (Cambridge, 1916), app. 8.
3. Andreas Kunz and John Armstrong, Introduction, *Inland Navigation and Economic Development in Nineteenth-Century Europe* (Mainz, 1995), p. 7.
4. Edwin A. Pratt, *A History of Inland Transport and Communication in England* (London, 1912), pp. 114–15.
5. Traffic on the Severn is described by G. Perry of Coalbrookdale in the *Gentleman's Magazine* (1758), pp. 277–78.
6. Joan Parkes, *Travel in England in the Seventeenth Century* (London, 1925), p. 109.
7. Ibid., pp. 97–98.
8. The River Severn has been known to rise eighteen feet within five hours, and there were times when the depth of water in the river was less than sixteen inches. Sir Alexander Gibb, *The Story of Telford* (1935), ch. 1.

9. T. S. Ashton, *The Economic History of England: The Eighteenth Century* (London, 1964), p. 72. According to T. S. Willan, the Severn was unusually free of flashes, floodgates, locks or sluices, 'The River Navigation and Trade of the Severn Valley, 1600–1750', *Economic History Review*, 7 (1954), pp. 68–69.

10. Bagwell, *Transport Revolution*, p. 13.

11. Pratt, *History of Inland Transport*, p. 128.

12. Joseph Priestley, *An Historical Account of the Navigable Rivers, Canals and Railways of Great Britain* (1831), p. 5.

13. Fiona Wood, 'Fuelling the Local Economy: The Fenland Coal Trade, 1760–1850', in Kunz and Armstrong, *Inland Navigation*, pp. 261–76.

14. H. J. Dyos and D. H. Aldcroft, *British Transport: An Economic Survey from the Seventeenth Century to the Twentieth* (Harmondsworth, 1974), p. 44.

15. W. H. G. Armytage, *A Social History of Engineering* (4th edn, London, 1976), p. 75. The pound lock has two sluice gates, one at each end of the 'pound'. Its chief advantage over the flash lock lies in its more economical use of water. The mitre gate, the invention of which is sometimes attributed to Leonardo da Vinci, consists of lock gates which meet in midstream, forming an apex, the gates themselves being held tight against each other by the downstream pressure of the water.

16. Charles Hadfield, *British Canals: An Illustrated History* (1969), pp. 21–22. Water wheels were still relied upon as a source of power until well into the second half of the nineteenth century, indeed they only reached their peak of technical efficiency *after* 1850, by which time the steam engine was well-established, Rondo Cameron, 'A New View of European Industrialization', *Economic History Review*, second series, 38 (1985), p. 5.

17. A good example is the battle to improve the River Medway in Kent, described by C. W. Chalklin in 'Navigation Schemes on the Upper Medway, 1600–65', *Journal of Transport History*, 5 (1961), pp. 105–15.

18. Another example of local opposition to river improvement can be found in K. R. Fairclough, 'The River Lea before 1767: An Adequate Flash Lock Navigation', *Journal of Transport History*, 10 (1989), pp. 130–32.

19. T. S. Willan, *River Navigation in England* (London, 1964), p. 133. Gerard Turnbull has questioned Willan's figures for the extent of navigability on English rivers in 'Canals, Coal and Regional Growth during the Industrial Revolution', *Economic History Review*, 40 (1987), pp. 539–40.

20. B. R. Mitchell and P. Deane, *Abstract of British Historical Statistics* (Cambridge, 1962), pp. 177–78.

21. This is the view of the geographer Michael Freeman, see his introduction to D. H. Aldcroft and M. J. Freeman (eds), *Transport in the Industrial Revolution* (Manchester, 1983).

22. James E. Vance, *Capturing the Horizon: The Historical Geography of Transportation* (New York, 1986), p. 85.

23. The Romans cut the first canal in England, the so-called Fossdyke, between the Trent, south of Gainsborough, and the River Witham at Lincoln.

24. Armytage, *Social History of Engineering*, p. 96.
25. The first modern British canal was built in Northern Ireland from the Tyrone coalfield to the port of Newry. Begun in the 1730s under the direction of the French Huguenot, Richard Castle, it was completed by the engineer Henry Steers in 1841. Charles Hadfield, *The Canal Age* (New York, 1969), p. 22.
26. For details on the Sankey Navigation's promoters, see J. R. Harris, 'Liverpool Canal Controversies, 1769–72', *Journal of Transport History*, 2 (1956), pp. 158–74.
27. Hadfield, *Canal Age*, p. 23.
28. Charles Hadfield and L. T. C. Rolt, *The Inland Waterways of England* (London, 1950).
29. C. P. Hill, *British Economic and Social History, 1700–1975* (4th edn, Cheltenham, 1977), p. 50.
30. Hadfield, *British Canals*, p. 79.
31. H. Thorpe, 'Litchfield: A Study of its Growth and Functions', *Transactions of Staffordshire Record Society*, 196 (1951–52), quoted in C. Hadfield, *Canals of the West Midlands* (1966), p. 36.
32. Hadfield, *Canals of the West Midlands*, ch. 2.
33. Hadfield, *British Canals*, pp. 91, 100.
34. The Manchester Ship Canal was thirty-five miles long, complete with locks, sluice gates, high-level railway bridges and the Barton Swing Aqueduct which carried the Bridgewater Canal over it. It was 'the greatest artificial waterway ever known' in Britain, cutting Manchester's dependence on Liverpool's docks and transforming the city into a major port, in the process lowering the cost of raw materials and exports, particularly cotton. Dyos and Aldcroft, *British Transport*, p. 219.
35. There were exceptions, such as the Trent and Mersey, which set up its own transport company. Gerald Crompton, 'Introduction: Rivers, Canals and Economic Development', in Gerald Crompton (ed.), *Canals and Inland Navigation* (Aldershot, 1996), p. xv.
36. Margaret C. Jacob, *Scientific Culture and the Making of the Industrial West* (New York and Oxford, 1997), p. 189.
37. Quoted in Asa Briggs, *The Age of Improvement, 1783–1867* (London, 1979), p. 30.
38. D. P. Gladwin, *The Canals of Britain* (1973), pp. 57–62.
39. Pratt, *History of Inland Transport*, p. 183.
40. J. R. Ward, *The Finance of Canal Building in Eighteenth-Century England* (Oxford, 1974).
41. Charles Hadfield, *British Canals*, pp. 158–59.
42. *Quarterly Review*, 22, quoted in Clapham, *Economic History*, i, p. 82.
43. Jackman, *Transportation in Modern England*, i, p. 426.
44. Ashton, *An Economic History of England: The Eighteenth Century*, pp. 84, 89.
45. Adam Smith, *The Wealth of Nations*, pp. 598–99.
46. John Phillips, *A General History of Inland Navigation* (1792).
47. Szostak argues that modern transport was a critical precondition for industrialisation. Rick Szostak, *The Role of Transportation in the Industrial Revolution:*

A Comparison of England and France (London, 1991), p. 6. Other historians are more sceptical and have judged with McCloskey that the cost savings created by transport improvements were insufficient to trigger any kind of 'revolution'. Donald McCloskey, '1780–1860: A Survey', in Roderick Floud and Donald McCloskey (eds), *The Economic History of Britain since 1700*, i, *1700–1860* (2nd edn, Cambridge, 1994), p. 259. Szostak's essentially monocausal thesis is criticised by Simon Ville in his review article, 'Transport and the Industrial Revolution', *Journal of Transport History*, 13 (1992), pp. 180–85. Michael Freeman sees transport developments as lagging behind industrialisation, an interpretation which would explain why early canal projects like Bridgewater's were such a resounding success, Freeman, *Introduction*, pp. 18–19.

48. Szostak, *Transportation*, p. 11.
49. T. Telford, *A Survey and Report of the Proposed Extension of the Union Canal from Gumley Wharf, in Leicestershire, to the Grand Junction Canal, near Buckby Wharf, in Northamptonshire* (1804), quoted in Hadfield, *British Canals*, pp. 33–34.
50. William Hutton, *An History of Birmingham* (1791; reprint 1976), p. 266.
51. Phillips, *A General History*, p. 598.
52. Roy Church, *Economic and Social Change in a Midland Town: Victorian Nottingham, 1815- 1900* (London, 1966), p. 5.
53. Turnbull, *Canals, Coal and Regional Growth*, p. 547.
54. Phyllis Deane, *The First Industrial Revolution* (Cambridge, 1969), p. 122.
55. Quoted in Ashton, *An Economic History of England: The Eighteenth Century*, p. 89.
56. C. W. Chalklin, *The Principal Towns of Georgian England* (London, 1974), pp. 39–41. Bradford, for instance, was a major beneficiary of the Leeds and Liverpool Canal to which it was linked in 1774 by a short spur. See G. Firth, 'Bradford Coal, Craven Limestone and the Origins of the Leeds and Liverpool Canal, 1765–75', *Journal of Transport History*, 4 (1983), pp. 50–62.
57. Crompton, *Introduction: Rivers, Canals and Economic Development*, p. xx; also John Armstrong, 'Inland Navigation and the Local Economy', in Kunz and Armstrong, *Inland Navigation*, pp. 307–10.
58. Sidney Pollard, *Peaceful Conquest: The Industrialisation of Europe, 1760–1970* (Oxford, 1981), pp. 5–7.
59. Final Report of the Royal Commission on Canals and Waterways.
60. Lionel B. Wells, 'A Sketch of the History of the Canal and River Navigations of England and Wales and of their Present Condition, with Suggestions for their Future Development', *Memoirs and Proceedings of the Manchester Literary and Philosophical Society*, fourth series (1893–94), p. 188.
61. Dyos and Aldcroft, *British Transport*, p. 214.
62. Church, *Victorian Nottingham*, pp. 173–74.
63. H. Pollins, 'The Swansea Canal', *Journal of Transport History*, 1 (1954), pp. 135–54.
64. Wells, 'A Sketch', p. 194.

65. From *Practical Treatise on Rail-Roads,* quoted in Pratt, *Inland Transport,* pp. 296–97.

66. J. Ginarlis and S. Pollard, 'Roads and Waterways, 1750–1850', in C. H. Feinstein (ed.), *Studies in Capital Formation in the United Kingdom, 1750–1920* (Oxford, 1988), p. 223.

67. The best account of canals in this period is found in the fourth volume of Reports by the Royal Commission on Canals, *Parliamentary Papers* (1907), 33, pt 2, p. 229 for particulars of the Aire and Calder Navigation. This company, jointly with the Sheffield and South Yorkshire, opened six miles of new canal in 1905.

68. Church, *Victorian Nottingham,* p. 368.

69. Dyos and Aldcroft, *British Transport,* p. 217.

70. Pratt, *Inland Transport,* pp. 298–99.

71. '. . . the railway companies have not used those branches which have come into their power for the purpose of developing traffic on the canals, but they have either suffered them to go into neglect ... or, I fear it may be said, in some instances they have actually desired to prevent the development of through systems of canal traffic, believing it would divert certain merchandise from their lines on to the canals'. Sir William Tomlinson, *Report of a Meeting Held at the Westminster Palace Hotel, 14 December 1904,* Mansion House Association on Railway and Canal Traffic for the United Kingdom, *Canals and Inland Navigations* (London, 1905), p. 6.

72. Gerald Crompton, 'The Role of Canals in British Industrialisation', Kunz and Armstrong, *Inland Navigation,* p. 15.

73. Andreas Kunz, 'Verkehr und Binnenhandel in Mitteleuropa, 1750–1850', in *Reich oder Nation? Mitteleuropa, 1780–1815,* ed. Heinz Duchhardt and Andreas Kunz (Mainz, 1998), pp. 184–87. Since the navigable German rivers (Rhine, Elbe, Oder) tend to run in a north-south direction, canal construction strove to connect them with east-west links. Frank Tipton, 'The Regional Dimension in the Historical Analysis of Transport Flows', Kunz and Armstrong, *Inland Navigation,* p. 169.

74. For canal developments in continental Europe, H. J. Habakkuk and M. M. Postan, 'Transport', *Cambridge Economic History of Europe* (Cambridge, 1965), chapter 4; also J. H. Clapham, *The Economic Development of France and Germany, 1815–1914* (4th edn, Cambridge, 1968), pp. 104–20, 350–55, and A. Milward and S. B. Saul, *The Economic Development of Continental Europe, 1780–1870* (London, 1973), pp. 112, 335–37.

75. Simon Ville, *Transport and the Development of the European Economy, 1750–1918* (Basingstoke, 1991), p. 43.

76. Pollard, *Peaceful Conquest,* p. 3.

77. See M. W. Flinn, *History of the Coal Industry,* ii, *1700–1830* (Oxford, 1984).

78. Crompton, *The Role of Canals,* p. 18.

79. Vance, *Capturing the Horizon,* p. 101.

80. Pleasure cruising on Britain's canals is not new. In June 1822 a Somerset vicar

hired a coal barge on the nearby Somerset Coal Canal, 'to convey the ladies to Combe Hay' (south of Bath). John Skinner, *Journal of a Somerset Rector, 1803–1834*, ed. Howard and Peter Coombs (Oxford, 1984), p. 190.

81. www. canaljunction. com

Notes to Chapter 2: Coastal Shipping

1. T. S. Willan, *River Navigation in England, 1600–1750* (London, 1964), p. 4.
2. John Armstrong, 'Introduction: The Cinderella of the Transport World: The Historiography of the British Coastal Trade', John Armstrong (ed.), *Coastal and Short Sea Shipping: Studies in Transport History* (Aldershot, 1996), p. xv.
3. One effect of this was that insurance costs were higher than for road transport, Gerard Turnbull, 'Scotch Linen, Stores, Wars and Privateers', *Journal of Transport History*, third series (1982), p. 62.
4. Armstrong, 'The Cinderella of the Transport World', p. xiii.
5. T. S. Ashton, *An Economic History of England: The Eighteenth Century* (London, 1964), p. 71.
6. Robert Tomlinson, 'Essay on Manning the Royal Navy', *Publications of the Navy Records Society*, 74, pp. 129–30, quoted Ashton, *An Economic History of England*, p. 70.
7. T. S. Willan, *The English Coasting Trade* (Manchester, 1967), p. 61.
8. For a study of Wiggins Key and the lighterage business in late seventeenth-century London, John Chartres, 'Trade and Shipping in the Port of London: Wiggins Key in the Later Seventeenth Century', *Journal of Transport History*, third series, 1 (1980), pp. 29–47.
9. *The Kentish Companion for the Year of Our Lord 1792* (1792), p. 160.
10. J. Swift, 'Hollyhead Journal', in H. Davis (ed.), *Jonathan Swift: Miscellaneous and Autobiographical Pieces, Fragments and Marginalia* (1962). p. 201.
11. John Armstrong, 'Government Regulation in the British Shipping Industry, 1830–1913: The Role of the Coastal Sector', Lena Andersson-Skog and Olle Krantz (ed.), *Institutions in the Transport and Communications Industries* (Canton, Massachusetts, 1999), p. 163.
12. R. P. Cruden, *The History of the Town of Gravesend in the County of Kent and of the Port of London* (1843), p. 484; *An Account of the Origin of Steamboats in Spain, Great Britain and America* (1831), p. 74; *Herapath's Railway Journal*, 28 May 1842, p. 535.
13. S. Middlebrook, *Newcastle on Tyne: Its Growth and Achievement* (1968), p. 184. W. Featherstone, 'How Steam Came to the Tyne', *Sea Breezes*, January 1965.
14. G. Chandler, *Liverpool Shipping* (1960), p. 50; A. C. Wardle, 'Early Steamships on the Mersey, 1815–20', *Transactions of the Historical Society of Lancashire and Cheshire*, 92 (1940), p. 85.
15. D. B. McNeill, *Irish Passenger Steamship Services*, i, *North of Ireland* (1969), p. 21.
16. *Edinburgh Evening Courant*, 25 June and 2 July 1821.
17. *Edinburgh Evening Courant*, 21 May 1821.

18. R. N. Worth, *History of Plymouth* (1890), p. 341.

19. W. I. Barry, *History of the Port of Cork Steam Navigation* (1915).

20. P. S. Bagwell, 'The Post Office Steam Packets, 1821–36, and the Development of Shipping on the Irish Sea', *Maritime History*, 1 (1971), D. B. McNeill, *Irish Passenger Steamship Services*, ii, *South of Ireland* (1971), pp. 13–21.

21. *Herapath's Railway Magazine*, 24 July 1841, p. 623.

22. Estimates are based on manuscript minutes of evidence of thirty-nine railway and harbour Bills, but principally the London & Cambridge, London & York, Bristol & Exeter, Edinburgh & Northern Glasgow, Kilmarnock & Ayr railways kept in the House of Lords Record Office. Figure for 1849 Edinburgh-London traffic taken from J. Thomas, *The North British Railway*, i (1969), p. 43.

23. *New Statistical Account of Scotland*, vi (1845), p. 202.

24. *Edinburgh Evening Courant*, 13 August, 3 September 1832.

25. J. Grant, *Old and New Edinburgh*, n.d., p. 211.

26. Post Office Records, packet 549/D (1828).

27. E. E. Allen, 'On the Comparative Cost of Transit by Steam and Sailing Colliers and on the Different Modes of Ballasting', *Proceedings of the Institute of Civil Engineers*, 14 (1854–55), p. 318.

28. *Edinburgh Evening Courant*, 5 January 1846, 1 January 1849; *Edinburgh Courant*, 1 January 1885.

29. Gloucester Record Office, House of Commons Select Committee on the South Wales and Great Western Direct Railway Bill, 22 May 1865, Minutes of Evidence of W. West, agent for Risca Colliery. Cardiff Chamber of Commerce, *Annual Reports*. C. Hadfield, *Canals of South Wales and the Border* (1960), p. 26.

30. House of Lords Record Office, Minutes of Evidence of House of Commons Select Committee on and Cambridge Railway, evidence of Thomas Evans, meat salesman, 18 April 1836, and Robert Herbert, agricultural reporter, 20 April 1836. G. Channon, 'The Aberdeenshire Beef Trade with London: A Study in Steamship and Railway Competition', *Transport History*, 2, March 1969; 1. W. MacCombie, *Cattle and Cattle Breeders* (1886), pp. 72–73, 82.

31. James Wilson, A *Voyage Round the Coasts of Scotland and the Isles*, i (1842), p. 56.

32. Numbers of Livestock Shipped from Ireland to Great Britain, *Parliamentary Papers* (1833), v, p. 630 (1870), lxi, p. 110.

33. G. R. Porter, *The Progress of the Nation* (1851), p. 344.

34. Freda Harcourt, 'Charles Wye Williams and Irish Steam Shipping, 1820–50', *Journal of Transport History*, third series, 13 (1992), p. 149.

35. Allen, *On the Comparative Cost of Transit by Steam and Sailing Colliers*, p. 321.

36. Journal of RMSP *Prince Arthur*, National Library of Ireland, MS 2818.

37. H. Benham, *Last Stronghold of Sail* (1948), p. 112.

38. Armstrong explores the reasons for this neglect in 'The Cinderella of the Transport World', pp. ix–xiii.

39. *Parliamentary Papers* (1843), lii, pp. 384–85, 398–99. Trade and Navigation Accounts, Board of Trade (Marine Library).

40. A liner is a ship which runs on a regular route to a published timetable. A tramp is a ship without a regular route which picks up cargoes where and when it can.

41. Royal Commission Canals and Inland Waterways, 4th Report, *Parliamentary Papers* (1910), xii, paras 293–94.

42. London Guildhall Library, MS 1667/123.

43. F. G. G. Carr, *Sailing Barges* (2nd edn, 1951), pp. 8–11; H. Benham, *Down Tops'l* (1951), p. 47.

44. T. Gray, 'Fifty Years of Legislation in Relation to the Shipping Trade and the Safety of Ships and Seamen', in Worshipful Company of Shipwrights, *Lectures at the Mansion House, 1886–7* (1887), p. 171.

45. S. Middlebrook, *Newcastle on Tyne: Its Growth and Achievement* (1968), p. 194. Earlier improvements in the area are examined in A. G. Kenwood, 'Capital Investment in Docks, Harbours and River Improvements in North-East England, 1825–50', *Journal of Transport History*, new series, 1 (1971).

46. J. Guthrie, *The River Tyne: Its History and Resources* (1880).

47. Middlebrook, *Newcastle on Tyne*, p. 235.

48. Anon., *Tales, Traditions and Antiquities of Leith* (1865), p. 322. Leith Dock Commission, *The Port of Leith* (1966).

49. J. W. Burrows, *Southend on Sea and District: Historical Notes* (1909), p. 180. House of Lords Record Office, Minutes of Evidence of House of Commons Select Committee on Southend Pier Bill, May 1835. Evidence of T. Ingram, waterman of Southend.

50. *Select Committee on Taxation of Internal Communication*, Minutes of Evidence, *Parliamentary Papers*, 1837, xx, evidence of Sir John Hall, Bart, question 321.

51. Petition of Mail Coach Contractors and Stage Coach Proprietors on the Great North Road (1838).

52. John Armstrong, 'Freight Pricing Policy in Coastal Liner Companies before the First World War', *Journal of Transport History*, third series, 10 (1989), p. 180.

53. Armstrong, *Government Regulation in the British Shipping Industry*, p. 154–55.

54. J. S. Maclean, *The Newcastle and Carlisle Railway* (1948), pp. 10, 24.

55. J. Graeme Bruce, 'The Contribution of Cross-Channel and Coastal Vessels to Developments in Marine Practice', *Journal of Transport History*, first series, 4 (1959), p. 65.

56. Bruce, 'The Contribution of Cross-Channel and Coastal Vessels to Developments', p. 67.

57. Committee of Privy Council for Trade, Report on Steam Vessels Enquiry, House of Lords Sessional Papers (1839), v, p. 25.

58. Omissions in the 1846 Act were partly made good by the Steam Navigation Act of 1848, the Mercantile Marine Act of 1850 and further legislation in 1851. D. O'Neill, 'Safety at Sea, 1850–1950', *Transactions of the Institute of Marine Engineers*, 62 (1950).

59. John Armstrong, 'The Role of Coastal Shipping in UK Transport: An Estimate

of Comparative Traffic Movements in 1910', *Journal of Transport History*, third series, 8 (1987), pp. 164–70.

60. John Armstrong, 'Climax and Climacteric: The British Coastal Trade, 1870–1930', D. J. Starkey and A. G. Jamieson (eds), *Exploiting the Sea: Aspects of Britain's Maritime Economy since 1870* (Exeter, 1998), pp. 37–58.

61. H. J. Dyos and D. H. Aldcroft, *British Transport: An Economic Survey from the Seventeenth Century to the Twentieth* (Harmondsworth, 1974), p. 311.

Notes to Chapter 3: Road Transport before the Car

1. B. R. Mitchell, *European Historical Statistics, 1250–1970* (1975), p. 24, B. R. Mitchell and P. Deane, *Abstract of British Historical Statistics* (1962), p. 5.

2. Mitchell and Deane, *Abstract*, p. 189.

3. P. Ambrose, *The Quiet Revolution: Social Change in a Sussex Village, 1871–1971* (1974), p. 26.

4. S. Bamford, *Passages in the Life of a Radical*, ed. H. Dunkley (1893), vol. 2.

5. G. L. Turnbull, 'Provincial Road Carrying in England in the Eighteenth Century', in D. Gerhold, *Road Transport in the Horse-Drawn Era* (1996), pp. 44–55.

6. B. Kerr, *Bound to the Soil* (1968), p. 85.

7. B. Austen, 'The Impact of the Mail Coach on Public Coach Services in England', in Gerhold, *Road Transport*, p. 207.

8. P. S. Bagwell, *The Transport Revolution, 1770–1985* (1988), p. 43.

9. D. Copeland, *Roads and their Traffic* (1993), p. 93.

10. D. Mountfield, *The Coaching Age* (1976), p. 60.

11. D. Austen, 'The Impact of the Mail Coach on Public Coach Services in England and Wales, 1784–1840', in Gerhold, *Road Transport*, p. 210.

12. Mountfield, *The Coaching Age*, p. 65.

13. Austen, *Impact of the Mail Coach*, p. 211.

14. Flora Thompson, *Lark Rise to Candleford* (1973), p. 18.

15. T. S. Ashton, *An Economic History of England: The Eighteenth Century* (1955), pp. 70, 78.

16. T. S. Ashton, *An Eighteenth-Century Industrialist: Peter Stubs of Warrington* (1939), pp. 86–88.

17. G. L. Turnbull 'Scotch Linen, Storms, Wars and Privateers: John Wilson and Son, Leeds Linen Merchants, 1754–1800', in Gerhold, *Road Transport*, pp. 25–44.

18. G. L. Turnbull, 'Provincial Road Carrying in the Eighteenth Century', in Gerhold, *Road Transport*, pp. 25–48.

19. The above account of the Exeter-London carrier trade is based on Dorian Gerhold, *Road Transport before the Railways: Russell's London Flying Wagons* (1993).

20. Gerhold, *Road Transport before the Railways*, p. 60.

21. Select Committee Appointed for the Purpose of Ascertaining how far the Formation of Railroads May Affect the Interests of the Turnpike Trusts and the Creditors of Such Trusts (1839), questions 40–47 and 132–48.

22. Ibid., p. 271.

23. Professor Alan Everitt and his team of researchers in the early 1970s were sure that they did. See Alan Everitt, 'Country Carriers in the Seventeenth Century', *Journal of Transport History*, second series, 3 (1976), pp. 179–202.

24. Ibid.

25. R. D. Blackmore, *Cripps the Carrier* (1886), p. 182.

26. M. J. Freeman, 'The Carrier System in South Hampshire', *Journal of Transport History*, second series, 4 (1977), pp. 61–85.

27. See the illustration of the Gloucestershire newspaper vendor in G. Mingay *The Victorian Countryside*, i (1981), p. 146.

28. P. S. Bagwell, 'The Decline of Rural Isolation'. in Mingay, *The Victorian Countryside*, p. 15.

29. B. Weinreb and C. Hibbert, *The London Encyclopedia* (1992), entry 'Smithfield Market', p. 812.

30. House of Commons Select Committee on Turnpike Trusts: Minutes of Evidence (1836).

31. W. Albert, *The Turnpike System in England and Wales, 1665–1840* (1972), pp. 14–22.

32. Albert, *Turnpike System*, pp. 30, 41, 42, 50 and 55.

33. Select Committee 1839, Report, p. 721.

34. B. and S. Webb, *The Story of the King's Highway* (1913), p. 125.

35. Lords' Committee to Examine Turnpike Returns (1833), p. 703.

36. T. Barker and M. Robbins, *A History of London Transport*, i (1963), p. 13.

37. Toll Reform Association, *Petition, Statement and Opinion on Metropolitan Turnpikes* (1848).

38. First Report of the Select Committee on the Road from London to Holyhead, 2 March 1819, p. 5.

39. Fifth Report Select Committee on the Road from London to Holyhead, 6 July 1819.

40. L. T. C. Rolt, *Thomas Telford* (1935).

41. Robert H. Spirpo Jr, 'John Loudon, M. McAdam and the Metropolital Turnpike Trust', *Journal of Economic History*, 2 (1956).

42. Barker and Robbins, *History of London Transport*, pp. 120, 122.

43. HMSO, *The Post Office* (1911), p. 12.

44. R. Watson and M. Gray, *The Penguin Book of the Bicycle* (1978), pp. 22–23.

Notes to Chapter 4: The Growth of the Railways

1. B. R. Mitchell, *British Historical Statistics* (1988), p. 247.

2. Mitchell, *British Historical Statistics*, pp. 305–6.

3. J. U. Nef, *The Rise of the British Coal Industry* (19); i, p. 247; M. J. F. Lewis, *Early Wooden Rialways* (1970), p. 90.

4. Lewis, *Early Wooden Railways*, p. 87.

5. H. Dickinson and A. Tilley, *Trevithick, the Engineer and the Man* (1934), p. 57.

6. *Enterprise: The Stockton and Darlington Railway, 1821–1863* (1993), p. 40. There is reproduction of the seal on p. 21.

7. Ibid., p. 2.

8. Ibid., pp. 67–68.

9. Ibid., p. 67.

10. M. W. Kirby, 'Stockton and Darlington Railway', in J. Simmons and G. Briddle (eds), *The Oxford Companion to British Railway History* (1997), p. 478.

11. W. T. Jackman, *The Development of Transportation in Modern England* (1962), p. 514–17.

12. Ronald Thomas, 'Liverpool and Manchester Railway', and Jack Simmons 'Excursion Train', in Simmons and Biddle, *The Oxford Companion to British Railway History* pp. 272–73 and 149–51.

13. Select Committee of the Amalgamation of Railway Companies (1872), xiii, p. xvii; Mitchell, *British Historical Statistics*, pp. 545–46.

14. Select Committee on Railways (1844), Minutes of Evidence, x, answer to question 1831.

15. Select Committee Appointed to Join with a Committee of the Lords to enquire into the subject of the Amalgamation of Railway Companies, Report, p. iii, BPP Committee Reports, xiii, pt l, sessions 6 February 1872 to 10 August 1872.

16. Select Committee on Communication by Railway, Second Report, 1839–40, *Parliamentary Paper* (1839), 517, p. vii.

17. H. G. Lewin, *The Railway Mania and its Aftermath* (1969), p. 1.

18. D. Alderman, *The Railway Interest* (1977), pp. 25–26.

19. Commons, *Hansard*, 3rd series, vol. lxxvi, 3 July 1844, col 484 Alderman, *Railway Interest*, p 17.

20. W. Galt, *Railway Reform* (1865), pp. xi–xiii.

21. Royal Commission on Railways, *Report, BPP*, 1867, xxxviii, p. 1.

22. Select Committee on Railways (1839), *Parliamentary Papers*, 1839, Minutes of Evidence, x, answer to question 5844.

23. *Hansard*, 5 February 1844, cols 246–54.

24. Enacted as 7/8 Victoria, cap. 85, 9 August 1844.

25. Report, Select Committee (1872), p. xvii.

26. W. E. Simnett, *Railway Amalgamation in Great Britain* (1923), p. 5.

27. Royal Commission on Railways (1865–67), Report p. xxi and p. 536, question 9899.

28. Charles Hadfield, *British Canals* (1950), p. 192.

29. Select Committee, Minutes of Evidence, 25 April 1872, question 3696.

30. Report, Select Committee (1872), p. xix.

31. John Armstrong, 'The Role of Coastal Shipping in UK Transport: An Estimate of Comparative Transport Movements in 1910', *Journal of Transport History*, third series, 8 (1987).

32. D. Rowland, *British Railways Wagons* (1985), p. 9.

33. T. C. Barker and C. I. Savage, *An Economic History of Transport in Britain* (1974), p. 74.

34. J. Simmons, *The Victorian Railway* (1991), chapter 3, 'The Pursuit of Reliability'.
35. Simmons and Biddle, *The Oxford Companion to British Railway History*, pp. 39–42.
36. Railway Companies' Association, meetings 22 February, 2 March 1899, *Minutes*, 2247 and 2257.
37. P. S. Bagwell, *The Railwaymen*, i (1963), chapter 4, 'A Chapter of Accidents'.
38. *Parliamentary Papers* (1899), vol. lxxxv, p. 695. Memorandum upon the use of automatic coupling on railway stock with special refeence to American experience.
39. J. Foreman-Peck and R. Millward, *Public and Private Ownership in British Industry, 1820–1990* (1994), p. 15.
40. Noted by, among others, E. A. Pratt, in *Railways and their Rates* (1905), pp. 91–97.
41. G. R. Hawke, *Railways and Economic Growth in England and Wales* (1970), p. 53. D. H. Aldcroft in 1972 put the estimate of economic and social saving as high as 10 per cent, arguing that in Hawke's analysis no evaluation was made of productive time savings as a result of faster travel by train. D. H. Aldcroft, 'Railways and Economic Growth: A Review Article', *Journal of Transport History*, 1 (1972), p. 238.
42. John B. Edmondson, *The Early History of the Railway Ticket*, Lancashire and Cheshire Antiquarian Society, Manchester (1968); Michael Farr, 'Thomas Edmondson', in *The Oxford Companion to British Railway History* (1997), p 141; *The Times*, 5 March 1984.
43. P. Bagwell, *The Railway Clearing House in the British Economy, 1842–1922* (1968), pp. 33–47, 114.
44. J. Simmons, *The Victorian Railway* (1991), p. 347.
45. C. A. Saunders, the Secretary of the Great Western Railway, asserted that the magnetic telegraph simplified the working of the railway, 'diminishing the need for stock of every variety'. Select Committee on Communication by Railway, Minutes of Evidence, 6 February 1840, question 366. See also J. Kieve, *The Electric Telegraph* (1973); R. D. Foster, 'Electric Telegraph' in *Oxford Companion to British Railway History* (1977), p. 502.
46. Select Committee on Railway Communication, 25 February 1840, question 2476.
47. Simmons, *The Victorian Railway*, p. 228.
48. A. Clinton, *Post Office Workers: A Trade Union and Social History* (1984), p. 36.
49. Alderman, *The Railway Interest*, p 20.
50. Foreman-Peck and Millward, *Public and Private Ownership*, p. 14.
51. See the account of each of these companies in Simmons and Biddle, *Companion to Railway History*.
52. Report of the Departmental Committee of the Board of Trade on Railway Agreements and Amalgamations (1911), Cmd 5631.
53. Select Committee on Amalgamation of Railway Companies (1872), appendix N, p. 835.

54. J. S. Didgson, 'Privatising Britain's Railways: Lessons from the Past', University of Liverpool Discussion Paper in Economics, 59 (1989), cited in Foreman-Peck and Millward, *Public and Private Ownership*, p. 88.
55. P. J. Cain, 'Railways, 1870–1914: The Maturity of the Private System', in M. J. Freeman and D. H. Aldcroft (eds), *Transport in Victorian Britain* (1988), pp. 108–117.
56. T. R. Gourvish, *Railways in the British Economy, 1830–1914* (1980), pp. 52ff.

Notes to Chapter 5: British Railways, 1914–1945

1. E. H. Dixon and J. H. Parmelee, *War Administration of the Railways in the United States and Great Britain* (1918), p. 106.
2. E. A. Pratt, *British Railways and the Great War* (1921), i, p. 75.
3. R. G. K. Ensor, *England, 1810–1914* (1952), p. 435.
4. Dixon and Parmelee, *War Administration*, p. 106; Pratt, *British Railways*, p. 41.
5. Pratt, *British Railways*, ii, p. 1147. *Hansard*, 141, 3 May 1921, col. 941, speech of Colonel Newman.
6. *Hansard*, 3 May 1921, cols 921–22.
7. Pratt, *British Railways*, i, pp. 126–31.
8. B. R. Mitchell, *British Historical Statistics* (1998), p. 726.
9. Pratt, *British Railways*, i, p. 142.
10. Dixon and Parmelee, *War Administration*, p. 117.
11. E. Larkin and J. G. Larkin, *The Railway Workshops of Britain, 1823–1988* (1983), p. 173.
12. Select Committee on Transport (1918), Minutes of Evidence, questions 746, 753.
13. Ibid., question 753.
14. Ibid., questions 825, 889.
15. Ibid., question 1043.
16. Ibid., questions 1534, 1535.
17. Bs Ref 1/4 Report of the Select Committee on Transport, para. 14.
18. Keith Grieves, *Sir Eric Geddes: Business and Government in War and Peace* (1987), p. 12.
19. Ibid., p. 33.
20. Ibid., p. 70.
21. *Hansard*, 24 February 1919, col. 1822.
22. *Hansard*, 24 February 1919, cols 1824, 1816.
23. PRO, MT 45/ 234.
24. PRO, MT 45/234.
25. PRO, MT 45/235.
26. P. B. Johnson, *Land Fit for Heroes* (1968), p. 42.
27. *Hansard*, 5th series, 117, 1 July 1919, col. 2121.
28. D. H. Aldcroft, *British Railways in Transition* (1968), p. 40.
29. Grieves, *Sir Eric Geddes*, p. 76.

30. A. K. Cline, 'Eric Geddes and the Experiment of Businessmen in Government', in K. D. Brown (ed.), *Essays in Anti-Labour History* (1974), p. 92.

31. Cmd, p. 787 (1920).

32. *Hansard*, 24 June 1920.

33. This railway map only gives a general impression. For more detail on the division of territories, see Ian Allan Ltd, *British Railway Maps of Yesteryear* (n.d.), pp. 36–38, 48, 52–56, 58–59.

34. C. Channon, Introduction to *Railways*, ii (1996), p. xvii.

35. P. Butterfield, 'Grouping, Pooling and Competition: The Passenger Policy of the London and North Easteren Railway, 1923–39', *Journal of Transport History*, third series, 8 (1985), pp. 21–47.

36. Aldcroft, *British Railways in Transition*, table 6, p. 50.

37. Quoted in *The Railway Magazine*, February 1998, p. 17.

38. Select Committee on Transport, 2nd Report (1918); Butterfield, *Grouping, Pooling and Competition*, p. 22.

39. Select Committee on Transport, 2nd Report, p. 28.

40. D. L. Munby, *Inland Transport Statistics Great Britain* (1978), table A22, p. 117.

41. Aldcroft, *British Railways in Transition*, p. 60.

42. K. H. Johnston, *British Railways and Economic Recovery* (1949), cited in Foreman-Peck and Millward, *Public and Private Ownership*, p. 248.

43. M. R. Bonavia, *The Four Great Railways* (1980), p. 99.

44. Foreman-Peck and Millward, *Public and Private Ownership*, p. 244.

45. Philip Bagwell, *The Railwaymen*, i (1963), pp. 511–13, 545–52.

46. Johnson and Long, *British Railways Engineering, 1948–1980* (1981), p. 17. Aldcroft, *British Railways in Transition*, pp. 73–74.

47. G. Channon, 'The Great Western Railway under the British Railways Act of 1921', *Business History Review*, 55 (1981).

48. G. Channon, *The Great Western Railway*, pp. 207, 211–212.

49. P. S. Bagwell, *Doncaster, 1853–1990: Town of Train Makers* (1991), p. 55.

50. J. Elliot and M. Esau, *On and Off the Rails* (1982); Bonavia, *Four Great Railways*, chap. 5.

51. Munby, *Inland Transport Statistics*, table 10, p. 55.

52. Bonavia, *Four Great Railways*, p. 131.

53. G. Crompton, 'Efficient and Economic Working: The Performance of the Railway Companies, 1923–33', *Business History*, 28 (1985), p. 228.

54. *Railway Gazette*, 10 February 1928.

55. H. J. Dyos and D. H. Aldcroft, *British Transport* (1969), pp. 318–19.

56. R. Bell, *History of British Railways during the War 1939–45* (1946), p. 5.

57. Bonavia, *Four Great Railways*, p. 187.

58. Bagwell, *Doncaster*, p. 67.

59. Aldcroft, *British Railways in Transition*, table 14, p. 99.

60. Ibid., p. 102.

Notes to Chapter 6: Motor Transport

1. T. C. Barker, editor's preface to *The Economic and Social Effects of the Spread of Motor Vehicles* (1987), p. ix. Professor Barker's substational introduction to this collection of essays is an invaluable aid to an understanding of the early development of motor transport and is used extensively in the first few paragraphs of this chapter.

2. R. Watson and M. Gray, *The Penguin Book of the Bicycle* (1978), chap. 4; C. F. Caunter, *History and Development of Cycles*, HMSO (1958).

3. Cited in T. R. Nicholson, *The Birth of the British Motor Car*, ii (1982), p. 186.

4. Barker, *The Economic and Social Effects of the Spread of Motor Vehicles*, p. 8.

5. C. F. Caunter, *Motor Cycles* (3rd edn, 1982), p. 1.

6. S. Koerner, 'The British Motor Cycle Industry during the 1930s', in M. Walshled, *Motor Transport* (1997), p. 101.

7. Ixion (of the *Motor Cycle*), *Further Motor Cycle Reminiscences: Being the Impressions of Thirty Years and Three Hundred Thousand Miles on the Road* (1928).

8. K. Richardson, *The British Motor Industry, 1896–1939* (1977), chap. 1.

9. Cited in Barker, *The Economic and Social Effects of the Spread of Motor Vehicles*, p. 18.

10. Ibid., p. 20.

11. Lady Troubridge and Archibald Marshall, *Lord Montagu of Beaulieu: A Memoir* (1985), pp. 81–84.

12. *Hansard*, fourth series, vol. 126, col. 1502.

13. *Hansard*, fourth series, vol. 126, col. 1505.

14. Royal Commission on Motor Cars, 23 November 1905, 10174–10215, 1906, xlviii.

15. Ibid., questions 12420–12448 and 1250–12580.

16. Ibid., questions 10047–10152.

17. Ibid., questions 82, 87, 170. For the subsequent history of the road lobby, see Mick Hamer, *Wheels within Wheels* (1987), chap. 3, and William Plowden, *The Motor Car and Politics, 1896–1970* (1971).

18. Royal Commission, questions 254, 285, 286, 535–36, 644.

19. *Hansard*, fifth series (1909), vol. 4, cols 496–98.

20. Ibid., col. 503. The new and raised taxes produced £600,000 a year initially, E. C. K. Ensor, *England, 1870–1914* (1936), p. 414.

21. J. B. F. Earle, *A Century of Road Materials: The History of the Roadstone Division of Tarmac Ltd* (1971), pp. xiv–xv.

22. B. R. Mitchell, *Abstract of British Historical Statistics* (1962), p. 230.

23. K. Grahame, *The Wind in the Willows* (1908), pp. 38, 42.

24. C. Wilson and W. J. Reader, *Men and Machines: A History of Napier and Sons Engineers Ltd, 1808–1958* (1958), p. 67.

25. Corinne Mulley, 'The Background to Bus Regulation in the 1930 Road Traffic Act: Economic, Political and Personal Influence in the 1920s', in M. Walsh (ed.), *Motor Transport* (1997), p. 125.

26. Record of a Meeting of the Board of Trade Advisory Council, 17 February 1928, Public Record Office, CP 49/28 in CAB 24/192.

27. PRO, CO 39 (28), in CAB 24/192.

28. Terms of Reference of Royal Commission on Transport (1928).

29. Royal Commission on Transport, Minutes of Evidence, memo no. 9 (1929).

30. Ibid., memo, no. 10 (1929).

31. Ibid., memo, no. 7. (1929).

32. Ibid., memo, question 1772 (1929).

33. Ibid., memo no 24, 20 March 1929.

34. BS 43/27, Cmd 3757 1931.

35. Royal Commission on Transport, minutes of evidence, question 4863.

36. Ibid., Report, para 5.

37. P. J. Pybus, 'Transport Policy', PRO, CAB 24/232, CP 286 (32).

38. The estimate is Peter Scott's, see 'The Growth of Road Haulage, 1921–58', *Journal of Transport History*, 19 (1998), p. 138.

39. This was the somewhat exaggerated view of George Glasgow, *General Strike and Road Transport*, preface by David Lloyd George (1926), p. 17.

40. D. G. Rhys, 'Concentration in the Inter-War Motor Industry', Walsh (ed.), *Motor Transport*, p. 67.

41. Mitchell, *Abstract of British Historical Statistics*, p. 230.

42. James Foreman-Peck, 'Death on the Roads: Changing National Response to Motor Accidents', in Barker, *The Economic and Social Effects of the Spread of Motor Vehicles*, p. 265.

   In the 1920s and early 1980s environmentalists were concerned about the danger to fish life in streams, especially those which flow over chalk, from the spraying of nearby road surfaces with liquid tar, although this threat was removed when a new product, Brotex, was discovered and tested in 1936–37.

43. G. L. Turnbull, *Traffic and Transport: An Economic History of Pickfords* (1979), p. 26.

44. J. Hibbs, *The History of British Bus Services* (2nd edn, 1989), p. 18.

45. Ibid.

46. Select Committee on Transport, Minutes of Evidence, 16 October 1918, question 1455.

47. Mulley, *The Background to Bus Regulation*, pp. 134–35.

48. Royal Commission on Transport, Minutes of Evidence, Sir Henry Maybury, Director-General of Roads, Ministry of Transport, 16 November 1928, question 787.

49. T. C. Barker and C. I. Savage, *An Economic History of Transport in Britain* (3rd edn, 1974), p. 182.

50. Hibbs, *The History of British Bus Services*, fig. 3, p. 122. See also Rhys, 'Concentration in the Inter-War Motor Industry'.

Notes to Chapter 7: Urban Transport

1. Most recently, John Armstrong, 'Transport', in Philip Waller (ed.), *The English Urban Landscape* (Oxford, 2000), p. 213.
2. T. C. Barker, 'Urban Transport', in M. J. Freeman and D. H. Aldcroft (eds), *Transport in Victorian Britain* (Manchester, 1988), pp. 142–43.
3. G. A. Sekon, *Locomotion in Victorian London* (London, New York, 1938), p. 8.
4. Ibid., p. 9.
5. W. J. Passingham, *The Romance of London's Underground* (London, 1932), p. 5.
6. Sekon, *Locomotion in Victorian London*, p. 81.
7. T. C. Barker and R. M. Robbins, *A History of London Transport: Passenger Travel and the Development of the Metropolis*, i, *The Nineteenth Century* (London, 1963), pp. 4–39, 56–98.
8. Sekon, *Locomotion in Victorian London*, p. 33.
9. Barker and Robbins, *A History of London Transport*, pp. 59, 98.
10. Herbert Morrison, *Socialisation and Transport* (London, 1933), pp. 14–15.
11. Michael F. Collins and Timothy M. Pharaoh, *Transport Organisation in a Great City: The Case of London* (London, 1974), p. 24.
12. Ralph Turvey, 'Road and Bridge Tolls in Nineteenth-Century London', *Journal of Transport History*, third series, 17 (1996), p. 150.
13. Ibid., p. 155.
14. Ibid., p. 159.
15. Quoted in Philip S. Bagwell, *The Transport Revolution, 1770–1985* (London, 1974), p. 123.
16. John R. Kellet, *The Impact of Railways on Victorian Cities* (London, 1969), pp. 354–65.
17. T. C. Barker, *Moving Millions: A Pictorial History of London Transport*, London Transport Museum (1990), p. 20.
18. Barker and Robbins, *A History of London Transport*, pp. 44–52, 99–165.
19. Ibid., p. 58.
20. Michael Barke, 'The Middle-Class Journey to Work in Newcastle upon Tyne, 1850–1913', *Journal of Transport History*, third series, 12 (1991), p. 121.
21. Collins and Pharaoh, *Transport Organisation in a Great City*, p. 25.
22. Sekon, *Locomotion in Victorian London*, p. 179.
23. The fifteen termini and their railway company owners were Paddington (Great Western Railway), Marylebone (Great Central Railway), Euston (London & North Western Railway), St Pancras (Midland Railway), King's Cross (Great Northern Railway), Broad Street, Liverpool Street (Great Eastern Railway), Fenchurch Street (London, Tilbury & Southend Railway), Cannon Street (South Eastern Railway), London Bridge (London, Brighton & South Coast Railway), Blackfriars and Holborn (London, Chatham and Dover Railway), Charing Cross (South Eastern Railway), Waterloo (London & South Western Railway) and Victoria (London, Brighton & South Coast Railway, and London,

Chatham and Dover Railway). Only Holborn (now known as City Thameslink) lies within the Circle Line area.

24. Brunel's tunnel was opened in 1842 after a long struggle to get it completed. For a recent account see Martin Worth, *Sweat and Inspiration: Pioneers of the Industrial Age* (Stroud, 1999), pp 102–7.

25. Arthur Elton, *British Railways* (London, 1945), p. 38.

26. Michael Reilly, 'Promoting the Subway: New York's Experience in an International Context, 1890–1914', *Journal of Transport History*, third series, 13 (1992), pp. 101, 104.

27. Quoted in Passingham, *The Romance of London's Underground*, p. 52.

28. The traction motors were distributed along the length of the train in the system devised by Frank J. Sprague, a control mechanism transmitted low voltage current to each of the individual motors. Michael Robbins, 'The Early Years of Electric Traction: Invention, Development, Exploitation', *Journal of Transport History*, 21 (2000), p. 98.

29. Reilly, *Promoting the Subway: New York's Experience in an International Context*, pp. 111–12.

30. T. C. Barker and Michael Robbins, *A History of London Transport*, ii (London, 1965), pp. 75–84.

31. Christian Barman, *The Man Who Built London Transport: A Biography of Frank Pick* (Newton Abbot, 1979), p. 27.

32. Introduction, in Stephen Glaister (ed.), *Transport Options for London*, Greater London Group, LSE (London, 1991), p. 3.

33. John P. McKay, *Tramways and Trolleys: The Rise of Urban Mass Transport in Europe* (Princeton, 1976), p. 218.

34. Craig R. Semsel, 'More than an Ocean Apart: The Street Railways of Cleveland and Birmingham, 1880–1911', *Journal of Transport History*, third series, 22 (2001), p. 48.

35. For cable and steam variants, see R. J. Buckley, *History of Tramways from Horse to Rapid Transit* (Newton Abbot, 1975), p. 26–44.

36. For Sprague's contribution to electric traction, see Robbins, *Early Years of Electric Traction*, pp. 92–101; Buckley, *History of Tramways*, pp. 59–62.

37. Robbins, *Early Years of Electric Traction*, pp. 93, 96; McKay, *Tramways and Trolleys*, pp. 50–51; Barker and Robbins, *History of London Transport*, i, pp. 296–300; ii, pp. 15–34.

38. McKay, *Tramways and Trolleys*, pp. 163–66. The British made considerable efforts to beautify their tram wire installations, see Semsel, 'More than an Ocean Apart: The Street Railways of Cleveland and Birmingham', pp. 51–52.

39. Barker and Robbins, *History of London Transport*, i, p. 179.

40. Ibid., p. 263.

41. Kerry Hamilton and Stephen Potter, *Losing Track* (London, 1985), p. 73.

42. McKay, *Tramways and Trolleys*, p. 69.

43. The longest tram route length was the North Metropolitan with fifty miles;

the shortest was the Highgate Hill with under one mile. Sekon, *Locomotion in Victorian London*, p. 107.

44. Hamilton and Potter, *Losing Track*, p. 72.
45. Morrison, *Socialisation and Transport*, pp. 12–13.
46. 'Metrolink Beats Patronage Forecast and Cuts 1m Car Journeys a Year', *Local Transport Today*, 20 January 1994.
47. Edwin Pratt, *A History of Inland Transport and Commerce in England* (London, 1912), p. 487.
48. Details from Vernon Sommerfield, *London Transport: A Record and a Survey*, London Transport (1934).
49. Morrison, *Socialisation and Transport*, pp. 20–21; Jack Simmons, *Transport* (London, 1962), p. 63.
50. The LPTB lasted until the establishment of the British Transport Commission in 1948.
51. K. J. Button, *The Economics of Urban Transport* (Farnborough, 1977), p. 57.
52. J. Michael Thomson, *Motorways in London: Report of a Working Party*, London Amenity and Transport Association (London, 1969), p. 15.
53. Hamilton and Potter, *Losing Track*, p. 106
54. Collins and Pharaoh, *Transport Organisation in a Great City*, p. 516.
55. Hugh McClintock, 'Post-War Traffic Planning and Special Provision for the Bicycle', in Hugh McClintock, *The Bicycle and City Traffic: Principle and Practice* (London, 1992), p. 20.
56. Ibid., p. 23.
57. Sean O'Connell, *The Car and British Society: Class, Gender and Motoring, 1896–1939* (Manchester, 1998), pp. 138–39.
58. Colin D. Buchanan, *Mixed Blessing: The Motor in Britain* (London, 1958), p. 190.
59. Ministry of Transport, *Traffic in Towns: A Study of the Long-Term Problems of Traffic in Urban Areas* (Buchanan Report) (London, 1963).
60. Tim Pharaoh and Dieter Apel, *Transport Concepts in European Cities* (Aldershot, 1995), pp. 41–43.
61. British Medical Association, Science Department, *Road Transport and Health*, BMS (September 1997), p. 7.
62. Phil Goodwin, 'Road Traffic Growth and the Dynamics of Sustainable Transport Policies', in Yoshitsugu Hayashi, Kenneth Button and Peter Nijkamp, *The Environment and Transport* (Cheltenham, 1999), p. 144.

Notes to Chapter 8: Nationalism

1. William Galt, *Railway Reform* (1865).
2. Philip Bagwell's copy (bought second-hand) is inscribed 'To G. Bernard Shaw, Esq., with the author's kind regards'. There is no immediate evidence of Shaw having read the book! Among the Fabians at that time Annie Besant was the person who dealt mainly with economic matters. See her essay 'Industry under

Socialism', in *Fabian Essays in Socialism*, Jubilee edition (1948), pp. 140–52, in which she makes no reference to transport in any form.

3. *Hansard*, 1946–47, vol. 431, 16 December 1946, col. 1658.

4. F. W. S. Craig, *British General Election Manifestos, 1900–1974* (1975), pp. 3, 63, 123.

5. Railway Clearing House, *Tables of Statistical Returns Relating to the Railways of Great Britain, 1938–46* (1947); J. Foreman Peck and R. Millward, *Public and Private Ownership of British Industries, 1820–1990* (1994), p. 276.

6. *Modern Transport*, 12 August 1939.

7. G. W. Crompton, 'Efficient and Economical Working? The Performance of the Railway Companies, 1923–1933', *Business History*, 27 (1988), pp. 222–37.

8. L. Hannah, *Electricity before Rationalisation* (1979), p. 352.

9. M. R. Bonavia, *The Nationalisation of British Transport* (1987), pp 5–6.

10. TUC and Labour Party Reports.

11. Gerald Crompton, 'Good Business for the Nation: The Railway Nationalisation Issue, 1921–47', *Journal of Transport History*, third series, 20 (1999). See also the same author's chapter in R. Millward and J. Singleton, *The Political Economy of Nationalisation in Britain* (1995).

12. University of North London, TUC Collections, 611.

13. T. R. Gourvish, *British Railways, 1948–73* (1986), p. 35.

14. A. J. Pearson, *The Railways and the Nation* (1964), p. 61–62.

15. *Hansard*, 16 December 1946, col. 1640.

16. *Hansard*, 16 December 1946, col. 1700.

17. *Hansard*, 17 December 1946, col. 1802.

18. Gourvish, *British Railways*, p. 27.

19. T. C. Barker and C. I. Savage, *An Economic History of Transport in Britain* (London, 1974), p. 215.

20. M. Bonavia, *The Organisation of British Railways* (1971), p. 55.

21. Gourvish, *British Railways*, p. 67.

22. M. Bonavia, *The Nationalisation of British Transport*, ch. 8.

23. Pearson, *The Railways and the Nation*, p. 112.

24. Gourvish, *British Railways*.

25. Ibid., p. 259.

26. Reappraisal of the Plan for the Modernisation and Re-Equipment of British Railways: Report, *Parliamentary Papers* (1958–59), xix, pp. 777ff.

27. Ibid., pt 2, sections 19 and 20.

28. Ibid., pt 3, section 62.

29. Report of the Select Committee on Nationalised Industries (1960), p. v.

30. Ibid., para. 420.

31. Central Transport Consultative Committee for Great Britain, Annual Report (1958), para. 52.

32. Ibid., para. 53.

33. Gourvish, *British Railways*, p. 325.

34. *Hansard*, 1961–62, vol. 649, cols 931, 959, 977–81.

35. Gourvish, *British Railways*, p. 414.

36. Barbara Castle, *The Castle Diaries, 1964–70* (1984), p. 372.

37. Mick Hamer, *Wheels within Wheels* (1987), p. 103.

38. Castle, *The Castle Diaries*, p. 110. In her Second Reading speech, introducing her Bill, Barbara Castle separated the country's 900,000 motor vans, which were exempt from registration (except for safety checks) from the 350,000 heavier lorries some of whose owners employed drivers 'under sweated conditions and low safety standards'. For this category of vehicle, each owner would have to obtain an operator's licence – what she called the 'quality licence'. This would only be granted when proper working and safety standards were assured.

39. DTER, *Transport Statistics Great Britain* (1999), table 1.24.

40. *Hansard*, 1967–68, vol. 756, col. 1302ff.

41. *Hansard*, 1967–68, vol. 756, col 1318.

42. D. D. Gladwin, *The Waterways of Britain: A Social Panorama* (1976), p. 221.

43. Ibid.

Notes to Chapter 9: Technology and Transport

1. See, for example, David S. Landes, *The Unbound Prometheus: Technological Change and Industrial Development in Western Europe from 1750 to the Present* (Cambridge, 1969), Nathan Rosenberg, *Inside the Black Box: Technology and Economics* (Cambridge, 1982), and Joel Mokyr, *The Lever of Riches:Technological Creativity and Economic Progress* (New York, 1990).

2. For a good introduction, see Richard Bessel, 'Transport', in Colin Chant (ed.), *Science, Technology and Everyday Life, 1870–1950* (London, 1989), pp. 162–99.

3. The social construction of technology presumes that social and cultural forces determine technical change. For an introduction see W. E. Bijker, T. P. Hughes and T. J. Pinch (eds), *The Social Construction of Technological Systems: New Directions in the Sociology and History of Technology* (Cambridge, Massachusetts, 1987); also Thomas P. Hughes, 'Technological Momentum', in Merrit Roe Smith and Leo Marx, *Does Technology Drive History? The Dilemma of Technological Determinism* (Cambridge, Massachusetts, 1994), p. 104.

4. H. W. Dickinson, *A Short History of the Steam Engine* (Cambridge, 1939), and H. W. Dickinson, 'The Steam Engine to 1830', in C. Singer, E. J. Holmyard, A. R. Hall and T. I. Williams (eds), *A History of Technology*, iv, *1750–1850* (London, 1958), pp. 168–98.

5. Aubrey F. Burstall, *A History of Mechanical Engineering* (London, 1963), pp. 267–278; Jack Simmons, *Transport* (London, 1962), p. 43. For an early illustrated treatment, Robert L. Galloway, *The Steam Engine and its Inventors: A Historical Sketch* (London, 1881).

6. Sean Day-Lewis, *Bulleid: Last Giant of Steam* (London, 1964), pp. 73–98. For a traditional account of British steam locomotive development up until 1930, G. Gibbard Jackson, *British Locomotives: Their Evolution and Development* (London, 1929).

7. R. H. Parsons, *The Steam Turbine and Other Inventions of Sir Charles Parsons OM* (London, 1945), p. 13; Dickinson, *Short History of the Steam Engine*, pp. 185–247.

8. W. J. Hughes, *A Century of Traction Engines* (Newton Abbot, 1968).

9. Percy Dunsheath, *A History of Electrical Engineering* (London, 1962), pp. 89–122.

10. Wilfried Feldenkirchen, *Werner von Siemens: Erfinder und internationaler Unternehmer* (Berlin and Munich, 1992), p. 112.

11. Dunsheath, *Electrical Engineering*, pp. 178–95; Buckley, *History of Tramways*, pp. 59–62.

12. Takeshi Yuzawa, 'The Introduction of Electric Railways in Britain and Japan', *Journal of Transport History*, third series, 6 (1985), pp. 2–5.

13. Jack Simmons and Gordon Biddle (eds), *The Oxford Companion to British Railway History: From 1603 to the 1990s* (Oxford, 1997), p. 143.

14. To run the A4 Pacifics the line had to be cleared of slower trains an hour in advance, thus disrupting the normal operating schedule of the railway. Stephen Potter, *On the Right Lines? The Limits of Technological Innovation* (London, 1987), pp. 7–14.

15. A comparison between British and French approaches to high-speed train technology was made by E. Roxanne Powell, 'The Frontiers of State Practice in Britain and France: Pioneering High Speed Railway Technology and Infrastructure, 1965–1993', unpublished Ph.D. thesis, University of London, 1995.

16. BR research engineers had calculated that a nine degree tilt would enable the APT to take curves up to 40 per cent faster than ordinary trains.

17. Potter, *On the Right Lines?*, p. 58.

18. Arthur Reed, *Britain's Aircraft Industry: What Went Right? What Went Wrong?* (London, 1973), pp. 34–41.

19. The critical problem with the Comet was insufficient knowledge on the part of the manufacturers of the dynamics of cabin pressurisation and the risks of metal fatigue in jet aircraft. It is noteworthy that, just as rival manufacturers made good use of the scientific findings from the investigation into the Comet crashes, so German and Italian engineers benefited from the work done on the APT's tilting mechanism when they came to build their own tilting trains, the Neitech-Zug and the Pendolino.

20. The TGV was designed to operate in the range from 250 to 300 kph and as early as 1972 a prototype reached 318 kph.

21. The various proposals are discussed in Keith Wilson, *Channel Tunnel Visions, 1850–1945: Dreams and Nightmares* (London, 1994). Its historical context is presented in P. A. Keen, 'The Channel Tunnel Project', *Journal of Transport History*, 3 (1958), pp. 132–44.

22. Michael Bonavia deals with the intriguing question of psychological preparation for the Tunnel in *The Channel Tunnel Story* (Newton Abbot, 1987).

23. Richard Gibb, 'The Channel Tunnel Project: Origins and Development', Richard Gibb (ed.), *The Channel Tunnel: A Geographical Perspective* (Chichester, 1994), p. 6.

24. Laurent Bonnaud, 'The Channel Tunnel, 1955–75: When the Sleeping Beauty Woke Again', *Journal of Transport History*, third series, 22 (2001), p. 11.

25. According to one report, the Eurostar held over 50 per cent of the London-Paris passenger travel market at the end of 2000, 'Europe's High-Speed Rail Network Challenges the Airlines', *International Herald Tribune*, 30/31 December 2000.

26. James M. Laux, *In First Gear: The French Automobile Industry to 1914* (Liverpool, 1976).

27. Ruth Schwartz Cowan, *A Social History of American Technology* (New York, 1997), p. 229; Wayne Lewchuk, *American Technology and the British Vehicle Industry* (Cambridge, 1987), pp. 33–65.

28. L. T. C. Rolt, *The Mechanicals: Progress of a Profession* (London, 1967), pp. 79–80; James Foreman-Peck, Sue Bowden and Alan McKinlay, *The British Motor Industry* (Manchester, 1995), pp. 6–34.

29. M. J. Freeman, 'Introduction', Michael J. Freeman and Derek H. Aldcroft (eds), *Transport in Victorian Britain* (Manchester, 1988), p. 1.

30. The diesel motor differs essentially from the petrol-driven internal combustion engine in that the heat of compression alone is sufficient to ignite the fuel. For a life of Rudolf Diesel and a technical history of his engine, Donald E. Thomas Jr, *Diesel: Technology and Society in Industrial Germany* (Tuscaloosa, 1987).

31. The British modernisation programme of the 1950s also brought such improvements as continuously welded track, concrete sleepers and coloured light signalling to replace the old semaphore arrangement.

32. Stephen Potter and Robin Roy, *Research and Development: British Rail's Fast Trains* (Milton Keynes, 1985), p. 10.

33. T. R. Gourvish, *British Railways, 1948–73: A Business History* (Cambridge, 1986), pp. 510–11.

34. Potter, *On the Right Lines?*, p. 104.

35. Charles H. Gibbs-Smith, *Aviation: An Historical Survey from its Origins to the End of World War II* (London, 1970), p. 100.

36. See Robert Schlaifer, *Development of Aircraft Engines* (Boston, 1950), pp. 156–98.

37. Keith Hayward, *The British Aircraft Industry* (Manchester, 1989), p. 14.

38. Sir Stanley Hooker, *Not Much of an Engineer: An Autobiography* (London, 1984), p. 64.

39. Virginia P. Dawson, 'The American Turbojet Industry and British Competition', in William M. Leary (ed.), *From Airships to Airbus: The History of Civil and Commercial Aviation*, i (Washington, DC, 1995), p. 127.

40. For an overview on the relationship between military technologies and their adoption in civil life, see William H. McNeill, *The Pursuit of Power: Technology, Armed Force and Society since AD 1000* (Oxford, 1983). For Britain before the First World War, R. C. Trebilcock. '"Spin Off" in British Economic History: Armaments and Industry, 1760–1914', *Economic History Review*, 22 (1969).

41. Two more Germans, Herbert Wagner and Helmut Schelp, were responsible for crucial research on turbines and compressors. For the race to get the jet

engine operational, Edward W. Constant II, *The Origins of the Turbojet Revolution* (Baltimore, 1980), p. 178–207. See also Hayward, *British Aircraft Industry*, pp. 29–36, and Ronald Miller and David Sawers, *The Technical Development of Modern Aviation* (London, 1968), pp. 157–61.

42. Rolt, *The Mechanicals*, pp. 101–12. For the revolutionary nature of the turbojet engine, see Constant, *Origins*; also George Basalla, *The Evolution of Technology* (Cambridge, 1988), pp. 28–29.

43. Superchargers had been around since the First World War and were especially applicable to aircraft engines because they substantially increased the intake of air at high altitudes where the air was thin. Their power was drawn from a turbine driven by the engine's exhaust gas and applied through gearing to the crankshaft. The technology of supercharger turbine construction progressed steadily through the inter-war years (mainly in the United States) and a range of new nickel alloys were created to build temperature-resistant fan blades; the same technology, with similar theoretical problems, as that required to build jet engine turbines.

44. Miller and Sawers, *Technical Development of Modern Aviation*, pp. 24–25.

45. By-pass engines add a stream of cold air, 'by-passing' the compressor and turbine, and joining the gas jet at the rear. This addition of colder, slower-moving air increases the mass of the jet and thus its thrust. These engines have a ducted fan at the front which, unlike an open propeller, can spin at the slower speed of the turbine – hence turbofan engine. See, for example, John Snow, 'Airliner Propulsion', Philip Jarrett, series editor, *Modern Air Transport: Worldwide Air Transport from 1945 to the Present* (London, 2000), pp. 62–64.

46. For the troubled history of the Rolls Royce RB211, Hayward, *British Aircraft Industry*, pp. 145–48.

47. For the financial implications of the Concorde project, Keith Hayward, *Government and British Civil Aerospace: A Study in Post-War Technology Policy* (Manchester, 1983), pp. 124–51.

48. 'Time and Money: Why Concorde was Never the Right Way to Speed up Air Travel', *Economist*, 19 August 2000. In July 2000 an Air France Concorde crashed outside Paris, killing over a hundred people. The type was immediately withdrawn by Air France and subsequently by British Airways. The Concorde's quarter century of operational life with the British and French flag-carriers seemed to be over, although a year later, in 2001, British Airways were planning to reintroduce the aircraft with new modifications.

49. For a 'green' critique of technology, see John Street, *Politics and Technology* (Basingstoke, 1992), pp. 138–56.

50. Liquid hydrogen, for example, has to be delivered to a car's fuel tank at such a low temperature that it cannot be handled by human beings and would need special 'robot-operated' filling stations.

51. Brian Richards, *Transport in Cities* (London, 1990), p. 67.

52. B. T. Collins, 'Transportation Developments in Nottinghamshire', *Chartered Institute of Transport Journal*, May 1975, pp. 249–55.

53. For a business history of the largest British bicycle manufacturer, see Roger Lloyd-Jones and M. J. Lewis, *Raleigh and the British Bicycle Industry: An Economic and Business History, 1870–1960* (Aldershot, 2000).

54. Philip S. Bagwell, *The Transport Crisis in Britain* (Nottingham, 1996), p. 2.

55. In Britain the 'killed or seriously injured' rate for cyclists per billion kilometres rose 80 per cent from 1954 to 1988 and was at a level twenty times that for car drivers, whose 'killed or seriously injured' rate was halved over the same period. Rodney Tolley, 'A Hard Road: The Problems of Walking and Cycling in British Cities', in Rodney Tolley (ed.), *The Greening of Urban Transport: Planning for Walking and Cycling in Western Cities* (London, 1990), p. 22.

Notes to Chapter 10: Air Transport

1. Roger E. Bilstein, 'Travel by Air: The American Context', *Archiv für Sozialgeschichte*, 33 (1993), p. 275.

2. See for example T. A. Heppenheimer, *Turbulent Skies: The History of Commercial Aviation* (New York, 1995).

3. 0.8 per cent in 1993. Transport Statistics of Great Britain, in Philip S. Bagwell, *The Transport Crisis in Britain* (Nottingham, 1996), p. 44.

4. For a traditional appraisal of airline operating costs and the problems of short-haul operations, see Hedley Crabtree, Reduction of Airline Costs, *Journal of the Royal Aeronautical Society*, 59 (1955), pp. 829–42, or Stephen Wheatcroft, 'Ten Economic Lessons from Short-Haul Airline Operation', *Journal of the Royal Aeronautical Society* (April 1961).

5. Charles Harvard Gibbs-Smith, *Aviation: An Historical Survey from its Origins to the End of World War II* (London, 1970), p. 154.

6. Eric Birkhead, 'The Financial Failure of British Air Transport Companies, 1919–24', *Journal of Transport History*, fourth series, 3 (1960), p. 138.

7. Report on Government Financial Assistance to Civil Air Transport Companies (Hambling Report), Cmd 1811, 1923; para. 14.

8. See R. W. Spurgeon, 'Subsidy in Air Transport', *Journal of the Institute of Transport* (November 1956), p. 16. The four airlines were Handley Page, Instones, Daimler Hire and the unsubsidised British Marine Air Navigation.

9. Surprisingly little has been written on Imperial Airways and the standard text remains Robin Higham's, *Britain's Imperial Air Routes, 1918 to 1939* (London, 1960). For a recent account see Peter Lyth, 'The Empire's Airway: British Civil Aviation from 1919 to 1939', in Guy Vanthemsche (ed.), *Revue Belge de Philologie et d'Histoire*, 78 (2001), pp. 865–87.

10. Sir Eric Geddes's Speech, First Annual General Meeting of Imperial Airways Limited, reported in *The Times*, Company Meetings, 30 December 1925.

11. *Air Subsidies to Civil Air Services*, Cmd 3143 (1928), note by the Secretary of State for Air on the principal provisions agreed to be embodied in a contract with Imperial Airways, Ltd.

12. Air Ministry, Directorate of Civil Aviation, *Annual Report on the Progress of Civil Aviation* (hereafter *ARPCA*), April 1923 to March 1924, Cmd 2210 (1924), p. 6.
13. *ARPCA*, April, 1922 to March 1923 (1923), Cmd 1900, p. 7, 13; *ARPCA*, 1929 (1930), p. 5.
14. Peter G. Masefield, 'Some Economic Factors in Air Transport Operation', *Journal of Institute of Transport*, 14 (1951), p. 83.
15. Imperial Airways had not entirely abandoned domestic services: it operated an experimental thrice-weekly service in 1930 on the route London-Birmingham-Manchester-Liverpool as a feeder into its London Airport (Croydon) terminus. Six hundred passengers were carried from June to September, *ARPCA*, 1930 (1931), p. 5.
16. For the history of Highland Airways, see A. J. Robertson, 'The New Road to the Isles: Highland Airways and Scottish Airways, 1933–1939', *Journal of Transport History*, 7 (1986), pp. 48–60.
17. An airline owned and directed by a competing form of transport was a phenomenon explicitly forbidden in the United States, although it is well known that the American railroads would have dearly liked to have taken a stake in the US trunk carriers formed in the 1930s.
18. Derek H. Aldcroft, 'The Railways and Air Transport, 1933–9', *Studies in British Transport History, 1870–1970* (Newton Abbot, 1974), p. 233.
19. RAS Memo to Maybury Committee, 1936, box 324, RAF Museum, Hendon.
20. *Report of the Committee to Consider the Development of Civil Aviation in the United Kingdom* (Maybury Committee), Cmd 5351 (1937), para. 125.
21. *ARPCA*, 1938 (1939), p. 80.
22. The railways proposed in their *Railway Plan for Air Transport* a scheme for a joint continental and British domestic service, operated by a railway-led airline. A copy of this document is in *British Railway Companies Plans for Air Transport*, June 1944; PRO, Kew, AVIA. 2/2462.
23. For BEA's creation and its relationship with independent airlines, Peter Lyth, 'The Changing Role of Government in British Civil Air Transport, 1919–1949', Robert Millward and John Singleton (eds), *The Political Economy of Nationalisation in Britain, 1920–1950* (Cambridge, 1995), pp. 65–87.
24. See, for example, Peter Fearon, 'The British Airframe Industry and the State, 1918–1935', *Economic History Review*, 27 (1974), pp. 236–51.
25. A. J. Jackson, *De Havilland Aircraft since 1909* (London, 1962), pp. 341–67.
26. Allied Airways (Gandar Dower), which flew between Aberdeen and the Orkney and Shetland Islands, did not join the AAJC and continued to operate independently for a while.
27. It is also added British South American Airways, but this airline failed within four years and was absorbed by BOAC.
28. The AAJC airlines acquired by BEA were: Railway Air Services; Great Western and Southern Air Lines; Highland Airways; Isle of Man Air Services; North

Eastern Airways; Scottish Air Services; West Coast Air Services; and Western Isles Airways; Allied Airways and Channel Island Airways were taken over in April 1947.

29. Lyth, 'The Changing Role of Government in British Civil Air Transport', pp. 80–81.

30. 'The Domestic Scene: Air Traffic in the United Kingdom', *Flight Magazine*, 8 April 1960, pp. 475–78. The biggest independents were BKS, Jersey Airlines and Silver City.

31. Spurgeon, 'Subsidy in Air Transport', p. 19.

32. J. L. Grumbridge, A. W. Tait and A. F. R. Carling, 'Fares Structures: Air, Rail, Road', *Journal of the Institute of Transport*, January 1960, p. 223.

33. *Economist*, 'BEA's Fares', 31 August 1957, p. 706.

34. Ibid., 'Nationalised Industries: How is it Done?', 31 August 1963.

35. 'The Airways Debate', *Flight Magazine*, 26 November 1954, p. 783, and the Civil Aviation Authority, *Air Transport in the Scottish Highlands and Islands* (London, 1974), p. 17.

36. Edwards recognised 'that exceptions are necessary in the cases of those services for which explicit subsidy is deemed desirable on grounds of social need or national policy. Nevertheless, as a general guideline for air transport regulatory policy, we strongly advocate the acceptance of the proposition that there should be no cross-subsidisation, in the long-term, of one route by another'. *British Air Transport in the Seventies*, Report of the Committee of Inquiry into Civil Air Transport (Edwards Report) (London, 1969), paras 665–67, also paras 761–69. For earlier critiques of cross-subsidisation see Report from the Select Committee on Nationalised Industries (SNCI) (Report & Accounts), HC 213 (1959), and again SCNI (Report and Accounts), HC 116 (1962).

37. BEA's Scottish manager, Robert McKean, said in 1966 that he did not want a subsidy because that would have brought 'governmental interference', 'BEA: Operation Outback', *Aeroplane Magazine*, 11 August 1966.

38. Masefield, *Some Economic Factors in Air Transport Operation*, p. 90. Peter Brooks, Masefield's assistant at BEA at the time, went as far as to forecast that 'perhaps within a few decades a majority of passenger journeys of more than twenty to thirty miles may be by helicopter'. Peter W. Brooks, 'Problems of Short-Haul Air Transport', *Journal of the Royal Aeronautical Society* (1952), p. 441.

39. Charles Woodley, *Golden Age: British Civil Aviation, 1945–1965* (Shrewsbury, 1992), p. 11.

40. 'BEA Helicopter Passenger Service', *Flight Magazine*, 2 March. 1950, p. 284.

41. The London South Bank helicopter service was the first city-centre helicopter station in Britain. The S55s were fitted with floats in case they had to put down on the Thames. Over three thousand passengers were carried in eight months. *BEA Report and Accounts*, 1955–56, p. 34.

42. Like many British aircraft projects in the 1950s, the Rotodyne design was too complicated, or too 'advanced', for its manufacturer. With turbo-prop engines

for forward propulsion, the upward lift was provided by a single large rotor driven by compressed air fed through jets at the tip of each rotor blade. Apart from being underpowered and suffering other problems, the noise from the rotor tip jets was unbearable.

43. 'What Happened to Helicopters?', *Economist*, 18 May 1963, pp. 682–83. The Land's End (Penzance) to Scilly Islands helicopter service continued and had carried 250,000 passengers by October 1968, *BEA Report and Accounts*, 1968–69, p. 63.

44. *BEA Report and Accounts*, 1965–66, p. 24.

45. British Eagle's and BUA's figures on the Edinburgh and Belfast routes were not as impressive as those on the Glasgow route, Edwards Report; para. 313, table 7.1.

46. 'It Starts on Sunday', *Flight International*, 31 October. 1963; 'Room for Independents', *Economist*, 9 November 1963, p. 584.

47. *Flight International*, 8 April 1960, pp. 483–84; also Submission of BEA to the Civil Air Transport Inquiry (Edwards Committee Report), 1968, box 341, RAF Museum, Hendon. In fact the Vanguard itself, which was not a success like the smaller Viscount, was prematurely moved by BEA from international to domestic operations in 1962.

48. *BEA Report and Accounts*, 1966–67, p. 19, also Edwards Committee Report, para. 320, table. 7.3.

49. 'Three Guinea War', *Economist*, 14 October 1961, p. 170; 'Three Guinea Bargain', *Economist*, 13 January 1962, p. 151.

50. See Peter Lyth, 'Chosen Instruments: The Evolution of British Airways', in Hans-Liudger Dienel and Peter Lyth (eds), *Flying the Flag: European Commercial Air Transport since 1945* (Basingstoke, 1998), p. 72.

51. For a detailed account see Kyohei Shibata, *Privatisation of British Airways: Its Managements and Politics, 1982–1987*, EUI Working Paper, EPU No 93/9, European University Institute, Florence, 1994.

52. 'Air Services: Going Provincial', *Economist*, 22 September 1973.

53. British Airways, *Annual Report and Accounts*, 1982/83, pp. 11–12, 1983/84, pp. 21–23.

54. British Airways, *Annual Report and Accounts*, 1976–77, p. 16; 1978/79, pp. 16–17; 1979/80, p. 19. The shuttle principle was pioneered in the United States by Eastern Air Lines between Boston, New York and Washington in the 1960s. The basic requirement is that a back-up aircraft must be provided for every flight in case all the seats on the first aircraft are filled.

55. 'The Law is BA's Market Force', *Economist*, 20 August 1983.

56. Duncan Campbell-Smith, *Struggle for Take-Off: The British Airways Story* (London, 1986), pp. 125, 142–43; also Civil Aviation Authority, *Airline Competition Policy*, CAP 500 (London, 1984). The CAA, which recommended that Manchester be created as major hub for BMA and another independent, Air UK, was ultimately overruled by a government anxious not to harm BA's prospects in the run-up to its privatisation. The Transport Secretary (Nicholas Ridley)

and the CAA were politically outgunned by the BA chairman (Lord King) and the Treasury, 'In the Wings with a Prayer', *Economist*, 6 October 1984.

57. British Airways, *Review of the Year*, 1984–85, p. 14.

58. British Airways, *Review of the Year*, 1985–86, p. 17, British Airways plc, *Annual Report and Accounts*, 1989–90, 'Leading the Transformation of the World's Airline Industry', p. 11.

59. In the five years until March 1987 revenue from BA's domestic services represented on average no more than 10 per cent of the BA Group's operating revenue. British Airways, Plc, *Annual Report on Form 20-F*, year ended 31 March 1987, p. 8.

60. In 2000, EasyJet's website listed regular services from its Luton airport base to Liverpool, Belfast, Glasgow, Aberdeen, Inverness and Edinburgh.

61. British Airways, *Fact Book 1991*, pp. 48–49.

Notes to Chapter 11: Privatisation

1. F. W. S. Craig, *British General Election Manifesto, 1959–1987* (1990), p. 267.

2. M. H. Macmillan, *The Middle Way* (1938). The second edition (1958) extended, but endorsed the main principles of the first. See first edition, p. 176, and second edition, p. 234.

3. P. S. Bagwell, *The Railwaymen*, i (1963), p. 654.

4. Craig, *British General Election Manifesto*, p. 217.

5. *Hansard* (1979–80), vol. 968, col. 248.

6. The source for the figure is a 1992 report by transport consultants Steer, Davies, Gleaver, *Financing Public Transport: How Does Britain Compare?*

7. J. S. Dodgson and N. Topham, *Bus Deregulation and Privatisation: An International Perspective* (1988), p. 1.

8. National Bus Company, *Annual Reports and Accounts*, 1980–83.

9. Financing of Public Transport Services: The 'Buses' White Paper (1981), ii, Minutes of Evidence, p. 147, *Parliamentary Papers* (1984), vol. 38.

10. Memorandum submitted by the Bus and Coach Council, 28 December 1981, to the Select Committee on Transport, second report, 1984.

11. *Transport Statistics*, Great Britain editions 1995 and 1996. Bus services: passenger journeys, Great Britain, table 5.2.

12. *Hansard*, 1984–85, vol. 73, col. 192.

13. Ibid., 1983–84, vol. 58, col. 758.

14. Ibid., vol. 58, col. 206.

15. Transport and Road Research Laboratory 'Some Early Effects of the 1985 Transport Act on Strathclyde', Research Report 168 by K. Perrett, J. Hopkin and D. Furgusol (1989). For Hereford, see Peter Fry's Commons speech, 12 November 1984.

16. *Transport Statistics*, Great Britain, 1996.

17. Central Transport Consultative Committee, *Annual Report*, 1989–90, pp. 9–11.

18. Commons Transport Committee, The Future of the Railways, HC Session 1992–93, HC 246/1, para. 20.
19. *Financial Times*, 15 July 1992.
20. Memorandum Submitted by the Institution of Civil Engineers to the Commons' Transport Committee, 11 November 1992, para. 4.
21. House of Commons Papers 879, Session 1992–93, *Future of the Railways*. Transport Committee, 11 November 1992, para. 420.
22. Central Transport Consultative Committee (CTCC), Memorandum to the House of Commons Transport Committee, 11 November 1992, section 8: Rolling Stock.
23. CTCC Memorandum, Section A2:2.
24. *Financial Times*, 8 December 1982.
25. Commons, Transport Committee, second report, Minutes of Evidence, question 112.
26. Commons, Transport Committee, Minutes of Evidence.
27. *Hansard*, 1992–93, vol. 218, col. 203.
28. D. and G. Butler, *British Political Facts, 1900–1994* (1994), pp. 298–99.
29. *Independent*, 30 November 1994.
30. *Daily Telegraph*, 22 May 1993.
31. *Hansard*, 1992–93, 2 February 1993.
32. Ibid., 2 February 1993, col. 203.
33. Ibid., 2 February 1993, col. 205.
34. *Hansard*, 5 July 1993, vol. 547, no. 164, cols 1069–70.
35. Ibid., 5 July 1993, col. 1095.
36. *Financial Times*, 14 April 1993
37. *Hansard*, 3 November 1993, vol. 549, col. 1098, and 5 November 1993, col. 1183.
38. *Observer*, business supplement, 1 May 1994; *Guardian*, 2 May 1994.
39. British Rail, *Rail Facts and Figures* (1992), p. 10.
40. British Railways Board, *Annual Report and Accounts, 1994–95*, p. 54.
41. *Financial Times*, 28 February 1996.
42. *Hansard*, 1995–96, vol. 275, col. 748.
43. Commons, Transport Committee, *Fourth Report*, Railway Finances, 5 July 1995, paras 162–64, p. 8.
44. Commons Transport Committee, *Fourth Report*, conclusions 'o' and 'p', p. iv.
45. *Financial Times*, 23 August 2000.
46. Health and Safety Executive, *Report*, 2 December 1999.
47. *Transport Statistics, Great Britain* (1998), table 5.26, p. 124.
48. Central Rail Users Consultative Committee, Annual Report, 1997–98, p. 10. D and R figures suggest a smaller advance from 32.1 billion kms to 35.1 billion kms. *Transport Statistics Great Britain* (1999), table 5.5.
49. *Transport Statistics, Great Britain* (1999), table 5.12.
50. Ibid., table 9.1.
51. Central Rail Users Consultative Committee, *Annual Report, 1998–99*, p. 32.
52. *Financial Times*, 9 October 2000.

Notes to Chapter 12: The Decline of Public Transport

1. John P. McKay, *Tramways and Trolleys: The Rise of Urban Mass Transport in Europe* (Princeton, 1976), pp. 173–91.
2. Quoted in T. C. Barker and C. I. Savage, *An Economic History of Transport in Britain* (London, 1974).
3. Herbert Morrison, *Socialisation and Transport* (London, 1933).
4. Quoted in H. J. Dyos and D. H. Aldrcroft, *British Transport: An Economic Survey from the Seventeenth Century to the Twentieth* (Harmondsworth, 1974), p. 381.
5. Charles Loch Mowat, *Britain between the Wars, 1918–1940* (London, 1968), p. 449.
6. Measured in ton miles. See Peter Scott, 'The Growth of Road Haulage, 1921–58: An Estimate', *Journal of Transport History*, third series, 19 (1998), pp. 138–55.
7. Kerry Hamilton and Stephen Potter, *Losing Track* (London, 1985), p. 49.
8. Philip S. Bagwell, *The Transport Revolution, 1770–1985* (London, 1974), pp. 328–32. For Lord King's 'preparation' of British Airways for privatisation in 1981–82, see Peter Lyth, 'Chosen Instruments: The Evolution of British Airways', in Hans-Liudger Dienel and Peter Lyth (eds), *Flying the Flag: European Commercial Air Transport since 1945* (Basingstoke, 1998), p. 75.
9. Stephen Plowden, *Towns against Traffic* (London, 1972), p. 12.
10. Colin Buchanan, *Traffic in Towns* (Harmondsworth, 1963).
11. Philip S. Bagwell, *The Transport Crisis in Britain* (Nottingham, 1996), p. 109.
12. Tim Pharoah and Dieter Apel, *Transport Concepts in European Cities* (Aldershot, 1995), p. 50–51.
13. In 1989 subsidies per 1000 kilometres were: Italy, £378 million; Belgium, £217 million; West Germany, £134 million; Holland, £133 million; France, £93 million; Britain, £38 million. 'How to Sell the Railways', *Economist*, November 1991, p. 39.
14. 'The Rail Billionaires', *Economist*, 3 July 1999, p. 85. Originally the journal was enthusiastic about privatisation of the railways. Consider this prediction from 1996: rail privatisation was likely 'to be a consumer's dream – the start of a new era which will revolutionise Britain's under-invested railway network ... even discounting the better management that privatisation should bring, assured levels of subsidy and a stable fare structure can hardly fail to deliver improved performance. Compared to their predecessors at British Rail, subject to constant ministerial interference, the new train operators have an easier task', 'Rail Privatisation: Slow Train to Success', *Economist*, 3 February 1996.
15. Matthew Engel, 'This Should be the End of the Line', *Guardian*, 12 October 1999.
16. Friends of the Earth (FoE), *Less Traffic, Better Towns*, a report for Friends of the Earth Trust by Tim Pharoah (London, 1992), p. 7.
17. Theo Kiriazidis, *European Transport: Problems and Policies* (Aldershot, 1994), p. 34.
18. CBI, *Trade Routes to the Future* (1989), p. 13.

19. *Transport and the Environment*, Eighteenth Report of the Royal Commission on Environmental Pollution, October 1994, Cmd 2674, para. 3.23; 30.
20. Bagwell, *The Transport Crisis in Britain*, pp. 4–5.

Notes to Chapter 13: Problems and Possibilities

1. Edward Hyde, Earl of Clarendon, *The History of the Rebellion and Civil War in England, 1703–1704* (1888), ii, p. 81.
2. Eric Hobsbawm, *On History* (1997), p. 33.
3. 1998 Comprehensive Spending Review, 'Transport: Poorjohn', *Economist*, 17 July 1999, p. 28.
4. Colin Buchanan, *The State of Britain* (London 1972), p. 58. The book comprised the three Chichele lectures given at Oxford University in 1971. Buchanan, who was a visionary thinker on the role of the motor car in society, was chiefly famous for his report *Traffic in Towns* (1963).
5. 'Fuel Taxes: Gordon's Giveaway', *Economist*, 11 November 2000, p. 58.
6. John Vidal, 'Earth Will Get Hotter than Expected', *Guardian*, 28 October 2000.
7. Michael Meacher, 'We've Got to Fix those Cars', *Guardian*, 31 October 2000.
8. Gordon Brown's speech to the Annual Conference of the Labour Party reported in *Local Transport Today*, 300, 12 October 2000. See also the same journal's feature article in issue 306, 11 January 2001.
9. *Financial Times*, 17 and 18 November 2000.
10. *British Rail Annual Report and Accounts*, 1993–94. Statement to the authors by Vernon Hince, Assistant General Secretary of the RMT union on 4 December 2000.
11. K. J. Button, *The Economics of Urban Transport* (Farnborough 1997), p. 38.
12. In Singapore a system of road tolls was introduced in 1975 along roads entering the city centre. The system reduced the number of cars entering the centre by 50 per cent, Brian Richards, *Transport in Cities* (London, 1990), p. 7.
13. Theo Kiriazidis, *European Transport: Problems and Politics* (Aldershot 1994), p. 30.
14. G. M. Trevelyan, *English Social History: A Survey of Six Centuries, Chaucer to Queen Victoria* (1942), introduction.

Bibliography

General

Aldcroft, Derek and Freeman, M. J. (eds), *Transport in the Industrial Revolution* (Manchester, 1983).

Bagwell, Philip S., *The Transport Revolution, 1770–1985* (London, 1974, 1988).

Barker, T. C. and Savage, C. I., *An Economic History of Transport in Britain* (London, 1974).

Berg, Maxine, *The Age of Manufactures* (Oxford, 1985).

Braudel, Fernand, *The Wheels of Commerce* (London, 1982).

Chaloner, W. H., *People and Industries*, 1963.

Clapham, J. H., *The Economic Development of France and Germany, 1815–1914* (Cambridge, 1921).

Court, W. H. B., *The Rise of Midland Industries, 1600–1838* (London, 1938).

Crafts, N. F. R., *British Economic Growth during the Industrial Revolution* (Oxford, 1985).

Deane, Phyllis, *The First Industrial Revolution* (Cambridge, 1965).

Dyos, H. J. and Aldcroft, D. H., *British Transport: An Economic Survey from the Seventeenth Century to the Twentieth* (Harmondsworth, 1974).

Flinn, M., *The History of the British Coal Industry*, ii, *1700–1830* (Oxford, 1985).

Girard, L., 'Transport', *The Cambridge Economic History of Europe*, vi (Cambridge, 1965)

Jackman, W. T., *The Development of Transportation in Modern England* (Cambridge, 1916).

Landes, David, *The Unbound Prometheus* (Cambridge, 1969).

Mantoux, Paul, *The Industrial Revolution in the Eighteenth Century* (New York, 1905, 1961).

Mokyr, Joel, *The Lever of Riches: Technological Creativity and Economic Progress* (New York, 1990).

Musson, A. E. and Robinson, Eric, *Science and Technology in the Industrial Revolution* (Manchester, 1969).

O'Brien, Patrick, 'Transport and Economic Development in Europe 1789–1914', in P. O'Brien (ed.), *Railways and the Economic Development of Western Europe* (London, 1983).

Pollard, Sidney, *Peaceful Conquest: The Industrialisation of Europe, 1760–1970* (Oxford, 1981).

Szostak, Rick, *The Role of Transportation in the Industrial Revolution. A Comparison of England and France* (Montreal, 1991).

Ville, Simon P., *Transport and the Development of the European Economy, 1750–1918* (London, 1990).

Coastal Shipping

Aldcroft, Derek H., 'The Eclipse of British Coastal Shipping, 1913–21, *Journal of Transport History*, 6 (1963).

Armstrong, John (ed.), *Coastal and Short Sea Shipping*, Studies in Transport History (Aldershot, 1996).

—, 'Freight Pricing Policy in Coastal Liner Companies before the First World War', *Journal of Transport History*, 10 (1989).

—, 'The Role of Coastal Shipping in UK Transport: An Estimate of Comparative Traffic Movements in 1910', *Journal of Transport History*, 8 (1987).

Bagwell, P. S. and Armstrong, J., 'Coastal Shipping', M. J. Freeman and D. H. Aldcroft (eds), *Transport in Victorian Britain* (Manchester, 1988).

Lee, C. H., 'Some Aspects of the Coastal Shipping Trade: The Aberdeen Steam Navigation Company, 1835–80', *Journal of Transport History*, 3 (1975).

Starkey, David J. (ed.), *Shipping Movements in the Ports of the United Kingdom, 1871–1913: A Statistical Profile* (Exeter, 1999).

Willan, T. S., *The English Coasting Trade, 1600–1750* (Manchester, 1938).

Inland Navigation

Barker, T. C., 'The Sankey Navigation: The First Lancashire Canal', *Transactions of the Historic Society of Lancashire and Cheshire* (1948).

Brindley, James, *The History of Inland Navigation* (1766).

Crompton, Gerald, 'Introduction: Rivers, Canals and Economic Development', Gerald Crompton (ed.), *Canals and Inland Navigation*, Studies in Transport History (Aldershot, 1996), pp. ix–xxii.

—, 'The Role of Canals in British Industrialisation', in Andreas Kunz and John Armstrong (eds), *Inland Navigation and Economic Development in the Nineteenth Century* (Mainz, 1995), p. 13–31.

Davies, C., 'Josiah Wedgwood and Canal Management', *Journal of Transport History*, i (1980), pp. 49–57.

Duckham, B. F., 'Selby and the Aire and Calder Navigation, 1744–1826', *Journal of Transport History*, 7 (1965), pp. 87–95.

Firth, G., 'Bradford Coal, Craven Limestone and the Origins of the Leeds and Liverpool Canal, 1765–75', *Journal of Transport History*, 4 (1983), pp. 50–62.

Freer, Wendy, 'Standards of Living among Canal People, 1840–1939', *Journal of Transport History*, 13 (1992), pp. 43–58.

Gladwin, D. D. and White, J. M., *English Canals*, ii, *Engineers and Engineering* (Lingfield, 1968).

Griffin, C. P., 'Transport Change and the Development of the Leicester Coalfield in the Canal Age: A Reinterpretation', *Journal of Transport History*, 4 (1978), pp. 227–238.

Hadfield, Charles, *British Canals: An Illustrated History* (Newton Abbot, 1950).

—, 'James Green as Canal Engineer', *Journal of Transport History*, 1 (1953).

—, *The Canal Age* (1968).

—, *The Canals of the East Midlands* (1966).

—, *The Canals of South Wales and the Border* (1960).

—, *The Canals of the West Midlands* (1966).

—, 'The Grand Junction Canal', *Journal of Transport History*, 4 (1959).

—, 'The Thames Navigation and the Canals, 1770–1830', *Economic History Review*, 14 (1944), p. 45.

Harris, J. R., 'Liverpool Canal Controversies, 1769–72', *Journal of Transport History*, 2 (1956).

Household, H., 'The Thames and Severn Canal', *Journal of Transport History*, 7 (1966).

Kunz, Andreas, 'The Economic Performance of Inland Navigation in Germany, 1835–1935: A Reassessment of Traffic Flows'; Andreas Kunz and John Armstrong (eds), *Inland Navigation and Economic Development in Nineteenth-Century Europe* (Mainz, 1995), pp. 47–77.

Phillips, John, *A General History of Inland Navigation* (1792).

Pratt, E. A., *A History of Inland Transport and Commerce in England* (London, 1912).

Priestley, Joseph, *Historical Account of the Navigable Rivers, Canals and Railways Throughout Great Britain* (1831, 1967).

Rolt, L. T. C., *The Inland Waterways of England* (1950).

Salis, H. R. de, *Bradshaw's Canals and Navigable Rivers of England and Wales* (1904).

Smith, George, *Our Canal Population* (1875).

Turnbull, Gerard, 'Canals, Coal and Regional Growth during the Industrial Revolution', *Economic History Review*, 40 (1987), pp. 537–60.

Vallancey, Charles, *A Treatise on Inland Navigation* (1763).

Ward, J. R., *The Finance of Canal Building in Eighteenth-Century England* (London, 1974).

Whitworth, Richard, *The Advantages of Inland Navigation* (1766)

Willan, T. S., *River Navigation in England, 1600–1750* (London, 1964).

Wood, A. C., 'The History of Trade and Transport on the River Trent', *Transactions of the Thoroton Society*, 54 (1950).

Wood, Fiona, 'Fuelling the Local Economy: The Fenland Coal Trade, 1760–1850', Andreas Kunz and John Armstrong (eds), *Inland Navigation and Economic Development in Nineteenth-Century Europe* (Mainz, 1995), pp. 261–75.

Road Transport before the Car

Albert, W., *The Turnpike Road System in England, 1663–1840* (Cambridge, 1972).

Austen B., 'The Impact of the Mail Coach on Public Coach Services in England and Wales, 1784–1840', *Journal of Transport History*, 2, March 1981.

Bates, A., *Directory of Stage-Coach Services, 1836* (1969).

Copeland, J., *Roads and their Traffic, 1750–1850* (Newton Abbot, 1968).

Gerhold, Dorian, *Transport before the Railways: Russell's Flying Waggons* (Cambridge, 1993).

—, *Road Transport in the Horse-Drawn Era* (Aldershot, 1996)

Goldsmith, Oliver, *She Stoops to Conquer*, Act 1 (1775).

Turnbull, G. L., 'Provincial Road Carrying in England in the Eighteenth Century', *Journal of Transport History*, 4 (1977).

—, *Traffic and Transport: An Economic History of Pickfords* (London, 1979).

The Growth of Railways

Brooke, D., *The Railway Navvy* (Newton Abbot, 1983).

Drummond, D., 'Building a Locomotive: Skill and the Work Force in Crewe Locomotive Works, *Journal of Transport History*, 8, March 1987.

Freeman, M. and Aldcroft, D. (eds), *Transport in Victorian Britain* (Manchester, 1988).

—, *The Atlas of British Railway History* (London, 1985).

Galt, W., *Railway Reform* (London, 1844, 1865).

Hawke, G. R., *Railways and Economic Growth in England and Wales, 1840–1870* (Oxford, 1970).

Irving, R. J., 'The Capitalisation of Britain's Railways, 1830–1914', *Journal of Transport History*, 7, March 1984.

Lewis, M. J. T., *Early Wooden Railways* (1970)

Pollins, H., 'Railway Contractors and the Finance of Railway Development in Britain', *Journal of Transport History*, 3 (1957).

Simmons, Jack, *The Railway in Britain* (3rd edition, London, 1990).

—, *The Railway in Town and Country, 1830–1914* (Newton Abbot, 1986)

—, *Victorian Railways* (London, 1991).

Simmons, Jack, and Biddle, N. (eds), *The Oxford Companion to British Railway History* (Oxford, 1998).

Vamplew R., 'Railways and the Scottish Transport System in Nineteenth Century', *Journal of Transport History*, 1 (1972).

Wooler, N., *Dinner in the Diner* (Newton Abbot, 1997).

British Railways, 1914–1939

Aldcroft, D., *British Transport since 1914* (Newton Abbot, 1975).

Alderman, G., *The Railway Interest* (Leicester, 1973).

Bonavia, M. R., *The Four Great Railways* (Newton Abbot, 1980).

—, *British Railway Policy between the Wars* (Basingstoke. 198?)

Channon G., 'The Recruitment of Directors to the Board of the Great Western Railway', *Journal of Transport History*, 17, March 1996; 20, March 1999.

Elliot, J., 'The Early Days of the Southern Railway', *Journal of Transport History*, 14, November 1960.

Larkin, E. J., and Larkin, J. G., *The Railway Workshops of Britain, 1823–1986* (Basingstoke, 1988).

MacDermot, E. T., *The History of the Great Western Railway*, 3 vols, ed. G. R. Clinker (1964).

Parris, H., *Government and the Railways in Nineteenth Century Britain* (1965).

Pratt, E. A., *British Railways and the Great War*, 2 vols (London, 1921).

Motor Transport

Buchanan, Colin D., *Mixed Blessing: The Motor in Britain* (London, 1958).

Caunter, C. F., *History and Development of Cycles* (HMSO, 1958).

—, *Motor Cycles* (HMSO, 1982).

Foreman-Peck, James, 'Death on the Roads: Changing National Response to Motor Accidents', in T. C. Barker (ed), *The Economic and Social Effects of the Spread of Motor Vehicles* (1997).

Freund, Peter and Martin, George, *The Ecology of the Automobile* (Montreal and New York, 1993).

Grahame, Kenneth, *The Wind in the Willows* (London, 1908).

Hamer, M., *Wheels within Wheels* (London, 1987).

Hibbs, J., *The History of the British Bus Services* (2nd edn, 1989).

Koerner, Steve, 'The British Motor Cycle Industry during the 1930s', Margaret Walsh (ed.), *Motor Transport* (Aldershot, 1997).

Mulley, Corinne, 'The Background to Bus Regulation in the 1930 Road Traffic Act: Economic, Political and Personal Influences in the 1920s', Margaret Walsh (ed.), *Motor Transport* (Aldershot, 1997).

Nicholson, T. R., *The Birth of the British Motor Car*, 2 vols (1982).

O'Connell, Sean, *The Car in British Society: Class, Gender and Motoring, 1896–1939* (Manchester and New York, 1998).

Plowden, W., *The Motor Car and Politics, 1896–1970* (London, 1971).

Richardson, K., *The British Motor Industry, 1896–1939* (Basingstoke, 1977).

Rhys, D. G., 'Concentration in the Inter-War Motor Industry', Margaret Walsh (ed.), *Motor Transport* (Aldershot, 1997).

Scott, P., 'The Growth of Road Haulage, 1921–58', *Journal of Transport History*, 19, September 1998.

Walsh, Margaret, 'Introduction: Mass Motoring, Missing from History', Walsh (ed.), *Motor Transport* (Aldershot, 1997), pp. ix–xxiii.

Wardroper, J., *Juggernaut* (London, 1981).

Watson, R. and Gray, M., *The Penguin Book of the Bicycle* (Harmondsworth, 1978), ch. 4.

Air Transport

Aldcroft, Derek H., 'Britain's Internal Airways: Pioneer Stage of the 1930s,' *Business History* (1964).

—, 'The Railways and Air Transport', in Aldcroft, *Studies in British Transport, 1870–1970* (Newton Abbot, 1974), pp. 226–42.

Air Ministry, Directorate of Civil Aviation, Report on the Progress of Civil Aviation, 1933–1938, HMSO (London).

Birkhead, E., 'The Financial Failure of British Air Transport Companies, 1919–24', *Journal of Transport History*, 4, May 1960.

Brooks, Peter W., 'A Short History of London's Airports', *Journal of Transport History*, 3, May 1957.

Davies, R. E. G., *Rebels and Reformers of the Airways* (Washington, DC, 1987).

Edgerton, David, *England and the Aeroplane: An Essay on a Militant and Technological Nation* (Basingstoke, 1991).

Fearon, Peter, 'The British Airframe Industry and the State, 1918–1935', *Economic History Review*, 27, May 1974, pp. 236–51.

Gibbs-Smith, C. H., *Aviation: An Historical Survey from its Origins to the End of World War 2* (London, 1970).

Higham, Robin, 'British Airways Ltd, 1935–1940', *Journal of Transport History*, 4, November 1959.

Humphreys, B. K., 'Nationalisation and Independent Airlines in the UK 1945–1951, *Journal of Transport History*, 3, September 1976.

Jackson, A. J., *De Havilland Aircraft since 1909* (London, 1962).

Lyth, Peter, 'Chosen Instruments: The Evolution of British Airways', Hans-Liudger Dienel and Peter Lyth (eds), *Flying the Flag: European Commercial Air Transport since 1945* (Basingstoke, 1998), pp. 50–86.

—, The Changing Role of Government in British Civil Air Transport, 1919–1949', Robert Millward and John Singleton (eds), *The Political Economy of Nationalisation in Britain, 1920–1950* (Cambridge, 1995), pp. 65–87.

Masefield, Sir Peter, 'Some Economic Factors in Air Transport Operation', *Journal of Institute of Transport*, March 1951.

Miller, Ronald and Sawers, David, *The Technical Development of Modern Aviation* (1968).

Robertson, A. J., 'The New Road to the Isles: Highland Airways and Scottish Airways, 1933–39', *Journal of Transport History*, 7 (1986), pp. 48–60.

Spurgeon, R. W., 'Subsidy in Air Transport', *Journal of Institute of Transport*, November 1956.

Wheatcroft, Stephen, 'Ten Economic Lessons from Short-Haul Airline Operation', *Journal of the Royal Aeronautical Society*, April 1961.

Wyatt, Sir Miles, 'British Independent Aviation: Past and Present', *Journal of Institute of Transport*, May 1963.

Urban Transport

Barker, T. C., *Moving Millions: A Pictorial History of London Transport* (London, 1992).

Barker, T. C., and Robbins, Michael, *A History of London Transport*, i, *The Nineteenth Century* (London, 1963); ii, *The Twentieth Century to 1970* (London, 1974).

Barman, Christian, *The Man Who Built London Transport: A Biography of Frank Pick* (Newton Abbot, 1979).

Burn, Charles, *On the Construction of Horse Railways for Branch Lines and for Street Traffic* (London, 1860).

McClintock, Hugh (ed.), *The Bicycle and City Traffic: Principles and Practice* (London, 1992).

MacKay, John P., *Tramways and Trolleys: The Rise of Urban Mass Transport in Europe* (Princeton, 1976).

Tolley, Rodney (ed.), *The Greening of Urban Transport: Planning for Walking and Cycling in Western Cities* (London, 1990).

Wood, Chris, *Street Trams for London* (London, 1994).

Technology and Transport

Armytage, W. H. G., *A Social History of Engineering* (London, 1961).

Berg, Maxine and Bruland, Kristine (eds), *Technological Revolutions in Europe: Historical Perspectives* (Cheltenham, 1998).

Gibb, Richard (ed.), *The Channel Tunnel: A Geographical Pespective* (Chichester, 1994).

Gunston, Bill, *The Development of Jet and Turbine Aero Engines* (2nd edn, Yeovil, 1997).

Hughes, Murray, *Rail 300: The World High Sped Train Race* (Newton Abbot, 1988).

Potter, Stephen, *On the Right Lines? The Limits to Technological Innovation* (London, 1987).

Nationalisation

Bonavia, Michael, *The Nationalisation of British Transport* (London, 1987).

Castle, Barbara, *The Castle Diaries, 1964–1970* (London, 1972)

Crompton, Gerald, 'Good Business for the Nation, 1921–47', *Journal of Transport History*, 20, September 1999.

Gourvish, Terry, *British Railways, 1948–73* (Cambridge, 1986).

Hillman M. and P. Whalley, *The Social Consequences of Rail Closures* (Leicester, 1980).

Johnson J., and Long, R. A., *British Railway Engineering, 1948–1980* (London, 1981).

Morrison, Herbert, *Socialisation and Transport* (London, 1933).

Mulley, Corinne, 'The Nationalisation of the Bus Industry: The Transport Act 1947, The Underlying Philosophy and Initial Progress', *Journal of Transport History*, 19, September 1998.

Parker, Peter, *For Starters: The Business of Life* (London, 1989).

Sharp, C. and Jennings, T., *Transport and the Environment* (Leicester, 1976).

Trade Union Congress (TUC), 'White Paper', *The Public Organisation of Transport*, University of North London, TUC Collection, 611.

Privatisation

Bradshaw, Bill, and Lawton Smith, Helen (eds), *Privatisation and Deregulation of Transport* (Basingstoke, 2000).

Dodson, J. S., *Bus Deregulation and Privatisation* (London, 1988).

Dudley, G. and Richardson, J., *Why Does Policy Change? Lessons from British Transport Policy, 1945–99* (London, 2001).

Glover, J., *National Railways: A Guide to the Privatised Railway* (Shepperton, 1996).

Hayashi, Yoshitsugu, Button, Kenneth and Nijkamp, Peter (eds), *The Environment and Transport* (Cheltenham, 1999).

Jack, I., *The Crash that Stopped Britain* (London, 2001).

McConville, James (ed.), *Transport Regulation Matters* (London, 1997).

Van de Velde, D. M. (ed.), *Changing Trains: Railway Reform and the Role of Competition. The Experience of Six Countries* (Aldershot, 1999).

Whitelegg, J., *Transport for a Sustainable Future* (London, 1993).

Index